REVISE FOR PRODUCT DESIGN:

Graphics with Materials Technology

John Halliwell
Barry Lambert

Consultant: Dave Webster

Success through qualifications

Heinemann Educational Publishers
Halley Court, Jordan Hill, Oxford OX2 8EJ
Part of Harcourt Education

Heinemann is a registered trademark of Harcourt Education Limited

© John Halliwell, Barry Lambert, 2004

First published in 2004

09 08 07 06 05 04
10 9 8 7 6 5 4 3 2 1

British Library Cataloguing in Publication Data is available from the British Library on request.

ISBN 0 435 630 938

Typeset by 𝓣 Tek-Art, Croydon, Surrey

Original illustrations © Harcourt Education Limited, 2004

Illustrated by 𝓣 Tek-Art, Croydon, Surrey

Printed and bound in the UK by Scotprint

Cover photo: © Powerstock

Picture research by Peter Morris

Acknowledgements
Every effort has been made to contact copyright holders of material reproduced in this book. Any omissions
will be rectified in subsequent printings if notice is given to the publishers.

The publishers would like to thank the following for permission to reproduce photographs:

(t = top, b = bottom, m = middle, l = left, r = right, second row = sr)

ALFA Robot page 159; Aviation Images page 83; Gareth Boden page 77 trm; Buro Happold page 123;
Peter Morris pages 13–14, 20, 41, 77 tl sr, 77 tr, 121; Nokia page 77 tlm sr; Pro-lok page 160; Rex Features
page 75; Science and Society Photo Library page 77 tl, page 77 tlm; Science Photo Library page 81.

The publishers would like to thank the following authors of *Product Design: Graphics with Materials
Technology (2nd edition)* – Barry Lambert, Lesley Cresswell, Alan Goodier and Jon Atwood – for allowing
their work to be used as reference material for this book.

There are links to relevant web sites in this book. In order to ensure that the links are up-to-date, that
the links work, and that the sites aren't inadvertently linked to sites that could be considered offensive,
we have made the links available on the Heinemann website at www.heinemann.co.uk/hotlinks When
you access the site, the express code is 0938P.

Contents

Part 1

Part 2 Advanced Subsidiary (AS)

Part 3 Advanced GCE (A2)

CONTENTS

Part 1

Introduction

How to use this book

To help you with your revision, this book is laid out to correspond with the student textbook, *Advanced Design and Technology for Edexcel, Product Design: Graphics with Materials Technology*. Units 1, 3, 4 and 6 are included as these are the units that are assessed by written examination papers rather than by coursework.

The Parts

Part 1, the Introduction, introduces you to revision strategy and to the examination papers. Part 2, Advanced Subsidiary (AS), and Part 3, Advanced GCE (A2), correspond to the units and sections found in the Specification and in the student textbook.

The sections

Each section starts with a short introduction and then is divided into topics. At the end of each section there are sample examination style questions for you to try.

The topics

'You need to' box

This provides you with a bulleted list of the key learning points that you need for each topic.

Key terms box

These are provided as they are important terms and you need to check you understand them. They are also shown in bold text the first time they are used in the topic.

KEY POINTS

These points summarise the learning you need to do. Each major heading reflects those provided in the 'You need to' box at the start of each topic.

Examination questions

Sample examination style questions are provided at the end of each topic so you can see the type of questions you could be asked on each topic.

Acceptable answers

These will help you to understand what is required in your answers. The points you need to make for each mark are shown in bold text.

> ### Examiner's Tip
>
> Experienced senior examiners have provided examination tips throughout the book to help you understand what is required in the questions and how to give a full answer for each question.

Do you want to improve your grade?

What is revision?

Revision involves preparing for an examination and is defined as 'reviewing previously learned material'.

Why revise?

The purpose of revision is to:

- refresh your knowledge and understanding of previously learned material
- improve your ability to recall and apply this knowledge and understanding to the questions in the examination.

How can I improve my grade?

You can improve your grade by revising thoroughly all that you have covered during your course. A copy of the Specification and other useful materials can be obtained from the Edexcel website (go to www.heinemann.co.uk/hotlinks and enter express code 0938P). Use this to check the areas that you have covered during your lessons. You can also ask your teacher to provide you with copies of past papers from Edexcel. By looking at these materials you will begin to develop a 'feel' for what is expected of you during the examination. They will also give you an impression of the style of questions asked.

Do I need to know about all the content in the Awarding Body Specification?

Yes. Over a period of years the awarding body is obliged to cover the whole of the Specification. However, this does not mean that you can predict which elements of the Specification are going to be covered the year you sit the examinations. Sometimes an element might occur two years in a row. It is therefore vital that you make sure that you are familiar with the whole subject area and you prepare fully by revising the whole Specification.

How does this book help me to improve my grade?

This book will help you in a number of ways. Firstly, it outlines clearly and logically all the topics that are covered in the Specification. It highlights key terms that will be useful to you in your revision and it gives hints and comments that have been written by senior examiners. Added together, these will give you a very good idea of what you really need to concentrate on when doing your revision. It will also give you a clear idea of what is required in the answers.

Revision strategy and explanation

Revising for the examinations

Revising thoroughly for each examination paper is a key part of your Product Design: Graphics with Materials Technology course. You need to understand and learn the subject matter for each examination paper and you need to practise by answering sample questions.

Examiner's Tips

- The more relevant and appropriate the material that you include in your responses in the examinations, the more marks you are going to get.
- It is important to get your revision strategy correct. Try to make your revision active. It is not a good idea just to read through a textbook or your notes. It is a better idea to make notes as you read. The act of writing down points will help to reinforce points in your mind and you can use the notes that you make as crib sheets later on.

As you revise you may struggle to understand some topics. Make a list of these and use your notes, textbook, this revision book and other resources to research the topic. If you need further assistance, ask your teacher for help as early as possible. Remember that you should not depend on your teacher alone to provide you with everything you need. It is important that you familiarise yourself with the subject using your own research and background reading.

> **Further information on the whole course and managing your own learning during the course can be found in** *Advanced Design and Technology for Edexcel, Product Design: Graphics with Materials Technology, Part 1.*

Preparing for the examination papers

To do well in Product Design: Graphics with Materials Technology examinations, you need to prepare yourself properly for each written examination. Make sure that you familiarise yourself with the structure of the various papers.

- What type of material is likely to be included in the various examinations?
- How is the paper laid out?
- How many sections and questions are there?
- How are the marks allocated?
- How much time will you have to answer each question?
- What is the examiner likely to be looking for?
- What equipment will be required for the exam?

Table 1 How your work at AS and A2 will be assessed

Level	Course units	Examinations	AS (%)	A2 (%)
AS level	**Unit 1** Product Analysis	$1\frac{1}{2}$ hour examination	30	15
	Unit 2 Coursework		40	20
	Unit 3A Materials Components and Systems **Unit 3B** Either Design and Technology in Society or CAD/CAM	Two 45-minute papers sat in a $1\frac{1}{2}$ hour examination	30	15
A2 level	**Unit 4A** Materials Components and Systems **Unit 4B** Either Design and Technology in Society or CAD/CAM	Two 45-minute papers sat in a $1\frac{1}{2}$ hour examination		15
	Unit 5 Coursework			20
	Unit 6 Design	3 hour examination		15

The following section will go some way towards helping you to start answering some of these questions.

The question papers

During this course you will be required to sit four externally assessed examination papers. At AS level you will take Unit 1 and Unit 3 and at A2 level you will take Unit 4 and Unit 6.

- Unit 1 is a Product Analysis Paper.
- Unit 3 and Unit 4 are theory papers divided into two sections, A and B. The section A questions cover Materials, Components and Systems and the section B questions cover the optional areas of Design and Technology in Society or CAD/CAM.
- Finally, Unit 6 is a design paper. This paper is referred to as *synoptic*. This means that this final unit is structured in such a way as to cover elements from both the AS and A2 courses. For this reason, Unit 6 must always be taken at the end of the course.

Unit 1 (AS) Product Analysis

In this paper you will be given a colour photograph or a number of photographs of a product that has both a graphical element and a resistant materials technology element. You will be required to make a thorough analysis of the product by responding to a number of questions that will be set out in sections a-g.

These sections remain similar year on year and will always follow the same basic format. This involves looking at the writing of specifications, the use of relevant materials, methods of production, manufacturing processes, quality, safety and the appeal of the product.

This paper will be marked out of a total of 60 marks. Three of those marks are given for the quality of written communication (QWC). The QWC mark is geared not only to the correct use of English but also to the correct use of technical language. You have $1\frac{1}{2}$ hours to answer this paper. All parts of this paper are compulsory.

Unit 3 (AS) and Unit 4 (A2) plus option papers

Unit 3 and Unit 4 are theory papers divided into two sections, A and B.

- Section A questions cover Materials, Components and Systems.
- Section B questions cover the optional areas of Design and Technology in Society or CAD/CAM.

Your teachers will make the choice of which optional area you will study. You cannot change your options between AS and A2: you must continue the option you studied during the AS course *and continue it into the A2 course.*

In Section A, Materials, Components and Systems, there will be 6 questions which will have a total allocation of 30 marks. However, you should note that the marks will not always be divided equally between the questions. For example, some questions may have more than 5 marks while others have less, depending on the complexity of the question. Section B, the option part of the paper, has two questions of 15 marks each, making a total of 30 marks.

You have $1\frac{1}{2}$ hours to answer *both* elements of each paper. (It is a good idea to divide the time equally between the two sections giving 45 minutes per section.) All parts of these papers are compulsory.

Unit 6 Design (A2 Synoptic)

This examination consists of one compulsory design question. As it is *synoptic*, this paper must be taken at the end of the course and will examine all the areas covered during the two years of your studies.

Pre-release research paper

Approximately six weeks before the examination, you will be given a pre-release research paper. This gives you an idea of the type of product to expect in your examination. This document outlines a context for the examination and suggests areas that you might consider researching. Take careful note of these points as they are designed to help you. The research you undertake during the preparation period is very important, as you will be expected to refer to it in the examination. The examination itself is 'open book'. This means you are able to take into the examination all the research material that you have undertaken. You can refer to this material throughout the examination. However, there are two things you are *not* permitted to do. Firstly you are not allowed to pre-draw any material. All the design work that you do must be done on the pre-printed sheets handed out on the day of the examination and secondly, you may not use ICT during the examination. This includes CAD or Internet research. Any material or research that you have gathered for the examination will not be collected or assessed by the examiner.

Examiner's Tips

- All the questions in all the papers are compulsory. In order to gain maximum marks you must attempt the entire question and answer all parts of that question.
- Before the examination, look at as many past papers as possible and work through them to give you an idea of the type of question to expect. Your teacher should be able to help provide these.
- At the start of each question, you may find it useful to jot down some notes about the points that you want to cover in your response. If you do not want these quick notes to be marked by the examiner, just put a line through them and the examiner will ignore them.
- The key word that appears in all the examiners' mark schemes is 'justification'. You need to justify all the points that you have made. It is a good idea to assume that the examiner knows nothing about the subject and that you should write down everything that you feel is relevant to your answer.

The Unit 6 examination

Unlike the other papers in the Design and Technology suite of examinations, where candidates write in examination answer booklets, the Design paper must be answered on the pre-printed, one-sided, A3 sheets provided. You should only use one side of each A3 sheet and should not need to use extra sheets. The design task is printed at the beginning, outlining the exact requirements of the design problem. The pre-printed A3 sheets also include clear statements at the top of each page outlining the requirements of each section together with suggested times. It is very important that you take note of the comments at the top of each sheet together with the number of marks available for each individual section. By doing this you should be able to understand more of what the examiner will be looking for and consequently gain more marks. Remember that this paper is part of the Graphics with Materials Technology course and you will be required to design a product that contains a materials element as well as a graphical element. The best approach to this examination is to think of it in terms of a mini-project rather similar to the coursework projects that you have produced for the course. This examination should contain the elements of research, analysis, the generation of ideas, the developing of solutions, representing and illustrating your final solution, the laying out of production plans and then testing and evaluating your designs.

You have three hours to answer this question. You must respond to all elements of the paper to gain maximum marks.

Examiner's Tip

When you are producing drawings it is often sensible to use coloured pencils. It is a good idea to colour code your work. For instance, if you are drawing something made of various materials, use a different colour for each material. Anything that makes your response easier for the examiner to understand is a good thing.

Answering the examination questions

To do yourself justice it is very important that you read the questions on the paper. Remember that all the questions must be answered. Firstly, make sure that you look carefully at the number of marks allocated to each section of each question. This will give a very *good* clue as to how many responses or points are required in your answers. There is a very strong likelihood that if four marks are indicated on the paper, the examiner will require four points in your answer. If you do not have the correct number of points you will not gain the marks.

In many of the questions you will be asked to produce notes and sketches or drawings. If they are needed, make sure that you include *good-quality*, well-annotated, clear sketches to back up your written responses. If you are asked for drawings and do not include them, you will not get the marks available and you won't do yourself justice. It is a good idea to adopt a colour coding system in your drawings. For example, you might think of using one colour for plastics, one colour for metals and another for woods. Stick to those colours throughout the paper.

When you write your responses you need to make sure that the examiner can understand your answer. For example, make sure that your responses are numbered correctly. If you have found it necessary to draw on extra sheets you should indicate clearly on your pre-printed answer sheets where the rest of the answer can be found.

There are some key words that appear in questions that give a clue to the type of response required. If you see the words *discuss*, *explain* or *outline*, the examiner is expecting a fairly detailed justification of your answer and not just single-word responses. The main thing to remember is to read the questions very carefully and think before you start to write. Examiners can only give credit for what you have written on the paper and not what they think you might mean.

Remember, thorough revision and preparation for your exams will give you the confidence to tackle the questions to the best of your ability so that you do as well as you can in each paper.

Part 2
Advanced Subsidiary (AS)

Industrial and commercial products and practices (G1)

In this unit you will demonstrate your understanding of industrial and commercial practices by analysing products. You need to develop a good understanding of product design, development and manufacture. The product you will be asked to analyse in the exam will incorporate two elements.

- A graphical element (such as brand identity, logos and packaging).
- A resistant material element (manufactured using materials such as wood, metal and plastic).

Basic product specification

You will be asked to develop a **product design specification**, which sets out the criteria that the product aims to achieve, for the illustrated product. You must provide *seven* different, justified design requirements. You must address at least *four* of the headings printed on the exam paper. Your statements can be written as bullet points. Each bullet-pointed response must be sufficiently detailed to justify the statement being made.

You need to

know how to develop the product design specification for a range of products using the following headings.

- ☐ **purpose/function**
- ☐ **performance**
- ☐ **markets**
- ☐ **aesthetics/characteristics**
- ☐ **quality and safety standards**

This unit will be assessed externally through a $1\frac{1}{2}$ hour Product Analysis examination. You will be given details and coloured illustrations of a product. You will then be expected to answer specific questions which relate to this product. You should use appropriate specialist and technical language in the exam along with accurate spelling, punctuation and grammar.

KEY TERMS
Check you understand these terms

Product design specification, Purpose/function, Performance, Market, Target market groups (TMGs), Marketing, Aesthetics/characteristics, Quality standards, Safety

Further information can be found in *Advanced Design and Technology for Edexcel Product Design: Graphics with Materials Technology*, Unit 1.

KEY POINTS

Purpose/function

The **purpose/function** of a product focuses on:

- the aim or end-use of the product

- how the product will be used or what it should do.

You should identify the properties of the product, materials or components and then explain why these make them suitable. It is not enough to provide unsupported statements such as 'because it is strong'. A chocolate box, for example, is:

- an enclosed container designed to hold the chocolates so that they can be sold as a set
- made from cartonboard which provides an excellent printing surface where graphics and text can be used to inform the customer and to help sell the chocolates.

Answers for this section and others can contain reference to other, less obvious features or materials of the product. The chocolate box, for example, contains a vacuum formed plastic tray.

- HDPS can be vacuum formed into individual compartments, presenting the chocolates attractively and preventing them from being damaged.

Performance

The **performance** of a product is related to the purpose/function of the product, the materials and components used. Performance can be defined as how well a product fulfils its purpose/function. Performance can also be related to the lifespan of the product. For example, a temporary point of sale display must be durable enough to remain in good condition for the length of the promotion.

Market

The **market** is made up of all the customers who are expected to buy the product. Many of these customers will have things in common such as age, lifestyle, income or tastes. Companies will divide these people into market segments and identify the largest segment so that they can concentrate their efforts on persuading them to buy the product. These targeted market segments are known as **Target Market Groups** (**TMGs**). **Marketing** encompasses all the activities involved in getting the product to the correct TMG and includes market research, pricing and distribution strategies. You need to be aware of market requirements and TMG requirements.

The requirements of the market

Should the product be designed to meet design/technological trends and developments? Think about the requirements of the retailers. For example, washing powder is sold in standard-sized boxes which makes them easy to stack and display on supermarket shelves.

The requirements of users and target market groups (TMGs)

For whom has the product been designed? How does it reflect the needs, preferences and aspirations of the target market group – for example male or female, young or old, able-bodied or disabled, expert or novice? For example, a push-along toy will be lightweight so that it can be moved easily by young children.

Aesthetics/characteristics

Aesthetics/characteristics are concerned with how the product, materials and components appeal to the customers' senses. Most important is the look of the product in terms of styling, shape, form, pattern, colour and finish. How does the product attract potential customers from the target market? How visually appealing is the product? A product, such as a CD cover designed for teenagers, will look very different to one which performs the same purpose/function but which is aimed at a different age group.

Quality standards

You should be prepared to explain how **quality standards** have been achieved in the product, materials and components through the use of Quality Control (QC), Quality Assurance (QA) and Total Quality Management (TQM). All statements must be specific to the product and thoroughly justified; they should, where appropriate, relate to size, dimensions and tolerances. For example, registration marks must be printed on a magazine to simplify the process of quality control, resulting in high-quality pictures.

Safety standards

You need to identify how **safety** of the product will be ensured in production and use. Statements should be justified and must be specific to the product, or refer to the processes used in production. Knowledge of specific British Standards, however, is not required. For example, food packaging should create an anaerobic atmosphere (be sealed airtight) to prevent biological contamination (germs).

Examiner's Tip

The specification headings will be reproduced on the exam paper. You are expected to address **at least four** of the specification headings in your answer. In this part of the question paper, it is sufficient to answer with bullet points and short sentences. Repeated points or general statements, such as 'lightweight' and 'colourful', may not be credited. There are 7 marks available for this part of the paper, so you need to provide 7 justified, explained or quantified points to achieve the full marks.

EXAMINATION QUESTION

Example question and answer

Fig. 1.1a A toy train and packaging

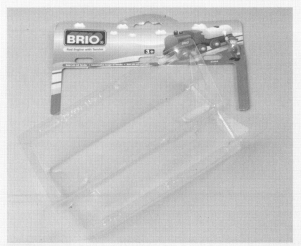

Fig. 1.1b Details of snap together PET and printed carton board packaging

Fig. 1.1c Details of instructions showing product range

Fig. 1.1d Details of wheels and magnets connecting the two parts of the train

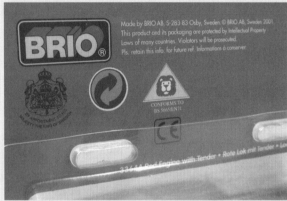

Fig. 1.1e Details of graphics on the reverse side of the printed cartonboard

 This product is part of a range of toys and consists of:
- *a hardwood (beech) train, finished with red and black water-based, non-toxic paint (the beech is from managed forests)*
- *injection moulded plastic wheels*
- *PET plastic, snap-together display packaging*
- *cartonboard packaging with printed graphics*
- *a full colour printed leaflet*
- *magnets, attached with screws, which connect the two parts of the toy train*

- *chrome-plated steel snap-on fastenings, which fix the wheels onto the axles.*

*a) Outline the product specification for the toy train and packaging. Address at least **four** of the following headings.*
- *function/purpose*
- *performance*
- *market*
- *aesthetics/characteristics*
- *quality standards*
- *safety.* **(7 marks)**

Acceptable answer (four from the following)
- *Function/purpose:* The packaging must be **easy to fix together** to **reduce assembly costs**.
- *Function/purpose:* The **plastic wheels must rotate** to allow the train to **roll along** the floor or along a track.
- *Performance:* The materials and finish of the toy train must be **durable and hard wearing** so that it will **survive knocks and bumps** as children play.
- *Market:* The packaging must **indicate a minimum age**, as the toy train contains small, moving parts, which may be **dangerous for very young children** (for example, choking hazard if detached).
- *Aesthetics/characteristics:* The toy train must be finished with **bright colours and simple graphics** so it will **appeal to children**.
- *Quality standards:* The colours on the packaging must be **properly registered** (aligned) to ensure that the **text is easy to read**.
- *Safety:* The toy train must not contain any **sharp, exposed edges** which could **cause damage or injury**.

Materials, components and their working characteristics

The selection of materials and components for a particular product is based on a number of factors, such as:

- the material's working properties
- the manufacturing processes involved
- the scale of production involved
- appropriate finishing techniques
- the required accuracy of the finished product
- cost.

The choice of a material or component will take into account a combination of these factors. It is not enough to simply identify the properties of the materials or components: you must explain why these properties make it a suitable choice.

You need to

understand how the properties and working characteristics influence the choice of materials and components used in a range of products.
- ☐ **paper, card and board**
- ☐ **plastics**
- ☐ **woods**
- ☐ **manufactured boards**
- ☐ **metals and alloys.**

understand the relationship between working characteristics, finishes, properties, quality and materials selection related to the product range.
- ☐ **aesthetic properties (the look of the material or product)**
- ☐ **physical and mechanical properties**
- ☐ **surface coating, decoration, self-finishing.**

KEY TERMS

Check you
understand these terms

boards, polymers, thermoplastics, thermosetting, elastomers, softwoods, evergreen, hardwoods, deciduous, ferrous, non-ferrous, alloys, physical and mechanical properties, surface finishes, self-finishing

KEY POINTS

Paper, card and board

The common properties and working characteristics of papers and boards

There are hundreds of different types of paper and **boards** to choose from. Board is the name for commercial cards, such as cartonboard, which start at approximately 220 microns. They are used extensively by the designer for modelling and as commercial packaging materials. The properties and working characteristics of papers and boards can be categorised by size; weight or thickness; colour; opacity (opaque, translucent or transparent); surface finish and texture; cost; ability to accept graphic media; and ability to be cut, shaped and formed.

Size

Paper and boards are usually supplied in standard sizes. Commercial papers and thin cards are also available on rolls, which are used in continuous 'web fed' processes such as the lithographic printing process used to produce newspapers.

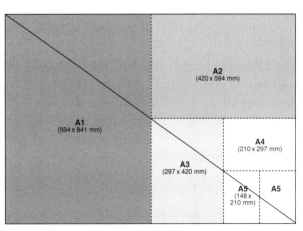

Fig. 1.2 Common 'A' sizes of paper and board

Weight and quantity

Papers and boards are usually described in terms of weight (gsm – grams per square metre) or thickness (microns – short for micrometres). Paper becomes a board after approximately 220 microns. Paper is normally supplied in standard quantities such as the ream (500 sheets) commonly used for standard office papers.

Table 1.1 Examples of papers and boards

Paper/Board	Description and properties	Uses
Bank, bond, tracing, cartridge and layout paper	45–150 gsm. A large number of papers are available displaying a wide range of properties.	A wide range of applications including drawing, painting and commercial applications
Card and board (including cartonboard and packaging laminates)	Various weights starting at 220 gsm. Commercial packaging board made up from various layers of card, paper, and in some cases metal foil and polymer sheet • Strong, durable; suitable for high quality, high speed printing and for cutting, creasing and gluing • Excellent printing surface • Excellent protection in structural packaging nets • Can be recycled • Relatively inexpensive to produce and process but costs depend on the product's weight, finish and quality.	Thin card used for photocopying and printing Card used for 3D modelling and packaging mock-up Widely used for boxes and cartons such as chocolate boxes Foil/polymer/card laminated cartonboard used for drinks cartons
Corrugated board/card	Fluted paper sandwiched between paper layers (liners), available in single, double or triple boards. Durable, good strength to weight, impact, puncture and tear resistant. Cost can be reduced by using recycled materials Good quality liners, such as Kraft papers, give good printing surface. Low cost, can be made using recycled materials.	Thinner corrugated card with fine flutes, used for perfume bottles Larger fluted corrugated card used for protective packaging

Plastics

Plastics are versatile materials that often require very little surface finishing. Plastics are sometimes referred to as **polymers** because they are formed from long chains of identical molecules. They can be vacuum formed, injection moulded and blow moulded. Plastics essentially fall into three main groups. **Thermoplastics** can be reformed by applying heat (and have a 'plastic memory'); **Thermosetting** plastics cannot be reformed using heat; **Elastomers** are plastics, such as rubber, which display elastic properties.

Many plastics can be identified by internationally recognised symbols, which are used to help the sorting process during recycling. Thermoplastics are often used as packaging materials because they share some common properties.

• versatile
• lightweight
• low cost
• tough and durable
• recyclable
• impact resistant
• most can be made translucent or transparent
• available in a range of colours
• available in a range of forms (such as sheets, tubes, granules)
• water-resistant
• can be thermoformed (shaped using heat)
• can be printed on.

Table 1.2 Examples of thermoplastics

Plastic	Recycling ID code	Significant properties	Uses	Advantages
PET (Polyethylene Terephthalate)	[1] PET	Excellent transparency, very tough, impenetrable to gases, can withstand a wide range of temperatures	Fizzy drink bottles, food containers, microwaveable food trays	Glass-like transparency allows product to be seen Does not affect flavour of food products Ideal for use as packaging for oven ready or microwaveable products
HDPE (High Density Polythene)	[2] HDPE	Excellent chemical resistance, good barrier to water	Bottles and containers for washing-up liquid and cosmetic bottles, thin sheet packaging	Very suitable for containers designed to hold a wide range of liquids which need to be tough, durable and flexible Very common form of packaging
PVC (Polyvinyl Chloride)	[3] PVC	Rigid – can be flexible if plasticisers are added Excellent chemical resistance Good barrier to weather/water/gases	Shrink wrapping and cling film Blister packaging Packaging for, toiletries, pharmaceutical products, food, confectionery, water, fruit juices	Very versatile can be used for a wide variety of products Chemical resistance makes rigid PVC suitable for products such as batteries or pharmaceutical products (drugs and medicines)
PS (Polystyrene)	[6] PS	RIGID POLYSTYRENES (HDPS, LDPS, HIPS)		
		RIGID POLYSTYRENE Wide range of colours including transparent Stiff and hard Can be made impact resistant – High Impact Polystyrene (HIPS)	Yoghurt pots CD cases Disposable cups and cutlery Bubble packs Prototype and architectural models	Very suitable for vacuum forming Very suitable for tough, durable and flexible containers designed to hold a wide range of liquids
		EXPANDED POLYSTYRENE (e.g. Styrofoam)		
		Limited range of colours – usually white, impact resistant, good heat insulator, durable, very lightweight – very buoyant on water, low water absorption	Take-away packaging, egg cartons, fruit, vegetable and meat trays, hot drink cups Protective packaging for electrical goods Expanded Polystyrene 'peanuts' are used to pack void spaces in boxes to prevent products moving in transit	Does not add any significant weight to a packaged product As a good heat insulator Expanded Polystyrene makes an excellent packaging material for hot food products Provides an excellent protective layer which absorbs impact, preventing damage to valuable and fragile products

Table 1.2 Examples of thermoplastics *(continued)*

Plastic	Recycling ID code	Significant properties	Uses	Advantages
Acrylic (Polymethyl methacrylate)	7 OTHER	Wide range of bright colours, glossy finish, hard, brittle, rigid, heavy	High quality containers or closures for perfume products Signage, windows Point of Sale displays	Available in a wide range of bright colours with a hard, glossy surface finish making it ideal for signage and products which require visual impact Little finishing required

Table 1.3 Examples of thermosetting plastics

Material	Significant properties	Uses	Advantages
Polyester	Heat, chemical and abrasion resistant; can be coloured	Photographic film, bottles, electrical casings, castings, fabrics, bonding agent for GRP, engineering components	Available in many different forms Good mechanical properties
Urea Formaldehyde	Stiff, hard, strong	Electrical fittings, adhesives	Heat resistant, range of colours

Woods

Wood is a natural resource and, because of this, quality can vary. If not handled and treated correctly, it can warp, twist and cup. It is also prone to decay and fungal attacks. Before the timber can be put to use, it must be converted, that is, cut into manageable sections. Then it must be seasoned to reduce the moisture content to an acceptable level. Woods can be cut, shaped and joined in many ways. A range of finishes can be applied to enhance the grain and figure of finished products. Woods can be divided into three groups: **Softwoods** – obtained from relatively fast-growing **evergreen** trees, inexpensive general purpose timber;

Hardwoods – obtained from **deciduous** trees, generally more expensive and durable than softwoods; Manufactured boards – large man-made boards with enhanced properties.

Manufactured board

Manufactured boards are available in large, wide sheets. The most common size is 2440 × 1220mm. They do not warp and twist in the same way as natural timbers but if left unsupported they will sag. Plywood and MDF can be manufactured with a natural timber finish in the form of veneers (thin layers of natural timbers), which create the impression of a solid wood finish.

Table 1.4 Woods

Wood	Classification	Properties	Applications/uses
Beech	Hardwood	Hard; tough; finishes well but is prone to warping; turns well	Workshop benches, kitchen implements, children's toys, furniture
Jelutong	Hardwood	Straight grained; soft; fine even texture	Pattern-making, carving, concept models
Pine	Softwood	Straight grained but knotty, easy to work, cheap and readily available, aesthetically appealing	Construction work, floor boards and roof trusses, interior joinery

Table 1.5 Manufactured Board

Material	Properties	Uses
Plywood	• Made up from a number of layers stacked at right angles, which enhances strength and stability • Can be produced with veneered external faces to resemble natural timber • Special waterproof grades used in the boat-building industry	General construction, marine grade plywood used for boat-building and outdoor construction
MDF	• A composite material with a uniform structure • Relatively strong, hard and heavy; no grain, very flat smooth surface • Machines well and is used extensively in flat-packed mass-produced furniture • Capable of taking a wide range of finishes • Easily joined using special knock-down fittings • Although prone to water damage it is very stable	General construction, furniture, model-making, patterns and formers

Composites

A composite material, such as MDF, is formed when two or more materials are combined/bonded together. These newly formed composite materials display improved mechanical properties.

Metals and alloys

Metals are used extensively in industry and can be categorised into three groups. **Ferrous** metals – made up from ferrite or iron (carbon can be added to produce steel); **Non-ferrous** metals – contain no iron, such as copper and aluminium and zinc; **Alloys** – mixtures of metals, or metals and non-metals, which display enhanced properties.

Table 1.6 A comparison of the properties and applications of metals

Material	Melting point (°C)	Properties	Applications/uses
Steel	1400	Ferrous alloy; tough, ductile and malleable, good tensile strength; easily joined by welding or brazing, can be hardened and tempered; poor resistance to corrosion (rusts)	Tin-plated steel used for aerosols, food tins, drinks cans, bottle tops, biscuit and paint 'tins', trays, 'tin' toys
Stainless steel	c. 1400	A range of ferrous alloys containing steel and other alloying agents, such as chromium and tungsten. Corrosion resistant, hard	Cutlery, kitchen sinks
Aluminium	660	Pure non-ferrous metal; good weight to strength ratio; surface oxidisation provides protective coating; malleable, ductile; good conductor of heat and electricity; properties of aluminium can be enhanced by alloying e.g. Duralumin	Castings, window frames, drinks cans, aerosols, cosmetic and toiletry products, screw caps, products, screw caps, foil laminates for cartons

Table 1.6 A comparison of the properties and applications of metals *(continued)*

Material	Melting point (°C)	Properties	Applications/uses
Copper	1083	Pure non-ferrous metal; malleable, ductile; excellent conductor of heat and electricity; corrosion resistant	Electrical cable, plumbing pipes, car radiators, PCBs, jewellery
Tin	232	Pure non-ferrous metal; soft, corrosion resistant	Tin plate (coating on steel 'tin' cans)
Zinc	420	Pure non-ferrous metal; ductile and easily worked; excellent corrosion resistance	Die casting alloys, protective coating for steel
Brass	927	Non-ferrous alloy of 65 per cent copper + 35 per cent zinc; corrosion resistant; good fusibility for casting, machines well	Marine and plumbing fittings, decorative products such as candlesticks

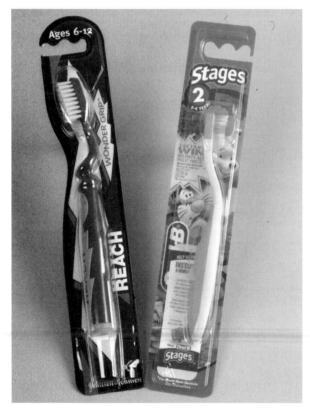

Fig. 1.3 Two toothbrushes aimed at different target markets, (two different age groups)

Aesthetic properties

Aesthetics is concerned with how the product appeals to the customers' senses. Many products perform identical functions and are only differentiated by their aesthetic appeal (styling). You should be able to explain how products are styled to appeal to different target markets.

Physical and mechanical properties

It is important to select materials with appropriate **physical and mechanical properties** and working characteristics.

Fusibility	– the ability to change into a liquid state when heated
Density	– the amount of matter within a material
Electrical resistance	– the ability to conduct electricity
Thermal resistance	– the ability to conduct heat
Environmental resistance	– the ability to withstand natural elements

Table 1.7 Terms used to describe aesthetic properties

Words related to 'texture'	Words related to 'colour'	Shape and form of the product
Hard, soft, abrasive, smooth, textured	Warm/cool, dull, bright/vivid, neutral, pastel/light, dark, eye-catching, associated	Functional, engineered, stylish, sleek, modern, traditional

	(for example, water, light and biological attack)
Optical	– the ability to conduct light properties (opacity, transparency, translucency)
Strength	– the ability to withstand force without breaking or permanent bending
Hardness	– the ability to withstand abrasion and indentation
Toughness	– the ability to withstand impact without breaking or fracturing
Elasticity	– the ability to deform, bend or flex and to return to the original state
Plasticity	– the ability to deform and retain a shape
Malleability	– the ability to deform under pressure
Ductility	– the ability to deform through bending, twisting or stretching

Other properties and characteristics may be identified, such as the suitability of paper or card for printing processes. Combining two or more materials can also enhance properties of some materials, as in the case of alloys, laminates, surface coatings and composite materials.

Surface coating, surface decoration, self-finishing

Surface coating and decoration offers an extensive range of **surface finishes** and treatments which can be applied to woods and metals.

Examiner's Tips

- Remember, repeated points or general statements may not be credited. All your points must be justified.
- In this part of your exam you will be asked to justify the selection of the materials or components used in the product. In answering the question, you need to refer to the properties/characteristics of the materials or component that make them appropriate for the function they perform or which make them suitable for manufacturing. One-word, or generalised answers, will not gain credit, as your answers must contain sufficient detail to provide adequate justification.
- When you are revising for the examination, choose a product that has both graphical and resistant material elements. Analyse the product using the exam headings.

Table 1.8 Finishes for wood, metal and plastics

Finish	Description	Properties
Paints	Oil- or water-based liquids which can be brushed, rolled or sprayed	Inexpensive, durable and waterproof – available in a wide range of colours; polyurethane paints are tough and scratch resistant
Varnishes	A plastic type of finish made from synthetic resins	Can provide a clear, glossy, tough, waterproof, heatproof and protective/wipe clean finish; available in a range of colours and finishes
Polish	Fine abrasives used to remove surface scratches	Enhances the aesthetic properties of wood, metals and plastics; can enhance protection
Electroplating	A metal coating process carried out by electrolysis	Can add more durable and decorative finish (e.g. chrome or silver) to materials such as brass and copper
Anodising	A chemical or electrolytic surface treatment for aluminium	Inhibits corrosion; the addition of coloured dyes can enhance aesthetic properties
Preservatives	Chemicals which are painted onto timber products	Provide timber products with protection from wet, fungus decay and pest attacks
Self-finishing	Processes such as injection moulding and laser cutting	Requires little or no finishing; different materials introduced together to form a single component

Table 1.9 Finishes applied to paper, card and board during manufacture or the printing process

Print finish	Description
Lamination	Combining materials in layers
Embossing	Raising part of the design above the surface of the flat material using an embossing die
Varnishes and lacquers	Liquids or films added during the printing process
Polishing	Some papers are 'polished' with special rollers during the production process
Coating	Minerals are used to coat papers
Colour	Print, dyes or lamination
Specialist papers	Specially finished papers such as marbled or textured paper

EXAMINATION QUESTION

Example question and answers. (This question refers to the photographs and product description on pages 13 and 14.)

b) Justify the use of:

i) beech, finished with water-based paints, for the toy train body　　**(3 marks)**

ii) printed cartonboard for the packaging.
　　　　　　　　　　　　(3 marks)

Acceptable answer

i) Beech is **hard** and so will **resist dents and abrasion**. This is important as children can be **heavy-handed**.

Using beech from managed forests **reduces** the impact on the environment and will **encourage environmentally aware customers to buy** the product.

Beech can be finished with water-based paints, which **do not use harmful solvents** so there is **less damage to the environment**.

ii) Cartonboard has **excellent printing properties** allowing the manufacturer to **promote the product** with **graphics and slogans**.

The cartonboard is relatively **inexpensive**, because it contains recycled material, which **helps to reduce costs**.

The card can be **recycled** and **turned into other paper or card products**.

Scale of production

Products are manufactured by different manufacturing systems. Market research provides the manufacturer with an indication of future sales. Scale of production is determined by the projected level of demand.

You need to

understand how and why products are manufactured using:

☐ one-off and batch production, high-volume and continuous production
☐ ICT in the manufacture of products: computer-integrated manufacture (CIM).

KEY TERMS

Check you
understand these terms

One-off production, Batch production, High-volume
production/continuous production, CIM

KEY POINTS

How and why products are manufactured using one-off, batch, high-volume and continuous production

When selecting materials and manufacturing processes, the designer needs to consider the scale of production. Costs are reduced as more products are produced. The scale of production will affect:

- the number of products manufactured
- the choice of materials and components
- the choice of manufacturing processes
- the choice of production planning techniques including just in time (JIT)
- production costs – including the benefits of bulk buying and the use of standard components.

Continuous production and other forms of high-volume manufacture are closely related. Continuous production, as the name suggests, operates 24 hours a day, 365 days a year. All operations such as equipment maintenance have to be carried out without interrupting the production line.

Table 1.10 Scale of production

Description	Examples of uses	Advantages	Disadvantages
One-off production (single item) Single, custom-made products requiring skilled, specialist craftspeople	Vinyl graphics for signs and transport livery; architectural models; movie props; shop and exhibition displays; packaging mock-ups; 3D prototype models; graphic design mock-ups such as posters, leaflets etc.	Product can be made to very exacting specifications; low tooling costs; low capital (setting up) costs; design can be changed easily during production	Slow; labour intensive; no economies of scale; skilled, specialist craftspeople often required; expensive materials and processes often used
Batch production Products produced in specified quantities. Production runs can be large or small. Companies can switch production to different products	Stationery; business cards; leaflets; brochures; posters; point of sale displays; promotional packaging	Flexible systems can be changed to produce different products easily; rapid response to changes in customer needs; easy to change size of batches; possible to adapt processes between batches; bulk buying of raw materials at lower prices	Advantages enjoyed by volume manufacture are sacrificed in order to achieve flexibility which leads to a slower, more expensive process and product
High-volume production Large numbers of products are produced on a production line making use of faster, more automated manufacturing processes and a largely unskilled workforce	Standard plastic bottles and containers; standard card and paper products	Less labour and more automation lead to higher efficiency; work can be divided into simple, repetitive tasks suitable for cheap unskilled labour; bulk buying of raw materials at lower prices; all the above lead to lower unit costs and a cheaper product	Very expensive to purchase and set up specialised machinery; difficult to make big changes during production; social issues due to fewer jobs created and reliance on unskilled labour performing boring, repetitive tasks

Table 1.10 Scale of production (continued)

Description	Examples of uses	Advantages	Disadvantages
Continuous production Where identical products produced continuously, in large quantities, along production lines which can work non-stop	Pharmaceutical products and packaging; aluminium cans; plastic bags	Shares the advantages of high-volume production; rapid, non-stop production makes optimum use of capital investment	Shares the disadvantages of high-volume production; difficult to maintain machinery

How and why products are manufactured using ICT: computer-integrated manufacture (CIM)

Computer-integrated manufacturing (CIM) systems

CIM describes planned systems in which sub systems are linked electronically. A CIM system uses ICT to integrate all aspects of a company's operations (production, business and manufacturing information) in order to create more efficient production lines.

CIM systems:

- Allow closer control over the production process, as all information is readily available and can be processed automatically
- Allow information about stock levels to be instantly available and many ordering operations can be automated
- Allow a number of people to work on a project at the same time (concurrent engineering)
- Allow the increased use of automated stock handling and manufacturing operations, for example through the use of robots and CNC equipment
- Increase the effectiveness of quality control using automated sensing systems
- Increase efficiency by combining CAD and CAM systems
- Increase flexibility and responsiveness by allowing changes to designs or production processes to be made quickly
- Allow better planning decisions to be made based on instantly available, accurate data
- Reduce operational costs by reducing the need for labour

Examiner's Tip

There are only four 'scales of production' to learn for this section: one-off, batch, high-volume and continuous production. One-word answers are not sufficient and each reason you give must be justified.

Table 1.11 Explaining why a scale of production has been chosen

One-off production of a sports trophy	It needs to be original and can be customised to reflect the sporting event. There will only be one winner at the sporting event so only one trophy is required. One-off production enjoys low capital (setting up) costs. Changes to the design can be incorporated more easily during production.
Batch production of sporting medals	There is only limited demand for the medals as the design will reflect the specific sporting event. Batch production is less labour intensive than one-off production, leading to lower costs. The metals and casting process is particularly suitable for batch production. Materials can be bought in bulk to reduce costs.

Table 1.11 Explaining why a scale of production has been chosen *(continued)*

High-volume production of novelty mascots	High-volume production can take advantage of more automation leading to higher efficiency and lower costs. Work can be divided into simple, repetitive tasks, which is suitable for cheap unskilled labour. As the sporting event will be televised, the market will be global leading to a high level of demand. It is cost effective to use automated quality control systems ensuring the production of high-quality products.
Continuous production of sports drinks bottles	Rapid, non-stop production makes optimum use of capital investment in machines and premises. The PET plastic bottles are a standard design which can be customised by adding appropriate labels. The large amount of materials required means that prices can be negotiated with the suppliers at lower rates. Minimal labour is required which reduces unit costs and human error.

EXAMINATION QUESTION

Example question and answer. (This question refers to the photographs and product description on pages 13 and 14.)

 *c) Give **four** reasons why the toy train and packaging is batch-produced.* **(4 marks)**

Acceptable answer

The train is part of a **large product range which changes** from time to time so it would be **uneconomic to set up for high-volume production**.

The plastic **wheels can be injection moulded** which means that they could be produced quickly in large numbers, relatively cheaply once the initial set up costs had been covered.

The clear PET plastic packaging is **suitable for vacuum forming** which is ideal for batch production requiring **little or no finishing** so there is less need for skilled labour **leading to reduced production costs**.

The cartonboard is suitable for the **offset lithography** printing process that would make it **easier to modify the design**, such as changing the **language** when exporting to a new country.

Manufacturing processes

In this part of the examination, examiners are looking for knowledge and understanding of the stages of manufacture of the product. You should use technical terms and diagrams wherever possible. Try to avoid making detailed references to quality control and safety testing here because you will be asked about these later in the exam. You should divide your time according to the marks available. These may change from year to year. When answering questions, it is vital that you refer to specific product materials, components, production processes and so on. General responses will receive little or no marks.

You need to

understand that one-off, batch and high-volume/continuous manufacture of products is achieved through:

☐ preparation
☐ processing
☐ assembly
☐ finishing.

KEY TERMS
Check you
understand these terms

Preparation, Stock control, JIT, Processing,
Assembly, Finishing

**Further information can be found
in *Advanced Design and Technology
for Edexcel Product Design: Graphics with
Materials Technology*, Unit 1.**

KEY POINTS

Preparation

Before manufacturing can start it is necessary to
prepare materials, tools, equipment and
components. **Preparation** deals with the
preparation for the manufacture of a given
product. *Do not refer to design and prototyping
stages.* You should refer to specialist tools or
equipment in your answer.

Stock control and just in time (JIT)

Companies are always seeking ways of reducing
costs. Maintaining high levels of products,
components and raw materials incurs
significant costs.

- Capital is tied up in raw materials,
  components, sub-assemblies and unsold
  products.
- Too much stock at the point of production
  can create safety issues and lead to
  deterioration.
- Storage of raw materials, components,
  sub-assemblies and unsold products costs
  money.

This is particularly significant for high-volume
manufacturers. On the other hand, stock
shortages in one section of the production line
can halt production altogether. **Stock control**
is the processes of managing raw materials,
components and finished products so that they
are available when needed. **JIT** is a
management philosophy which seeks to
minimise costs. In the automotive industry
some components are manufactured by
suppliers literally hours before they are
required at the factory. They are delivered to
the production line so that each component
arrives in the correct order. The result is that
each product is manufactured to the
specification of an individual customer.

Table 1.12 Examples of preparation for manufacture

Stock control and JIT	Raw materials and pre-manufactured standard components are ordered and stored on delivery. Quality control: materials and pre-manufactured standard components in stock are inspected for defects. JIT systems are planned with suppliers so materials/components will arrive as required on the production line.
Production of specialist tools and equipment	Moulds are machined for injection moulding/vacuum forming/blow moulding. Dies are made for cold forming/die casting/die cutting/embossing. Formers are constructed for glass reinforced plastic/carbon fibre forming processes. Patterns are constructed for casting processes. Jigs are made to simplify repetitive manufacturing processes.
Print planning	Paper, card, ink and standard components are bought in and inspected for defects/level of quality. Paper or card is cut to the correct size and shape suitable for the printing press. The printing plates or silk screens are manufactured and checked for quality. Printing machines are cleaned and set up for the new print run. Dies are made and assembled into the die cutting machines. Printing presses are set up and adjusted for the print run – inks, plates and finishing materials are introduced. An initial test run is performed to check colour registration/colour quality/quality of print finishes.

Standard components

Standard components can be regarded as those components which have been 'bought in' from specialist suppliers. It makes economic sense for manufacturers to buy in some components rather than invest in machinery to make what are sometimes very specialised components. Standard components can be separated into three categories.

Processing

The **processing** stage starts at the point where manufacturing begins and should not be confused with the earlier preparation stage or later assembly stage.

Table 1.13 Components

Component	Examples
Standard components	Nuts, bolts, washers, nails, screws, rivets, self-tapping screws
Specialised components	Gears, bushes, bearings, cams, closures (such as bottle tops)
Sub-assemblies	Complete printed circuit boards, gearbox assemblies, cam mechanisms

Table 1.14 Black and white and full colour printing processes

Process	Description	Uses	Advantages
Offset lithography	Based upon the principle that water and oil do not mix; rollers apply image to paper; not suitable for all types of paper due to water use. • The plates are dampened and then inked, one for each colour. • The paper is fed into the printing press. • The image is transferred to a blanket cylinder and onto the paper or card. • Special print effects or finishes are applied (such as hot foil blocking, spot varnishing).	Business cards and stationery; brochures; posters; magazines; newspapers; packaging including plastics, paper and boards	• Wide range of machines available, small and large, so suitable for short and long runs • Good-quality photographic reproduction although colour can vary due to water and dyes used • Inexpensive process • High speed
Screen printing	Colours are forced through screens which contain stencils to produce areas of colour. • The prepared screen is placed over the material to be printed. • Ink is introduced and forced through the screen using a squeegee. • The image is allowed to dry and the process is repeated for the other colours.	T-shirts; sports bags; posters; card, plastic and metal signage; control panels; point of sale displays; binders and document wallets; mouse mats	• Thick opaque inks are good for simple designs with blocks of colour rather than fine detail • Inexpensive to set up so suitable for short runs • Fast, commercial machines available • Suitable for most materials
Letterpress (and flexography)	Relief printing process using a metal or flexible polymer plate; high cost; slow process so usually employed for short runs. Number of colours limited. • Ink is transferred onto the plate cylinder or platen. • Paper or card is fed into the press. • Pressure is applied to transfer the image and the printed sheets are ejected.	Text in books; letterheads and business cards; flexography is widely used to print on 'difficult' surfaces such as plastic bags or corrugated card	• Dense, opaque inks can be used to produce very high-quality prints so ideal for products such as business cards which need visual impact but do not require a range of colour

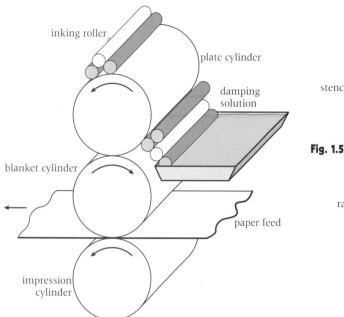

Fig. 1.4 Offset lithography printing process

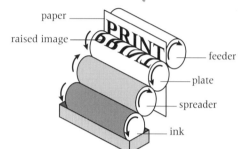

Fig. 1.5 Screen printing process

Fig. 1.6 Letterpress process

Table 1.15 Print finishes

Process	Description	Uses
Die cutting	Die cutting is a machine process that involves punching out, scoring and creasing. The die is a sharp metal blade, which can be manufactured to any shape in order to cut the appropriate shape or hole. Blunt blades are used for creasing.	Pop up cards and books, packaging nets, gift cards
Cutting	Guillotines are used in both manual and automated cutting processes. **CNC** cutting machines use adjustable gauges to position the material and more than one blade.	Most printed sheet materials such as posters, flyers, menus
Folding	Folding can be a manual or automated process. Publications produced in volume use automated folding machines where pages are forced into a slot along the fold, which is compressed by rollers. In books this process produces signatures (a section of a book printed from one plate which is cut, folded and collated).	Books, leaflets, packaging
Varnishing	Liquid coatings are applied during or after the printing process to enhance aesthetic or mechanical properties. Spot varnishes are applied to enhance areas of the design.	Glossy book covers, glossy packaging, glossy highlights
Laminating	Paper, aluminium foil and/or plastic (polythene or PET) layers are bonded to paper and card products in order to enhance their properties. Hot foil blocking is used to apply metal foils to areas of the design.	Orange juice cartons and vacuum packed coffee packs, chocolate bar wrappers and chocolate boxes
Embossing	An embossing die is used to produce raised features.	Book covers, food and confectionery packaging
Hot foil blocking	A heated die is used to apply the thin metal foil to the appropriate areas of the design.	Book covers, prestige packaging

Injection moulding

Liquid plastic is forced into a mould which is cooled to produce a wide range of products such as casings for electronic products and closures for packaging. The injection moulding process is described as follows: granules are poured into the hopper; the granules are heated; the screw pushes the softened granules forward; the plasticised (melted) material is forced into the mould; the mould is cooled (water flowing through mould); the ram is withdrawn, the mould opens; the hardened product is ejected from the mould with ejector pins; the mould closes and the process is repeated.

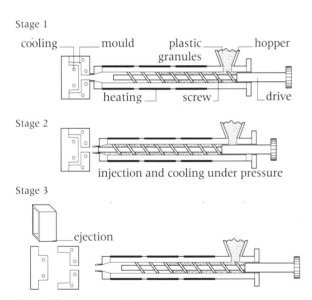

Fig. 1.7 The injection moulding process

Blow moulding

This process is used to produce hollow containers such as plastic bottles. The blow moulding process is described as follows: An extruded parison is inserted into a split mould; the spilt mould closes, sealing the parison at one end; hot compressed air forces the plastic into the shape of the mould; the mould is cooled and the plastic hardens; the mould

opens and the product is ejected; the process is repeated.

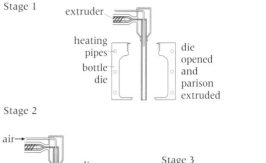

Fig. 1.8 The blow moulding process

Vacuum forming

The vacuum forming process is used to produce trays and containers such as chocolate box trays, yoghurt pots and blister packs. This process is also available in schools and is commonly used to form HDPS sheet. The

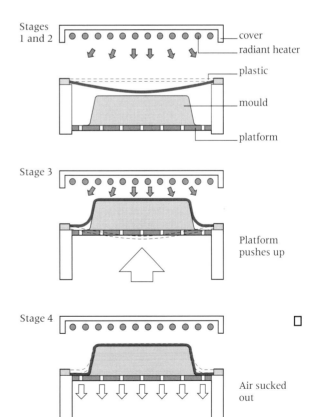

Fig. 1.9 The vacuum forming process

vacuum forming process is as follows: A mould is placed on the platen which is lowered (the mould must be tapered – draft angle – without undercuts, so that it can be removed); a plastic sheet is clamped into place above the mould; the heater is pulled over this plastic sheet; when the plastic sheet has softened the platen is raised; a pump expels the air which creates a vacuum causing the plastic to be forced over the mould; the platen is lowered and the mould is removed; waste material is trimmed.

The casting process

A cavity is created using a pattern (sand casting or die casting). Metal is then heated onto a molten state and poured or forced into the empty cavity; the molten metal then solidifies and the product is extracted and cooled. Sand casting is used to make products such as workshop vices, sculptures and brass name-plates. Die casting is used to make products such as pencil sharpeners and toys.

Making aids for accurate production

As part of the preparation process, manufacturers need to produce or order various pieces of equipment which will be used in the manufacturing stage. Using these will enhance the quality and accuracy of the final product. This equipment is shown in Table 1.16.

Table 1.16 Examples of making aids and standard components used to produce accurate products

Process/ equipment	Description
Jigs	Devices used to locate and hold work and to guide cutting tools.
Patterns	Either templates used to mark out materials (often sheet material such as fabric), or, specially produced equipment used to create a cavity for casting.
Templates	Marking out guides used by drawing around the pre-cut shape.
Formers	Used for forming materials to a desired shape, such as when bending plastics or metals to a set angle.
Moulds	The equipment used to form liquid materials, such as molten plastic in injection moulding.
Standard components	Standard, 'bought in' components are often used because they are tried and tested accurate designs.

Cutting and abrading (wasting and bending)

Materials can also be formed by manual or automated cutting and abrading processes. For example:

Table 1.17 Shaping materials

Method	Description	Tools or processes
Cutting	Cutting involves tools such as saws, which use teeth, or scissors which use a shearing action to cut through materials.	Hack saws, tenon saws, scissors, guillotines, die cutters, guillotines
Wasting	Tools which shape material by turning unwanted parts into unusable waste.	Files, surforms, wood planes, saws, drills, chisels, turning tools, files, milling and screw cutters
Abrading	Tools which shape or finish material by a grinding or 'rubbing' action. Some forms of engraving employ miniature grinders.	Glass paper (wood), emery cloth (metal), wet and dry paper (plastic), polishing, disc grinder
Bending	Many materials can be bent to form new shapes. Sometimes heat is applied to soften the material or, in the case of card, the material is weakened by creasing or scoring.	Line bending of plastics, cold/heat bending of metals, scoring and creasing of cards e.g. buckle folding machine

- castings need to be cleaned up using cutting equipment or grinders to remove unwanted material
- printed material needs to be cut to size using guillotines.

The use of ICT in the processing stage

Computer technology is used extensively to manage and control production. CNC (Computer Numerical Control) machines are controlled by computers which generate instructions called G and M codes. These G and M codes translate the design drawn on the computer screen into a language that will be understood by the CNC machine. Examples of computer controlled machinery include CNC milling machines, lathes, routers, laser cutters; CNC engraving machines; computer controlled printing processes; computer controlled guillotines; CNC plotter cutters/vinyl cutters and computer controlled die cutting machines.

Assembly

Assembly starts after all the component parts have been manufactured. Designers will incorporate features to simplify the process of assembly such as slot and tabs in card packaging. A schedule is created which determines the order in which components are assembled. More complex products require collation (collating), which involves organising the components into the correct order and quantity. Much of the process is carried out manually on production lines although the use of automated machinery is becoming more common. Careful checks and tests are also carried out against the specification at this stage to ensure that all parts are fitted correctly and accurately.

Examiner's Tip

The examiner will be looking for *good-quality* sketches in this section. Make sure that you include well-annotated diagrams that enhance your answers. Remember that there will be marks allocated for clear and appropriate diagrams.

Table 1.18 Examples of assembly processes

Mechanical	Adhesives	Binding (such as books and magazines)
• Product components are assembled using appropriate components such as screws, self-tapping screws, rivets, nuts and bolts. • Knock-down fittings are the standard components used to join flat-pack furniture. • Injection moulded polymer components can be designed to slot together without the need for additional fastenings. • Boxes and cartons can be folded and assembled using slots and tabs. • Inserts/trays/protective packing are inserted into packaging.	• Permanent adhesives are applied to appropriate points and used to bond packaging together. • Promotional materials such as cosmetic samples or CDs are glued onto the cover of magazines using semi permanent adhesives. • PVA is a strong adhesive for papers and woods. • Solvent welding cements are used to join thermoplastics such as polystyrene and acrylic. • Thermosetting adhesives (epoxy adhesives) are heat resistant and provide high-strength joints for dissimilar materials.	• The pages are folded and collated so that the pages are correctly ordered. • Perfect binding is used on magazines and paperbacks. The folded sections have the back fold trimmed off and glue is spread down the spine before the cover is glued on. • In saddle stitching a booklet is opened over a 'saddle' and stapled along the back fold before final trimming. • Sewn binding is used for hard-back books, which are sewn with threads down each section.

There are three methods of assembly:

- mechanical
- adhesives
- binding.

These assembly processes can be divided into semi-permanent and permanent fastenings.

- Semi-permanent or temporary fastenings include nuts, bolts, screws and some temporary adhesives or bindings. These are used where the joint has to be dismantled.
- Permanent fastenings are those in which one or more of the components has to be destroyed to separate the joints. In packaging this creates a tamper-evident product. In other products the use of strong adhesives prevents the product from coming apart.

> ### ✏ Examiner's Tip
>
> Remember, repeated points or general statements may not be credited. All your points must be justified.

Finishing

Finishing products

Products can be enhanced using a range of **finishing** processes. In general, finishes should be colourfast with a uniform colour and texture; not run, peel or blister; resist environmental and operating conditions (corrosion or mistreatment); resist physical damage (wear or scratching); resist staining or discoloration; and be easy to keep clean.

Examples of finishes applied to materials and products include:

- Surface coating – dip coating; paints; anodising; preservatives; lamination
- Applied finishes – varnish; lacquer; paints
- Self-finishing (requires little or no finishing in some instances) – hand-shaped plastics; some laser-cut plastics; injection moulding; blow moulding; vacuum forming; die casting
- Surface decoration – engraving; etching; vinyl transfer

- Print finishes – lamination, embossing; varnishing; cutting; die cutting; folding

Finishing ready for distribution

Final checks take place at this point, and you may refer to these in your answers for this section. For example:

- final quality control checks/inspections against the original specification take place
- adhesive labels or tags are applied to some products to show that the product meets UK or international standards.

Once a product has been processed, assembled and finished it is necessary to prepare it for despatch. The following processes are all designed to provide extra protection for the products during transit, and to make them easier to handle.

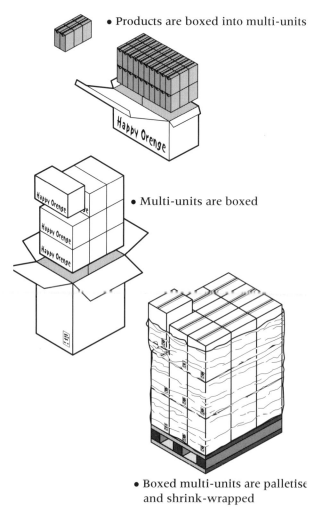

- Products are boxed into multi-units

- Multi-units are boxed

- Boxed multi-units are palletise and shrink-wrapped

Fig. 1.10 Finishing ready for distribution

- packing into multi-units with other products into more manageable packages
- boxing of units or multi-units
- palletising of units or multi-units
- shrink-wrapping of multi-units or boxes
- transporting pallets to warehouse for storage or distributed to customers/suppliers/retailers.

Examiner's Tips

It is possible that the same answer could be used more than once in this section but *you will not be awarded marks for repeating answers.* Make a quick check to ensure that you have not used the same answer more than once.

- Look carefully at the marks allocated to each section. This will give you a good idea of how many points to include in your response.

Table 1.19 Examples of finishing processes

Finishing processes	
Anodising	The aluminium components of a product are anodised to prevent oxidation, and dyes are added to enhance visual impact.
Preservatives	The wood parts of a product are painted with preservative to provide resistance from fungal and insect damage.
Varnishing	The cover of a publication is spot varnished to enhance aspects of the design.
Paints	The steel parts of a product are painted to protect against rust (corrosion) and to enhance aesthetic qualities.
Lamination	A poster is laminated to increase its strength and durability, and to allow it to be wiped clean.
Shrink-wrapping	Multi-units are shrink wrapped allowing them to be handled more easily.

EXAMINATION QUESTION

Example question and answer. (This question refers to the photographs and product description on pages 13 and 14.)

 Q1 *d) Describe, using notes and sketches where appropriate, the stages of manufacture of the toy train and packaging under the following headings.*

- *preparation (of tools, equipment and components)* **(5 marks)**
- *processing* **(5 marks)**
- *assembly* **(3 marks)**
- *finishing.* **(3 marks)**

*Include reference to industrial manufacturing methods in your answer. It is **not** necessary to include detailed reference to quality control and safety testing in this section.*

Acceptable answer

Moulds are **machined for injection moulding** of the wheels. **Paper, card, ink and standard components are bought in** and inspected for defects/level of quality. **Dies** are made and **assembled into the die cutting machines**. The **mould/former** is made for **vacuum forming clear plastic bubble**. **Lithographic printing presses** are set up and **adjusted** for the print run of the leaflet.

The **card is printed** using **lithography**. Print finishes, such as **varnishing**, are applied. The **printed cartonboard** is **die-cut** to shape. The **wheels** are **injection moulded**. The **clear PET, snap-together packaging** is **vacuum formed**.

The **wheels** are **attached to the axles** and **assembled onto the toy train** using snap-on fasteners. The **magnets** are **screwed securely** to the body of the train. The **product and leaflet are inserted** into the packaging before it is **sealed**.

The **packaged toys** are **multi-packed** into suitable boxes for ease of handling. The **boxes** are **palletised and shrink-wrapped** so they can be transported easily using forklift trucks. The **palletised boxes** are **stored** ready for distribution.

Quality

In this part of the examination, you need to make reference to a specific stage of manufacture, explain what exactly is being checked and how it is being checked. Remember to avoid discussing safety in this part of the examination.

You need to

☐ **understand quality control in production**
☐ **understand quality standards.**

KEY TERMS

Check you understand these terms

Quality assurance (QA), Total quality management (TQM), Quality control (QC), Sampling, Quality standards (QS)

Further information can be found in *Advanced Design and Technology for Edexcel, Product Design: Graphics with Materials Technology*, **Unit 1.**

KEY POINTS

Quality control in production

Quality assurance (QA)

Quality assurance is an overall approach adopted by a company to ensure that high-quality standards are maintained throughout an organisation. The use of QA ensures that identical products are manufactured on time, to specification and budget. All activities within a company – standards, procedures, documentation and communication systems – are established and monitored. Quality becomes everyone's responsibility.

Total quality management (TQM)

This is an approach to management which seeks to establish the highest possible standards of quality within every part of a company and in every stage of manufacture from designing a product to obtaining feedback from customers. The features of **total quality management** include:

- a commitment to continuous improvement for the complete lifestyle of a product
- control over raw materials, a record at every production stage to aid product/process improvement and a reduction in waste/reworking and customer satisfaction
- quality is built in and monitored at every stage of production, to enable the product to be made 'right first time'
- the reputation of the company is enhanced, resulting in repeat orders and increased profitability
- manufacturers of batch and high-volume products who demonstrate the use of a total quality management (TQM) system throughout the company can apply for ISO 9000, the international standard of quality.

Quality control (QC)

Quality control is the practical part of quality assurance. It ensures high standards during production and aims to create a system with zero faults. It is achieved by setting up a system of inspection, checks and tests which will be carried out at critical control points (CCPs) during manufacturing. It is often impossible to inspect every component against standards and specifications, so **sampling** is used where inspection takes place at planned intervals. These specifications and standards need to provide clear details about materials, dimensions and tolerances, processes and assembly.

Most quality control checks will be made during the processing, assembly and finish stages and include:

- continuous, automated inspection using sensors and electronic devices
- visual inspection of random samples against predetermined test specifications (for example, testing critical dimensions)

- inspections and testing of components or products (for example, using x-ray or ultrasound)
- inspections and testing of specific machinery
- testing samples to destruction.

Quality control during final print run

Automated printing processes make use of a variety of quality checking methods. Visual checks form an important part of the quality control process but accurate testing can only be carried out with the use of sensors and electronic equipment. Quality control checks are carried out on the printed control strip incorporated on the waste areas of the printed sheet. Checking registration marks, greyscale values and colour bars periodically, ensures correct image registration and colour/tonal balance. Colour density (thickness) can be measured on the colour bar using a device called a densitometer. Crop marks are also printed on the waste areas to show where the paper or card should be cut after printing. It is a simple task to check that cutting operations and crop marks match.

Meeting specifications and tolerances

Quality is measured against the product specification and agreed quality standards. Each specification point must be measurable so that valid checks can be made. Because most products will function perfectly well with small imperfections, tolerances are used. Tolerance is the 'margin of error' or degree of imperfection allowed in a product or component. Tolerances can be checked manually through visual inspections or by using sophisticated probes and sensors. Tolerances can be set for any property including size, weight, colour and strength.

Examiner's Tip

In order to score marks in this section, it is important to be specific in your answers. Ask yourself: what steps does the manufacturer have in place to ensure quality? You must identify the nature of the quality check and the procedure under inspection.

Table 1.20 Examples of quality control in production

Preparation	Suppliers are contacted to ensure that they are registered ISO 9000 companies to ensure the supply of quality raw materials. Moulds for the injection moulding process are checked by eye for manufacturing flaws. CNC milling machines are calibrated and tested manually to ensure that they are working within tolerances. All lithographic plates are inspected manually for flaws prior to printing the first proofs (test pages).
Processing	Colour density of printing process is checked using a densitometer/visual inspection. Colour registration is checked automatically using sensors to ensure plate alignment. Dies from die cutters are inspected manually at regular intervals to check sharpness of cutting edges. Critical dimensions of the component are measured to check that they are within tolerance.
Assembly	Samples of packaging are checked manually for faults in permanent closures. Magazine inserts and semi permanent adhesives are inspected manually to check that they do not fall out. Visual inspections of book bindings are made to make sure that pages are held securely. The contents are checked through sampling to ensure that the correct quantity have been included.
Finish	Samples of the finished, printed and varnished product are inspected to check for smudges. Visual inspection of the vinyl lettering is carried out to check for accuracy of alignment. Visual inspections are made of the polished plastic to check for defects such as scratches. The painted surface of the product is checked by eye to make sure there are no runs.

Quality standards

Most **quality standards** are set at the request of industry or government to ensure that products are safe and reliable. Standards organisations establish:

- safety and product specifications
- testing procedures
- quality assurance techniques.

Products which meet the appropriate standards are permitted to carry recognised logos such as the BSI 'Kitemark' or the CE logo, but companies need to demonstrate that quality control systems are in place to ensure that products will continue to meet these standards.

Standards organisations include:

- BSI: The British Standards Institute (the Kitemark logo)
- CEN: The European Committee for Standardisation (the CE logo)
- ISO: International Standards Organisation (ISO 9000 is a commonly used QA standard).

Fig. 1.11 Standards symbols – the Kitemark logo and the CE logo

Products must meet aesthetic, performance and price requirements in order to reach appropriate quality standards.

Examples of quality standards checks

- The functions of the product are tested to ensure that it performs to an acceptable standard.
- Filled boxes are weighed to ensure that quantities of the product fall within tolerances.
- Mechanical components are checked over time to ensure that wear and tear does not interfere with performance, over the specified lifespan of the product.
- Cast components are measured to check that critical dimensions fall within tolerances.
- Components are tested to destruction to ensure that they meet acceptable standards for strength and durability.

EXAMINATION QUESTION

Example question and answer. (This question refers to the photographs and product description on pages 13 and 14.)

Q1 *e) Discuss the quality issues associated with the toy train and packaging through:*

- quality control in production **(4 marks)**
- quality standards. **(4 marks)**

Acceptable answer
Quality control in production:

The **moulds** used for the injection moulding process need to be **inspected visually for wear and tear** at regular intervals between production runs. **Samples** of the toy trains should be taken periodically and **checked** to ensure that the **beech is sufficiently durable (using impact tests)** and **free from defects such as knots**. During the lithographic printing process, used to print the cartonboard packaging, **colour density** needs to be **inspected using a densitometer**. It is also important to avoid product rejection due to **inaccurate die cutting**: the cartonboard packaging should be **checked visually** on the production line through periodic **sampling**.

Quality standards:

The PET plastic, snap-together packaging needs to be **checked manually** to ensure that it **locates** accurately during assembly, enabling the product to fulfil its performance requirements. The **finish** on the toy train should be **inspected visually** to ensure that there are no **scratches or imperfections** resulting from manufacturing or handling. The packaging should be **tested for strength** to ensure that it will protect the toy trains and will not come apart during transit and while on display. The running mechanism is **tested, using a specialist machine, continuously over an extended period to simulate a child playing** with the train. The mechanism must be **sufficiently durable to operate for a pre-determined length of time, without failure,** in order to meet the appropriate quality standard.

Health and safety

In this part of the examination, you should show that you understand the principles of health and safety legislation and good manufacturing practice.

You need to

☐ **understand the safe use of the product**
☐ **understand safety procedures in production.**

KEY TERMS

Check you
understand these terms

Legislation, Health and safety, Risk assessment, Hazards

Further information can be found in *Advanced Design and Technology for Edexcel, Product Design: Graphics with Materials Technology*, Unit 1.

KEY POINTS

Safe use of the product

As consumers and workers we are protected by:

• national **legislation** (laws)

• national and international safety, quality and testing organisations such as the BSI.

We have a right to expect that manufacturers and advertisers will not mislead us and that their products will not harm us when used in accordance with instructions. We also expect these products to function properly and to be of sufficient quality to last for a reasonable length of time. Where hazards cannot be eliminated, manufacturers have a responsibility to identify them clearly.

The following are some examples of safety issues applying to the use of the product.

• Products which conform to recognisable national and international standards organisations such as BSI can be regarded as safe.
• Small, easily detachable components can cause a choking hazard and should be identified where appropriate.
• Sharp edges can cause severe injuries and should be removed during manufacture if possible.
• Flammable material should be minimised, especially in building materials and furniture.
• Toxic substances must be clearly identified using recognisable symbols (COSHH).
• Hazardous products must include detailed and clear instructions for storage and use.

- All products must be clearly labelled providing any important safety information.
- Food ingredients must be clearly identified to reduce the risk of allergic reactions.
- Children's products should give some recommendation for age range, and appropriate safety instructions.
- Plastic packaging can cause suffocation and should carry appropriate warnings.

Safety procedures in production

Employers, manufacturers and retailers have a duty of care to protect us from potential hazards (sources of potential harm). Where the use of dangerous products or materials is unavoidable, manufacturers have a duty to warn users of potential hazards and to provide adequate protection and training. Legislation (laws) and regulations exist to ensure that employers fulfil their responsibilities. These include:

- legislation such as the Factories Act (1961) and the management of Health & Safety at Work regulations (1992)
- regulations and codes of practices (such as COSHH).

The Health and Safety Executive (HSE) is the regulatory body that ensures that companies comply with this legislation. They have the power to enter and inspect premises in relation to **health and safety** matters.

Risk assessment

It is a statutory requirement for employers and other organisations such as schools to carry out **risk assessments** in order to eliminate or reduce the chances of accidents happening. There are five steps involved in risk assessment.

1 Identify the **hazard** (danger).
2 Identify people at risk.
3 Evaluate the risk.
4 Decide on control measures.
5 Record assessment.

The investigation and analysis of such hazards would take into account some of the following aspects when looking at the production of a product.

- Adhering to appropriate health and safety regulations in line with company policy on working practices.
- Organising appropriate training of staff using machines and handling of tools and materials.
- Guarding machines, especially those which involve human intervention or control.
- The installation and maintenance of appropriate space, ventilation, heating, light and noise levels.
- The incorporation of fail-safe devices and emergency stops on all automated machinery.
- The regular inspection and servicing of machines, and the keeping of log books.
- The installation of appropriate health and safety notices around the factory and near machines.
- Ensuring the correct use of personal protective equipment (PPE).
- Ensuring that risk assessments have been carried out.
- Making sure that COSHH data is provided along with appropriate first aid instructions.
- Ensuring that hazardous substances are stored appropriately.
- Providing healthy working conditions for employees including adequate breaks.

Examiner's Tip

When you are discussing safety in the workplace, do not be tempted to write a long list of clothes: apron, safety shoes, gloves etc. The examiner will treat these as one answer, and you will only receive one mark for mentioning safety clothing.

EXAMINATION QUESTION

Examination question and answer. (This question refers to the photographs and product description on pages 13 and 14.)

 f) Discuss the health and safety issues associated with the production of the toy train and packaging under the following headings.

- safe use of the child's toy and packaging **(4 marks)**
- safety procedures in the production of the child's toy and packaging. **(4 marks)**

Acceptable answer

The manufacturer must **check that the product meets European standards** and can be sold across the EU in order to **display the CE mark**. It is important to ensure that **all the materials and finishes** used are completely **non-toxic**. The toy should be finished to **remove all sharp and** **protruding edges** which could **cause cuts**. The product and packaging should **not cause any environmental harm** and should be suitable for **recycling**.

The plastic components are **injection moulded** and it is important that the operators of the equipment are **fully trained**. Suitable **ventilation and extraction** should be installed and maintained to remove toxic fumes generated by the injection moulding process. **Risk assessments** should have been completed for **all equipment and machines** identifying any potential risks so that hazards can be eliminated. While no hazardous materials are used directly in the manufacture of the toy, other potentially **dangerous chemicals, fumes and substances used during production, such as oils and solvents** must be **carefully controlled, handled and stored according to COSHH regulations** so that the workplace remains safe for all the employees.

Product appeal

In this part of the examination, you will explain the appeal of the product. Remember that the examiner is not asking whether you would buy the product. In order to be objective you need to explain why the product would appeal to the target market group.

You need to

☐ **know the influences on the design, production and sale of products.**

 KEY TERMS
Check you understand these terms

Form, Function, Trends/styles, Cultural issues

 Further information can be found in *Advanced Design and Technology for Edexcel Product Design: Graphics with Materials Technology*, **Unit 1.**

KEY POINTS

Influences on the design, production and sale of products

It is not easy to evaluate the potential success of a design because judgements are necessarily influenced by personal tastes. However, it is possible to identify factors which influence a design and to predict how these will influence sales to the target market or target market group (TMG). The company will hope to persuade the TMG to buy the product.

The factors which influence design, production and product sales include:

- artistic factors influenced by the work of artists
- cultural factors influenced by cultural customs and beliefs
- economic factors influenced by the prevailing economic conditions and customer wealth
- environmental factors influenced by environmental issues

- ethical and moral factors influenced by values and beliefs
- political and social factors influenced by the political situation and social conventions
- the target market and market trends: the influence of tastes, fashions and trends of the TMG
- lifestyle and demographic factors influenced by market research profiling of populations and their lifestyles
- aesthetic factors such as style and colour influenced by prevailing fashions for certain colours
- cost, performance and after-sales factors influenced by customer expectations and competition.

In the exam you are being asked to decide how the product has been designed to appeal to the target market under the following headings.

Form

Form is the three-dimensional size and shape of an object. You need to describe how the form of a product appeals to the target market group.

Function

You need to explain how well the product performs its **functions**. Do not forget that the separate materials and component parts also have individual functions within the product. Remember to consider the packaging and whether it clearly informs the customer of the contents and displays prominent safety warnings.

Trends and styles

You need to explain how market **trends** (such as changes in sales/buying behaviour) and **styles** (fashions) are reflected in the product and how these help to attract the TMG.

- How does the style of the product appeal to the TMG?
- How does it fit in and enhance the lifestyle/image of the TMG?
- Does the colour/style meet with current market trends?

Cultural

The way we live as a society, our attitudes, our religions and customs can be defined as our culture. You need to explain how the product reflects **cultural issues**.

- Is the product recyclable or has it been made from recycled materials to appeal to environmentally concerned consumers?
- Does it have any special features, such as decoration, which are based on cultural elements? Is it designed to appeal to any particular cultural groups?
- Where will it be sold? What sort of retail outlet is likely to offer it for sale?
- Is it an inexpensive product of mass or global appeal or an expensive, luxury product which will appeal to a small number of customers?

Examiner's Tips

- Do not repeat yourself within this section. Do not make unspecific, unsupported or generalised comments. One-word answers are not sufficient. You should not simply rewrite the specification.
- The total marks available for each category will change depending upon the product chosen. Some categories may be left out completely. The marks for each section should tell you the number of justified points you should make. Remember, repeated points or general statements may not be credited. All your points must be justified.
- You may include negative comments if you are able to justify them. Check the marks for each category and make one justified point for each. For some products the examiner may remove one or more of the categories: form, function, trends/style and cultural issues. In these cases the 8 marks will be divided between those categories remaining.
- Three marks are awarded overall for the quality of written communication. In order to achieve all three marks, your written work must be clear, coherent and relevant. You should also take care to include appropriate specialist and technical language along with accurate spelling, punctuation and grammar.

EXAMINATION QUESTION

Example question and answer. (This question refers to the photographs and product description on pages 13 and 14.)

 g) Discuss the appeal of the toy train and packaging under the following headings.

- form   **(2 marks)**
- function   **(3 marks)**
- trend/styles   **(2 marks)**
- cultural issues.   **(1 mark)**

Acceptable answer

Form – The toy is **ergonomically designed** so that it is just the **right size and weight for a young child's hands**, and so will appeal to children. The design and form of the **packaging will appeal to retailers and customers** because it **protects the product** from damage during transit and display.

Function – The toy train is designed to **be used with other products** and will **appeal** to customers who **collect this brand of toy**. The **packaging incorporates a hole** and will **appeal** to retailers because it can be **displayed easily**. The **printed cartonboard** of the packaging will **appeal** to customers and retailers because it **displays clear and useful product information**.

Trends/styles – The use of **natural timbers, water-based paint and recycled packaging** materials is **becoming more important to customers and will encourage them to buy** the product. The product should **sell well because toys based on trains**, such as Thomas the Tank Engine, are **very popular**.

Cultural – The design of the **graphics** on the toy train and packaging should **not cause offence** to any cultural groups.

PRACTICE EXAMINATION STYLE QUESTION

Figure 1.12 shows an illustration of a multi-pack bottled drink product. Figure 1.13 shows detail of the closure (top) from one of the bottles.

Fig. 1.12 A multi-pack bottled drink product

Fig. 1.13 Detail of the closure from one of the bottles

The product consists of:
- a bottle
- a screw-on top which incorporates a resealable mouth-piece
- a tamper evident cover which needs to be broken before use
- printed cartonboard (card) multi-pack packaging
- a printed label around the bottle.

a) Outline the product specification for the illustrated fruit juice bottle, bottle top, packaging and label. Address at least **four** of the following headings.
   - function/purpose
   - performance
   - market
   - aesthetics/characteristics
   - quality standards
   - safety.   **(7 marks)**

b) Justify the use of:
   - PET for the bottle   **(3 marks)**
   - cartonboard (card) for the
     multi-pack packaging.   **(3 marks)**

c) Give **four** reasons why the fruit juice bottle is mass-produced.   **(4 marks)**

d) Describe, using notes and sketches, the stages of manufacture of the multi-pack packaging under the following headings.
   - preparation (of tools, equipment and components.)   **(4 marks)**
   - processing   **(6 marks)**
   - assembly   **(4 marks)**
   - finishing.   **(2 marks)**

   Include reference to industrial manufacturing methods in your answer. Do **not** include the production of card, cartonboard or plastics in your answer. Do **not** include detailed reference to quality control and safety testing in this section.

e) Discuss the quality of the fruit juice bottle, bottle top, multi-pack packaging and label under the following headings.
   - quality control in production   **(4 marks)**
   - quality standards.   **(4 marks)**

f) Discuss the health and safety issues associated with the fruit juice bottle, bottle top, multi-pack packaging and label and its production under the following headings.
   - safety of use of the fruit juice bottle   **(4 marks)**
   - safety procedures in the production of the fruit juice bottle.   **(4 marks)**

g) Discuss the appeal of the fruit juice bottle, bottle top, multi-pack packaging and label under the following headings.
   - form   **(3 marks)**
   - function   **(3 marks)**
   - trend/style   **(1 mark)**
   - cultural.   **(1 mark)**

   Quality of written communication: **(3 marks)**

Note: 3 marks are awarded overall for the quality of written communication. In order to achieve the full marks, your written work must include appropriate specialist vocabulary and excellent spelling, punctuation and grammar to communicate consistently with clarity, relevance and coherence. The quality of written communication also includes the correct and appropriate use of technical language.

Total for this question paper: **60 marks**

UNIT 3A Materials, components and systems (G301)

Unit 3 is divided into two sections.

- Section A: Materials, components and systems (compulsory for all candidates)
- Section B: Consists of two options (of which you will study only **one**).

Section A will be assessed during the $1\frac{1}{2}$ hour, Unit 3 examination. You should spend half of your time answering all of the questions for this section. It is important to use appropriate specialist and technical language in the exam along with accurate spelling, punctuation and grammar. Where appropriate, you should include clear, annotated sketches to explain your answer.

Much of the knowledge covered in this unit builds upon material covered in Unit 1. You should refer back to the previous chapter in order to prepare yourself fully for this examination.

Paper, cards and boards

You need to

- ☐ **know the sources and structure of paper, cards and boards**
- ☐ **know about the classification of paper, cards and boards.**

KEY TERMS
Check you
understand these terms

Wood pulp, Bonding agents, Sizing agents, Fourdrinier machines, Opacity

Further information can be found in *Advanced Design and Technology for Edexcel, Product Design: Graphics with Materials Technology*, Unit 3A, section 1.

KEY POINTS

The sources and structure of paper, cards and boards

Paper, cards and boards consist of processed wood fibres. However, other materials, such as cotton, straw and hemp, can also be used to create a product with modified properties. Softwoods produce longer fibres resulting in a stronger product whereas the shorter hardwood fibres produce a smoother, more opaque product.

The pulping process is designed to separate the wood fibres, which are bound together with a natural substance called lignin. Additives are used to improve the properties of most **wood pulps**. There are three basic methods of producing wood pulp: see Table 3.1.

Table 3.1 Methods of producing wood pulp

Pulping process	Process	Characteristics
Mechanical pulp	The timber is soaked, debarked, ground and screened	Inexpensive; high yield; lower quality; additives such as bleach (peroxide or sodium hydroxide) can be used to improve properties
Chemical pulp	The timber is debarked, cut into small chips, pounded and screened. The pulp is treated with chemicals (acids or alkalis) which remove unwanted constituents	Expensive; lower yield; higher quality due to lower level of impurities and formation of longer fibres
Waste pulp (recycled)	Recycled paper and card are pulped; impurities such as inks are removed chemically and/or mechanically	Low quality because recycling results in shorter fibres; properties can be improved with the addition of virgin fibres, **bonding agents, sizing agents** and pigments

Producing paper from wood pulp

Paper is produced on **Fourdrinier machines**. These are huge machines which produce paper in volume using a continuous process. The main stages of production are described in Fig. 3.2.

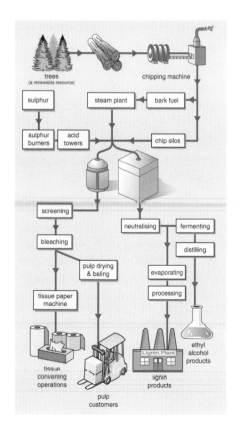

Fig. 3.1 The mechanical and chemical production of woodpulp

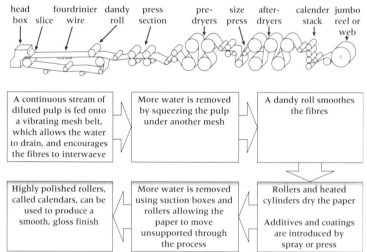

Fig. 3.2 Paper production on a Fourdrinier machine

The classification of paper, cards and boards

The common properties and working characteristics of papers and boards

There are hundreds of different types of paper and boards to choose from. They are used extensively by designers for modelling, and as materials for commercial packaging. The properties and working characteristics of papers and boards can be categorised by their size, weight or thickness, colour, **opacity** (opaque, translucent or transparent), surface finish and texture, cost, ability to accept graphic media, and ability to be cut, shaped and formed. Classifications of paper, card and board include:

- uncoated paper – for example, copier paper (80 gsm, lightweight, smooth, bright white or coloured, inexpensive) and newsprint (40–52 gsm, off-white, high proportion of recycled material)
- coated papers – for example, coated inkjet paper (80–150 gsm, bright white, high density, smooth, expensive) and photo glossy inkjet paper (140–230 gsm, bright white, very expensive)
- specialist papers – for example, embossed paper, wrapping paper and marbled paper (various types and weights, decorative surface or texture)
- card and board – for example, mounting board (1000–1500 microns, very thick, high quaity, very expensive, smooth or textured colour layer applied to one surface) cartonboard and corrugated board.

Additives and coatings

Additives and coatings are used to enhance the properties of paper: see Table 3.2.

Table 3.2 Additives and coatings to enhance the properties of paper

Bleach	Used to reduce colour impurities
Bonding agents	Used to help bind fibres together
Sizing agents	Used to improve paper quality by reducing absorbency (e.g. starch, resin, alum)
Pigments	Used to improve colour quality
Coatings	Used to improve paper quality
Laminates	Used to improve paper quality, strength and/or durability

EXAMINATION QUESTIONS

Example questions and answers

Using your knowledge of your specific area of study:

 *a) Give **two** methods of enhancing paper, card or board quality during manufacture.* **(2 marks)**

Acceptable answer
1 Bleaching
2 Laminating.

b) Outline the main stages of the Fourdrinier process used to manufacture paper in volume. **(8 marks)**

Acceptable answer
A **continuous stream of diluted pulp is fed onto a vibrating mesh belt**, which **allows the water to drain**, and encourages the **fibres to interweave**. More water is removed by **squeezing the pulp under another mesh and by using suction boxes and rollers** allowing the paper to move unsupported through the process. **Rollers and heated cylinders dry the paper.** At this stage **additives and coatings can be introduced by spray or press.** Finally, highly **polished rollers, called calenders**, can be **used to produce a smooth, gloss finish.**

Woods

KEY TERMS

Check you
understand these terms

Conversion, Seasoning, Softwoods, Hardwoods, Veneers, Cellular structure, Heartwood, Sapwood, Fibres, Grain

Further information can be found in *Advanced Design and Technology for Edexcel, Product Design: Graphics with Materials Technology*, Unit 3A, section 1.

KEY POINTS

Sources, classification and structure of woods

The structure of woods can be affected by a wide range of factors including:

• species of tree
• growing conditions
• natural features such as knots
• method of **conversion** (sawing timber into useable forms)
• method of **seasoning** (removing excess moisture from converted timber)
• storage environment faults and defects
• insect and fungal attack.

Softwoods are relatively fast-growing trees with straight trunks. As a result they are easier to manage and produce less waste. **Hardwoods** are generally more durable than softwoods. This is due to their denser grain structure. They offer much more variety in terms of colour, texture and figure (grain pattern). Since they take longer to grow, they are generally more expensive than softwoods. The most expensive and exotic species are often turned into **veneers** (thin sheets of timber) and used as laminates. Man-made boards are covered in Unit 1.

Table 3.3 The classification of wood

Classification	Sources	Structure and properties	Examples	Uses
Softwoods	Northern hemisphere coniferous forests (often managed) in the colder climates of North America and northern Europe	Fast growing (20 years); straight and tall trees; relatively inexpensive	Scots pine, red cedar, spruce	General building and constructional work; waste is used to produce paper and card; vacuum forming moulds; architectural models
Hardwoods	Most temperate regions of Europe, Japan and New Zealand; tropical/sub tropical areas of the world such as Central and South America, Africa and Asia	Slow growing (80 years); relatively expensive; durable	balsa, teak, jelutong, oak, ash, beech, mahogany	General constructional work; veneers

Table 3.4 The properties and uses of hardwoods and softwoods

Timber	Hard/soft	Origin	Properties/characteristics	Uses
Oak	Hardwood	Europe, USA	Hard and tough; Durable; Finishes well; Heavy; Contains an acid which corrodes steel	High-quality furniture; Garden benches; Boat building; Veneers
Mahogany	Hardwood	Central and South America	Easy to work; Durable; Finishes well; Prone to warping (going out of shape)	Indoor furniture; Interior woodwork; Window frames; Veneers
Beech	Hardwood	Europe	Hard and tough; Finishes well; Prone to warping; Turns well	Workshop benches; Children's toys; Interior furniture
Ash	Hardwood	Europe	Tough; Flexible (good elastic properties); Works and finishes well	Sports equipment; Ladders; Laminated furniture; Tool handles
Birch	Hardwood	Europe	Hard wearing	Plywood veneers
Pine (Scots)	Softwood	Northern Europe	Easy to work; Knotty and prone to warping	Constructional wood work (joists, roof trusses); Floorboards; Children's toys

Cellular structure, fibres and grain direction

The tree consists of two major parts, the **heartwood,** which gives the tree strength and rigidity, and the outer layers or **sapwood,** which are where the growth occurs. Growth takes place on a seasonal basis and results in the annual rings. One ring represents one year's growth. As the tree ages, the wood tissue develops in the form of long tube-like cells which vary in shape and size. These are known as **fibres**, which grow parallel to the trunk. The fibres give rise to the general **grain** direction and patterns in the wood. It is this variation in cell size and make-up which leads to the botanical distinction of hardwoods and softwoods.

Conversion

Conversion is the term given to the process of sawing logs into useable timber. The timber is cut in one of two ways: slab sawn or radial 'quarter' sawn. The method of conversion chosen is reflected in the price and affects the quality of the figure (grain pattern) and the dimensional stability of the timber.

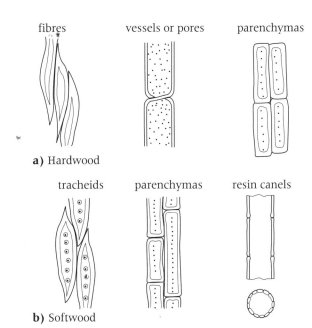

fibres   vessels or pores   parenchymas

a) Hardwood

tracheids   parenchymas   resin canels

b) Softwood

Fig. 3.3 The structure of hardwood and softwood cells

Table 3.5 The conversion of timber

Advantages of slab (plain or through and through) conversion	Advantages of quarter (radial) conversion
Quicker, simpler process; Less labour intensive; Less waste; Cheaper	More aesthetically pleasing; More stable: less likely to move, warp, bow or twist
a) slab sawn **Fig. 3.4a** Slab conversion	b) radial (quarter) sawn **Fig. 3.4b** Quarter conversion

Seasoning

The **seasoning** of wood is the process of reducing the excess water and moisture from the cell walls. Moisture content is reduced to less than 20 per cent so that the timber becomes:

- less prone to rot and decay
- less corrosive to metals
- stronger and more dimensionally stable.

EXAMINATION QUESTION

Example question and answer

 Q1 a) Outline **two** differences between hardwood and softwood. **(4 marks)**

Acceptable answer

Hardwoods are **derived from broad-leafed trees** which usually produce a **harder, stronger and denser grain**. Softwoods generally **come from faster-growing, coniferous trees** which makes the wood **cheaper.**

b) Explain the term 'conversion', using notes and sketches. **(3 marks)**

Acceptable answer

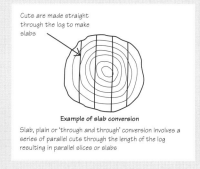

Cuts are made straight through the log to make slabs

Example of slab conversion

Slab, plain or 'through and through' conversion involves a series of parallel cuts through the length of the log resulting in parallel slices or slabs

Fig. 3.5a Slab conversion

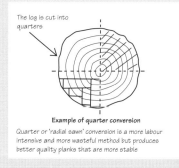

The log is cut into quarters

Example of quarter conversion

Quarter or 'radial sawn' conversion is a more labour intensive and more wasteful method but produces better quality planks that are more stable

Fig. 3.5b Quarter conversion

Metals and alloys

You need to

☐ **know the sources, classification, structure and processing of metals**
☐ **know about specialist metals.**

KEY TERMS
Check you understand these terms

Ferrous, Non-ferrous, Alloys

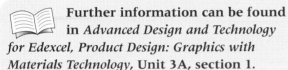

Further information can be found in *Advanced Design and Technology for Edexcel, Product Design: Graphics with Materials Technology*, **Unit 3A, section 1.**

KEY POINTS

The sources, classification, structure and processing of metals

The sources, classification and processing of metals

With the exception of gold, all metals are found in the form of oxides and sulphates. Metals are divided into three basic categories: **ferrous** metals, **non-ferrous** metals and **alloys**.

Table 3.6 The classification and processing of metals

Group	Properties	Processing	Source
Ferrous metals	Contain ferrite or iron; almost all are magnetic	The ore, coke (fuel) and limestone (to remove impurities) are heated to 1600°C in a blast furnace. The resulting pig iron is refined further and the carbon content is adjusted. Steel is produced in a basic oxygen furnace and poured into castings or ingots. The steel ingots are heated and rolled into standard sections. BDMS is oiled and cold drawn through dies. Other materials such as chromium and tungsten can be added to improve or change the properties of the ferrous metal.	Iron ores
Non-ferrous metals	Do not contain iron	Ores are crushed, processed, heated and refined. Pure metal is finally extracted using electrolysis. This is very expensive due to the high energy costs involved.	Bauxite (aluminium); copper ore
		Aluminium is the most abundant metal on the planet but large amounts of energy are needed to extract it from the ore (bauxite). Bauxite is mined, crushed and dried. The bauxite is dissolved in hot caustic soda and filtered to produce aluminium oxide. The aluminium oxide is roasted in a 'rotary kiln' to produce alumina. The alumina is dissolved in molten cryolite. A powerful current is passed between the carbon lined furnace (the electrolytic reduction cell) and carbon rods producing pure aluminium. The aluminium is tapped off and cast into ingots for further processing.	
Alloys	Ferrous and non-ferrous	Alloys are produced by melting together two or more metals, or occasionally metals and non-metals.	Metals and non-metals

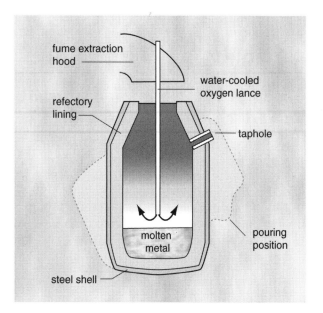

Fig. 3.6 The production of steel using a basic oxygen furnace

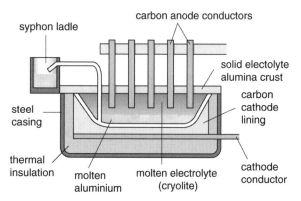

Fig. 3.7 Electrolytic reduction cell

The microstructure of metals

With the exception of mercury, all metals are solid at room temperature. In their molten statc, thcy arc wcak and flow easily. As the metal cools and solidifies small seed crystals are formed and the atoms arrange themselves in a regular pattern: a lattice structure. Finally small crystals and grains are formed. The properties of a metal will be affected by its crystalline structure.

Specialist metals

The properties of metals may be modified by combining them with other metals or non-metals. For example, carbon is added to iron to produce steel which is a much more versatile material.

Table 3.7 The microstructure of metals

Structure	Properties	Examples
Close-packed hexagonal (CPH)	Weak, poor strength to weight ratio	Zinc, magnesium
Face-centred cubic (FCC)	Ductile, good electrical conductor	Gold, copper, silver, aluminium
Body-centred cubic (BCC)	Hard, tough	Chromium, tungsten

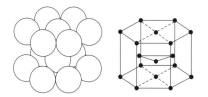

Fig. 3.8a Closed-packed hexagonal (CPH)

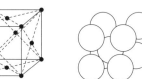

Fig. 3.8b Face-centred cubic (FCC)

Fig. 3.8c Body-centred cubic (BCC)

EXAMINATION QUESTIONS

Example questions and answers

 Q1 *a) The working properties of metals can be improved by alloying. Explain the term alloying and give a specific example of its use.* **(3 marks)**

Acceptable answer

Alloying is where **two or more elements** are added to a metal to **improve the parent**

metals qualities. For example, **copper and zinc might be alloyed to make brass** or brazing metal to produce a 'new' metal that has a **lower melting point** than the original copper.

*b) Iron and carbon are two elements in stainless steel. State **two** other alloying elements.* **(2 marks)**

Acceptable answer

Chromium and **tungsten**.

Plastics

You need to

☐ **know the sources, classification, structure and manufacture of polymers**
☐ **know about monomers, polymerisation and cross-linking**
☐ **know about thermosetting and thermoplastic polymers.**

 KEY TERMS

Check you understand these terms

Thermoplastics, Thermosetting plastics, Elastomers, Hydrocarbon naphtha, Monomers, Polymerisation, Van der Waals forces, Covalent bonding

---

Further information can be found in *Advanced Design and Technology for Edexcel, Product Design: Graphics with Materials Technology*, Unit 3A, section 1.

KEY POINTS

The sources, classification, structure and manufacture of polymers

Plastics fall into two categories.

• natural (from plants and animals)
• synthetic (man-made).

Classification of plastics

Synthetic plastics are by far the largest group and are derived largely from crude oil. Plastics are sub-divided into three groups: **thermoplastics, thermosetting plastics** and **elastomers**. The differences in the molecular structures of these groups lead to differences in properties and working characteristics.

The manufacture of plastics

1 Crude oil is refined in a fractioning tower to produce **hydrocarbon naphtha**.
2 The hydrocarbon naphtha is then 'cracked' (controlled breakdown of naphtha into **monomers**) to produce ethylene and propylene.
3 These simple molecules link up to form long chains through **polymerisation** (the formation of large chains of molecules).

Monomers, polymerisation and cross-links

Thermoplastics

Thermoplastics consist of long tangled chains of molecules with a limited number of smaller cross-links. The polymer chains are held weakly together by mutual attraction known as **Van der Waals forces**. The introduction of heat weakens the bonds and the material becomes pliable and easier to mould or form. When the heat is removed, the chains reposition and the material becomes stiff once again.

Thermosetting plastics

Thermosetting plastics are set with heat and thereafter have little plasticity. During polymerisation the molecules link side to side and end to end. This is known as **covalent bonding** and results in a very stiff and rigid microstructure. Once formed, they cannot be re-formed by heating.

Fig. 3.9a Thermoplastics — Van der Waals bonding

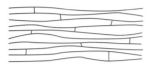

Fig. 3.9b Thermosetting plastics — covalent bonding

Thermosetting and thermoplastic polymers

Many plastics can be identified by internationally recognised symbols, which are used to help the sorting process during recycling. Thermoplastics are often used as packaging materials because they share some common properties. They are versatile, lightweight, low cost, energy saving,

Table 3.8 Properties of thermoplastics

Plastic	Significant properties	Uses	Advantages
LDPE (Low-density polythene) — 4 LDPE	Soft, flexible; excellent chemical resistance; good barrier to water but not gases	Stretch wrapping; liquid-proof coatings for card such as milk cartons; carrier and other plastic bags	When combined with card, LDPE becomes a very versatile and cost effective material; plastic bags perform well as an inexpensive method of producing a thin, protective layer for a wide range of goods
PP (polypropylene) — 5 PP	Very flexible; will withstand repeated folding; can be sterilised	Food containers; bags for dry food products such as pasta; bottle crates; slot-together boxes; yoghurt and margarine tubs; sweet and snack wrappers; video cases	Excellent chemical resistance means PP can be used where other plastics would be unsuitable; extremely tough and durable so will not break if dropped; flexibility and resistance to fatigue (wearing out) means that this material can be manufactured into boxes with 'integral' hinges which can be folded repeatedly without snapping or tearing
Acetate (cellulose triacetate – produced by reacting cellulose and acetic anhydride with sulphuric acid as a catalyst) — 7 OTHER	Thin, transparent sheet; flexible; low flammability	Cinema films; animation overlays; OHP films; printing; LCD screens for prototype models; windows for architectural models; windows in packaging; protective cover for two-dimensional presentation drawings	Flexible; easily joined using hot melt glue; easily cut; transparent (available in clear or a range of tints); certain forms can be used in printers and photocopiers

tough and durable, recyclable, impact resistant, and water-resistant. They can be made translucent or transparent, are available in a range of colours and forms (such as sheets, tubes, granules), can be thermoformed (shaped using heat) and printed.

EXAMINATION QUESTIONS

Example questions and answers

 a) Explain the term 'polymerisation'. **(2 marks)**

Acceptable answer
Polymerisation is the **formation of large chains of molecules** where the **molecules link side to side and end to end**.

b) Outline the difference between the structures of thermoplastics and thermosetting plastics. **(4 marks)**

Acceptable answer
Thermoplastics consist of **long tangled chains of molecules** with **small cross-links**. The chains are held together by **mutual attraction, known as Van der Waals forces** and as such they tend to be rather **flexible**. Thermosetting plastics **set with heat** and thereafter have **little plasticity** since the **molecules link side to side and end to end**. This is known as **covalent bonding** and results in a **very stiff and rigid microstructure**.

Composites and laminates

You need to

☐ **know about the manufacture of composite materials.**

 KEY TERMS
Check you understand these terms

Composites, MDF, Bonding, Laminates, Glass reinforced plastic (GRP), Carbon fibre

 Further information can be found in *Advanced Design and Technology for Edexcel, Product Design: Graphics with Materials Technology*, **Unit 3A, section 1.**

KEY POINTS

The manufacture of composite materials

Composites, such as **MDF**, are created by bonding two or more materials together. Reinforcing materials are held in a matrix by a **bonding** agent to produce a material that enhances the properties of its constituents.

Laminates consist of sheet materials built up in layers and impregnated with a bonding agent. 'Formica' consists of layers of paper bonded with a thermoset plastic resin. In industry manufacturers use fast, automated methods of production. This is essential for more cost effective, larger runs.

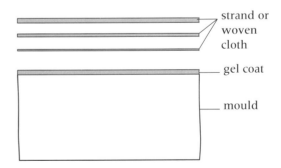

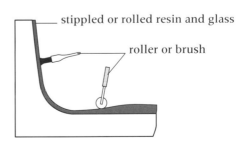

Fig. 3.10 The production of GRP components

Table 3.9 Composites and laminates

Material	Composition	Properties	Uses
Glass reinforced plastic (GRP or fibre glass)	A tapered mould is made taking care to avoid undercuts and sharp corners. Sealant and releasing agent are applied to the mould. Hardener and pigment are added to polyester resin. A 1mm-thick resin 'gelcoat' is applied to the mould and allowed to dry for around 30 minutes. Glass fibre matting is laid over the mould and pressed into the resin using rollers or by stippling with a brush. Alternate layers of resin and glass fibre are built up to an appropriate thickness. Excess material is removed. The resin is allowed to cure (24 hours) before the mould is separated, and the edges are finished when fully hardened.	Very good strength to weight ratio; tough glossy, water-resistant finish on surfaces in contact with mould; large, complex shapes possible; safety equipment must be used to protect from fumes and fine fibres	Sailing boat hulls; canoes; signage; garden pond liners
Carbon fibre	The production of carbon fibre products follows a similar process to that used for GRP, replacing the glass fibre matting with sheets of carbon fibre and a different resin.	Excellent strength to weight ratio; tough glossy finish on surfaces in contact with mould; large, complex shapes possible; safety equipment must be used	Aerospace components; sporting equipment such as fishing rods, rackets and skis; body armour

Other forms of lamination include:

- decorative products made from coloured layers of acrylic bonded with Tensol cement
- packaging laminates incorporating plastics and metal foils to enhance the properties of card.

Composites have revolutionised many industries. Carbon fibre is widely used in the production of aircraft components due to its excellent strength to weight ratio.

EXAMINATION QUESTIONS

Example questions and answers

 *a) Name **one** specific composite material.*
(1 mark)

Acceptable answer
Medium Density Fibreboard (MDF)

b) Describe the structure of your chosen composite material. **(2 marks)**

Acceptable answer
Wood waste is reduced to fibres and **bonded** together using heat, pressure and a **synthetic resin adhesive.**

*c) Name **one** product manufactured using your chosen composite material.* **(1 mark)**

Acceptable answer
Exhibition stand

d) Give one reason why your chosen material is a suitable choice for the manufacture of this product. **(2 marks)**

Acceptable answer
MDF is a suitable choice for an exhibition stand because it **machines well** which allows the manufacturer to add **machine decorative edges.**

Components

KEY TERMS

Check you understand these terms

Graphite, Overhead projector (OHP)

📖 **Further information can be found in** *Advanced Design and Technology for Edexcel, Product Design: Graphics with Materials Technology*, **Unit 3A, section 1.**

KEY POINTS

Pencils, pens and marker pens

Design professionals use a range of specialist equipment. Pigments are combined with other materials allowing them to be used on a range of surfaces.

Projected images using light

In order to communicate information it is often helpful to be able to project enlarged images or text on to a suitable surface or screen.

Table 3.10 Drawing tools and equipment

Equipment	Description	Uses
Pencils	Hard pencils (H to 9H) contain progressively more clay and less **graphite than soft pencils (HB to 9B)**.	Detailed artwork and technical drawings, sketching and shading, general rendering
Technical Pens	Fragile, interchangeable, tubular steel nibs (0.13–2.0 mm in diameter) supplied by refillable cartridge. Ink flows due to gravity/capillary action providing a consistent flow of ink resulting in a precise line	Detailed artwork and technical drawings where accuracy and precision is important
Ballpoint Pens	Ink is transferred by a nylon, ceramic, steel or tungsten carbide ball	Handwriting
Plastic Tip Pens	A network of fine channels feeds the plastic nib producing accurate line widths	Handwriting, drawing and sketching
Fibre Tip Pens	Nib is constructed from nylon or vinyl fibres bonded in resin to enhance durability	General rendering, fine nibs used as technical pens, handwriting
Fountain Pens	A fine channel feeds a metal nib producing a variety of line widths and shapes	Handwriting, calligraphy
Markers	Available as spirit (quick drying) or water (inexpensive) based. Chisel, bullet, round, square, fine or brush point. Felt, fibre, nylon or foam nibs. Available in a wide range of colours.	General rendering, rapid design concepts, presentation drawings

Table 3.11 Projected images using light

Equipment	Description	Uses
Overhead projector (OHP)	OHPs consist of several simple components. • bulb (light source) • glass plate (to hold acetate in position) • lens (to enlarge the image) • mirror (to direct the image onto the screen) • casing (to hold and position the components). Image size and focus is adjusted by altering the distance between the OHT and the lens. Acetate transparencies (OHTs) are prepared using permanent/non-permanent fibre tip pens or printed (specialist transparencies required).	Presentations of information to an audience or class; used to trace enlarged images onto vertical surfaces such as walls (murals) by artists or designers
Slide projectors	Used to project photographic slide transparencies onto a screen. The distance from the projector to the screen determines the size of the image. The lens assembly can be used to adjust the focus.	Presentations of information to an audience or class
LCD projectors	Used to send images from a computer screen electronically, through a projector, onto a suitable surface. By using an interactive white board or a specialised input device, the computer can be controlled remotely.	Presentations of information to an audience or class; PowerPoint

EXAMINATION QUESTIONS

Example questions and answers

a) Name the **two** main constituents of the 'lead' in pencils. **(2 marks)**

Acceptable answer
Graphite and **clay**.

b) A range of equipment is available to the designer. Describe the purpose and use of the following.

• spirit markers
• technical pens. **(4 marks)**

Acceptable answer
1 Spirit markers are **quick drying and are used to colour large areas quickly**. As they are quick drying, **different tones can be built up easily by overlaying colours**.
2 Technical pens are available with a **wide range of interchangeable nibs**, which are ideal for **producing precise and consistent lines** in accurate working drawings.

Working properties of materials and components related to preparing, processing, manipulating and combining

You need to

understand the working properties and functions of materials and components, relating to the composition and structure of materials.
☐ aesthetic properties
☐ functional properties
☐ mechanical properties.

KEY TERMS
Check you understand these terms

Aesthetic properties, Functional properties, Mechanical properties

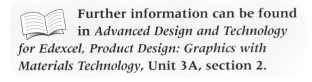

Further information can be found in *Advanced Design and Technology for Edexcel, Product Design: Graphics with Materials Technology*, Unit 3A, section 2.

KEY POINTS

Aesthetic properties

When we talk about the look of a material or product we are referring to its **aesthetic properties**.

Table 3.12 Aesthetic properties of materials and components

Property	Description	Example
Colour	Materials are selected because of their natural colour. Colour can be enhanced through treatments such as heat, chemicals, pigments, dyes or natural finishes.	Acrylic is often chosen to make signs because it is available in a wide range of bright colours requiring little finishing
Style	Dictated by fashions. Recognisable by form or decorative details.	An architect restoring an old cottage may choose traditional materials rather than modern materials
Texture	Materials are selected because of their natural textures. Added to materials during manufacturing to improve product appeal, e.g. moulding, embossing or by adding other materials.	A foam model for a new camera design can be enhanced by adding small, self-adhesive, paper circles which can be sprayed to give the impression of moulded details

Functional properties

The **functional properties** of materials are those physical properties which affect how a material will react to forces and other environmental conditions.

Table 3.13 Functional properties of materials and components

Property	Description	Example
Strength	Ability to withstand force without breaking or permanent bending. Tensile strength – resistance to stretching forces Compressive strength – resistance to pushing forces Bending strength – resistance to bending forces Shear strength – resistance to sliding/cutting forces Torsional strength – resistance to twisting forces.	Plastics are much stronger than glass, which is very fragile and breaks easily. As a result, plastic bottles can be made much lighter than their glass counterparts.
Durability	Ability to withstand wear and tear. Factors influencing the choice of materials include the required lifespan of the product, the frequency of use of the product and the demands placed upon the product (e.g. weather, corrosion).	Polythene plastic bags used for shopping will last longer and resist wear more effectively than paper bags.
Flammability	Ability to catch fire. Flammability is affected by, for example, the material structure, moisture content, shape and form and air circulation. Regulations exist which establish minimum safety standards.	Highly flammable foams and textile products used in home furnishings must be treated with fire retardant chemicals.

Mechanical properties

Mechanical properties those which involve the application of a force applied to the material.

Table 3.14 Mechanical properties of materials

Property	Description	Example	Example of a standard performance test
Plasticity	The ability to deform permanently under pressure.	Thermoplastics can be moulded when heated	squeeze in engineer's vice — ball bearing — specimen
Malleability	The extent to which a metal will deform in all dimensions without failing (cracking or rupture).	Aluminium can be formed into complex shapes for some car bodies	
Ductility	The extent to which materials can be drawn down to progressively smaller diameters in one direction without fracturing.	Copper is formed into long wires	
Hardness	The ability to withstand wear, scratching and indentation.	Steel and glass are hard to dent or scratch	**Fig. 3.11** An Indentation test to measure the hardness of materials

EXAMINATION QUESTIONS

Example questions and answers

a) Name **one** aesthetic property of copper which makes it suitable for making jewellery.   **(1 mark)**

Acceptable answer
Copper is an **attractive colour** when polished.

b) Copper is ductile and malleable. Explain the meaning of these two mechanical properties, referring to common uses of copper.   **(4 marks)**

Acceptable answer
Ductile
Ductility is the extent to which materials can be **drawn down to progressively smaller diameters without fracturing**. This property of copper, which is also highly conductive, makes it a **highly suitable material for the manufacture of electrical cable**.

Malleable
Copper can be used to make **decorative containers**. Because copper is malleable it can be **formed permanently into complex shapes without cracking**.

Hand and commercial processes

You need to

know about hand and commercial methods of preparing, processing, manipulating and combining materials and components to enhance their properties including associated tools,

Further information can be found in *Advanced Design and Technology for Edexcel, Product Design: Graphics with Materials Technology*, Unit 3A, section 2.

machinery and equipment including CAD/CAM in relation to:

- ☐ drawing
- ☐ computer graphics
- ☐ typography
- ☐ modelling and prototyping
- ☐ photography and photographic processing
- ☐ production of nets
- ☐ cutting, wasting, abrading, shaping, bending, casting and moulding
- ☐ joining and preparation for finishing.

KEY TERMS

Check you understand these terms

Pictorial drawings, Working drawings, Information drawings, Enhancement, Two-dimensional modelling, Three-dimensional modelling, Desktop publishing (DTP), Prototyping, Typography, Virtual modelling, CAD/CAM, Block models, Photographic processing, Wasting, abrading, casting, moulding

KEY POINTS

Drawing – pictorial, information and working drawings

Sketching is used for the rapid communication of ideas in two and three dimensions.

There are many formal drawing techniques. They can be categorised as **pictorial, working** or **information drawings**. Each technique follows accepted rules or conventions. Often it is necessary to use specialist equipment and drawing aids to produce accurate drawings.

Drawings can be **enhanced** by the use of:

- line
- tone
- texture
- colour.

Computer graphics

Computers can be used to represent images in two and three dimensions. **Two-dimensional models** might be printed out to show a single pictorial view of a building. **Three-dimensional models** can be manipulated on screen to show the building from different views.

Table 3.15 Computer software applications

Software	Description	Uses	Advantages
Desktop publishing (DTP) Examples: Microsoft Publisher Serif PagePlus Adobe PageMaker Quark XPress Adobe InDesign	Desktop publishing applications allow designers to lay out publications. Text is word processed. Photographs, images and graphics are created digitally or commissioned from an illustrator and scanned to create digital images. The overall layout style is created in a DTP programme and all the elements are combined. A proof copy is printed and checked (proof-read) before being sent digitally to a commercial printing company which produces the printing plates.	Books, newspapers, magazines, leaflets, business cards, posters, printed packaging designs, web pages	Text and images can be manipulated within a programme; wide choice of typefaces and clipart; layout tools such as grids and guides can be used to maintain a 'house style'; manual processes such as zoom, cut and paste can be reproduced electronically, pre-designed templates can be used and a house style template can be created to produce standardised documents; documents can be spell checked.

Table 3.15 Computer software applications *(continued)*

Software	Description	Uses	Advantages
2D computer graphics Examples: Microsoft Paint CorelDraw Serif DrawPlus Serif PhotoPlus Adobe Photoshop Macromedia Freehand JASC Paint Shop Pro Adobe Illustrator	There is a wide range of software available to the designer working in 2D. Digital images may be used or non-digital images may be scanned. The software comes with a wide range of tools such as drawing tools and filters which may be used to construct and manipulate images.	Web graphics; logos; magazine illustration; advertising images; photograph retouching; 2D models	Designs can be modified easily; wide choice of typefaces and clipart; manual processes such as zoom, cut and paste can be reproduced electronically; a wide range of tools is available to create interesting effects automatically; the image can be built up in layers which can be modified individually; most applications now include features to help in the creation of web graphics.
3D computer graphics Examples: PTC ProDesktop 3D Studio Lightwave	Objects can be built up in 3D to create a true and accurate representation of the subject. Tools can be used to enhance the object including: • shading • ray tracing • radiosity • light source • camera angles • animation.	3D modelling and **prototyping**; virtual products; CGI (cinema animation)	Speed; accuracy; repeatability; ease of modification; ease of storage; ease of transport; ease of testing; range of tools; can be downloaded directly to a CNC device to create a prototype.

Typography

Typography is the art of designing communication through the printed word. It is often associated with the design of fonts/typefaces.

Layout

In any publication consistency of design is important. Desktop publishing (DTP) is used to plan the organisation of any new publication including page size, margins, columns, page numbers, footers.

Text

Fonts/typefaces are designed by professional designers. Many fonts are related and grouped together as a 'family'. Aesthetic appearance and legibility are the main factors that are considered when selecting a font. This is also affected by the designer's choice of font size, leading, tracking and kerning.

Fig. 3.12 The structure of a font

Headings and subheadings

Appropriate headings and subheadings are selected to break up the text and draw attention to important sections. Decisions have to be made about the application of size, italics, lower/upper case, colour, character style (serif/sans serif), character width (expanded/condensed), density (solid/outline/positive/negative), external and internal subheadings.

Captions/breakouts

Captions are used to identify or comment upon images. Breakouts are short passages of text which need to be emphasised. The style and use of both needs to be consistent throughout the publication.

Spacing

Tracking allows the designer to adjust the space between all letters within a document. Kerning allows the designer to adjust the space between certain pairs of letters. The space between lines of text can be changed by adjusting the leading.

Modelling and prototyping

Modelling and prototyping are an effective means of communicating design proposals and testing ideas. Prototypes are original, working models used to test ideas. A great deal of money and time is invested at this stage of development to avoid costly mistakes in tooling and machinery. Models and prototypes can be produced in different ways.

- material modelling – shaping materials to produce solid 3D models
- **virtual modelling** – creating digital models on-screen using a computer
- **CAD/CAM** modelling – using computer-aided design and manufacture to produce 3D models.

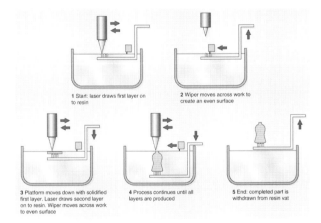

Fig. 3.13 The process of stereolithography

Photography and photographic processing

Focusing

The focus can be adjusted automatically or manually, using the focus ring, to produce a sharper picture.

Table 3.16 The use of three-dimensional modelling in the development of products

Model type	Description
Sketch models	These are the first models made during the early stages of product development. They are rapidly assembled from easily shaped, low-cost materials such as foam and card. They are used to explore initial ideas.
Block models	Block models are designed to test aesthetics and ergonomics. They are detailed and finished to a high standard so that the designers and clients can literally 'get a feel' for the product. Compliant materials are used, such as styrofoam and jelutong.
Working models	Working models start to show internal details and moving parts.
Prototypes	This is the last stage of development. Materials specified for the final product are used and all external and internal details are incorporated in a fully functional model. Extensive testing of accurate prototypes may lead to adjustments to the design to avoid costly changes once manufacturing has started.
Architectural models	Architects commission specialist model makers to produce scale models of buildings and interiors. Block and sheet modelling materials are combined with specialist components such as scaled models of people, vehicles, trees and so on.
Rapid prototyping	Stereolithography is a relatively new form of prototyping which can convert digital drawings into complex solid models. The technology converts CAD drawings to build up the prototype in layers using a laser to solidify liquid resin.

Shutter speed and aperture

These two functions control the amount of light reaching the film. The shutter speed (measured in sixtieths of a second) determines how long the film is exposed to light and the size of the aperture ('f-stops') can be adjusted to allow more or less light into the camera while the shutter is open.

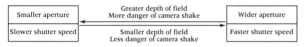

| Smaller aperture | Greater depth of field More danger of camera shake | Wider aperture |
| Slower shutter speed | Smaller depth of field Less danger of camera shake | Faster shutter speed |

Fig. 3.14 The relationship between aperture size and shutter speed

The speed of the film is another factor which will affect exposure settings. Fast moving subjects require a fast shutter speed and therefore need a wide aperture to allow enough light in to expose the film.

Photographic processing

Turning exposed photographic film into negatives is called **photographic processing**. There are many different types of film. Most have different processing requirements. For example, colour film consists of three layers sensitive to different parts of the spectrum. This makes colour processing a much more complicated process.

Production of nets

Constructing nets

Nets (also known as developments) can be produced from almost any sheet material such as paper, card and board, metal and plastic. Most nets, now, are developed using CAD and should show: cut lines – a continuous line; fold lines – a broken line; tabs; and annotation.

Structural packaging design

Cartonboard is the most common material used for producing boxes for the packaging of consumer products. Costs and mistakes can be reduced by:

- using standard pre-drawn nets
- using internationally recognised diagrams and symbols to communicate designs.

Table 3.17 The stages in film processing and printing

Processing stage	Description
Development	The film is loaded into the development tank in darkness. The correct temperature needs to be maintained and the tank should be agitated regularly.
Wash or stop bath	The film is immersed into this chemical solution which arrests the developer.
Fixation	This solution fixes the processed negative image.
Washing and drying	The film is washed thoroughly and hung to dry in a clean atmosphere.
Printing	Photographic prints are produced from negatives in a dark room under filtered light. The negative image is projected onto light-sensitive paper using an enlarger. A test strip is produced to determine exposure and the enlarger adjusted to produce the desired size and focus. The exposed paper is immersed into the developer, followed by the fixer and finally washed and dried.

Commercial production of packaging nets

After the cartonboard has been through the printing and print finishing processes it needs to be turned into containers. The entire process can be automated.

1 An accurate die is made.
2 The die is mounted into the die cutting machine.
3 The cartonboard nets are trimmed on a power guillotine.
4 A test sheet is produced.
5 The printed cartonboard is fed into the die-cutting machine and stamped out.
6 Waste is directed away using ejector pins or rubbers.

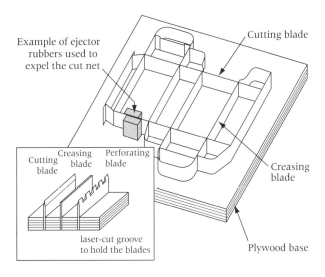

Example of ejector rubbers used to expel the cut net

Cutting blade

Cutting blade · Creasing blade · Perforating blade

laser-cut groove to hold the blades

Creasing blade

Plywood base

Fig. 3.15 A cutting die

7 The cut nets are removed and stacked.
8 The nets are pre-folded on a folding machine.
9 Glue is sprayed onto appropriate tabs, triggered by a sensor on the conveyor belt.
10 The joins are carefully compressed together between two conveyor belts, allowing the adhesive to cure.
11 The containers are shipped to the manufacturer to be filled.

Cutting, wasting, abrading, shaping, bending, casting, moulding

You will need to refer to Unit 1 in this book to refresh your knowledge of previously studied material. You will also need to be able to describe, using notes and sketches, the processes of cutting, **wasting**, **abrading**, shaping, bending, **casting**, injection **moulding**, blow moulding and vacuum forming.

Joining and preparation for finishing

Joining techniques are numerous and it is important to select appropriate methods. They are categorised as permanent, temporary and adhesives.

- Permanent – nails; rivets; mechanical joints; soldering and brazing; welding
- Temporary – nuts and bolts; screws; knockdown fittings
- Adhesives – glue sticks; spray mounts; hot melt glue; PVA; contact adhesive; tensol cement; synthetic resin; double-sided tape; polystyrene cement

EXAMINATION QUESTIONS

Example questions and answers

 *Name **three** camera settings which need to be adjusted before a photograph is taken. These may be automatic functions or set manually.*

(3 marks)

Acceptable answer
- **Focus**
- **Aperture**
- **Shutter speed**.

 *Describe **four** main stages involved in the production of a film negative. (You should not include the processes involved in the development of photographic prints from negatives.)* **(4 marks)**

Acceptable answer
1 **Development**: The film is **loaded into the development tank in darkness. The correct temperature needs to be maintained and the tank should be agitated regularly.**
2 **Wash or stop bath**: The film is immersed into this chemical solution **which arrests the action of the developer.**
3 **Fixation**: The film is immersed into this chemical solution which **fixes the processed negative image into a permanent image.**
4 **Washing and drying**: The film is **washed thoroughly and hung to dry in a clean atmosphere.**

Finishing processes and product manufacture

KEY TERMS

Check you understand these terms

Anodising, Varnishes, Self-finishing, Engraving, Vinyl stickers, Inkjet, Laser, Offset lithography, screen-printing, letterpress printing, Photocopying, Finishing and binding

Further information can be found in *Advanced Design and Technology for Edexcel, Product Design: Graphics with Materials Technology*, **Unit 3A, section 3.**

KEY POINTS

Surface coating

Anodising

Anodising is used to enhance aluminium and aluminium alloys. The whole product is immersed in a sulphuric acid solution. The product being anodised is turned into an electrical anode and lead plates in the tank are used as cathodes. As a direct current (DC) is passed through the solution, a thin oxide film forms on the product surface. Coloured dyes can be added before the surface is lacquered to produce an attractive and protective finish.

Painting

There is a wide range of paints available to the designer used to enhance aesthetics and protect materials. Preparation requirements vary depending upon the material. Some specialist paints such as 'Hammerite' require very little preparation. Most paints, however, require a smooth, clean, grease and dust free surface. Primer and/or undercoats are often used to prepare surfaces. Topcoats can be divided into three categories.

- oil-based (including gloss)
- emulsion
- polyurethane.

Varnishing

Varnishes are a form of synthetic resin which produce a hard, durable finish. Two common types are polyurethane varnishes, available in a range of finishes and colours, and acrylic varnishes which are quick drying and solvent free.

Self-finishing

Some materials are **self-finishing**. Processes such as injection moulding, casting and laser cutting produce plastic products which require little or no finishing. The moulding process also allows:

- different materials to be introduced together to form a single component
- low-relief lettering, decoration and texture
- colouring through the use of dyes or chemicals.

Surface decoration

Engraving and etching

Engraving and etching are forms of surface decoration used predominantly on hard materials such as glass, metal and stone. The engraving process involves the use of specialist hand tools, specialist engraving machines and grinders or automated CNC equipment. The surface of the material is cut away, sometimes to reveal a different coloured layer underneath.

Etching makes controlled use of acids which eat away at the material surface to produce a design. Masks are used to protect areas of the material.

Vinyl stickers

Vinyl stickers are self-adhesive characters or symbols which can be purchased in sets or manufactured using CNC plotter/cutters.

Computer printers

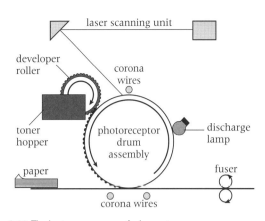

Fig. 3.16 The basic components of a laser printer

Table 3.18 Computer printers

Hardware	Description	Use	Advantages
Inkjet printer (output device)	The print head produces heated bubbles of ink which burst, spraying the ink onto the page. A vacuum is created as the nozzle cools which draws a new bubble. The image is printed in strips using four colour reservoirs (CMYK). It is relatively slow. Cartridges have relatively low capacity. Liquid inks require short drying time. Expensive coated papers are available for higher-quality prints.	Used widely at home and in schools	Low-cost printer available; high-quality images at high resolutions; relatively low cost for average user; cheap method of obtaining colour prints
Laser printer (output device)	Available in black/white and colour. Faster models tend to be more expensive (measured in pages per minute: PPM). Laser printers use the same technology as photocopiers. A laser beam draws the negative image on a rotating drum causing it to lose its electrical charge. The electrically charged areas of the drum attract toner powder which is transferred to the paper using pressure and heat. In colour laser printers this process is repeated for all four colours.	Used more in busier computer suites and offices	Very high-quality print and very high resolutions; fast; will not smudge; more cost effective over long term and more suitable for heavy usage

Offset lithography, screen-printing, letterpress, black and white printing

Refer to Unit 1 to refresh your knowledge of **offset lithography, screen-printing, letterpress**, and black and white printing.

Examiner's Tip

Remember, a good-quality, well-annotated drawing can put as much information across as a whole page of written notes.

Table 3.19 Photocopying

Description	Uses	Advantages
Photocopying is a dry printing process which relies on particles of toner being attracted to charged areas of the paper which is then heated to fix the image. Inexpensive for short black and white runs. Colour copying is expensive. No setting up time required. Suitable for copier paper and heat resistant acetate.	Reproduction of images and short documents; enlarging or reducing images and documents	As there is no need to spend time or money on setting up the process, the photocopier is an ideal means of producing single sheets and short documents

Finishing and binding ready for distribution

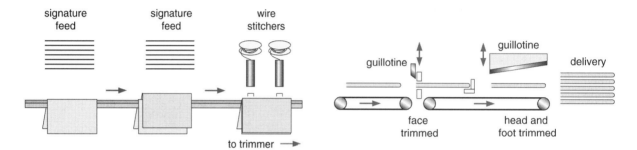

Fig. 3.17 The folding, binding and trimming process

Table 3.20 Finishing and binding techniques

Finishing and binding	Description
Decorative **finishing** techniques	There are a number of finishing techniques that can be used to enhance the format of paper, card and boards. • laminating, varnishing, embossing, hot foil blocking • encapsulating – similar to laminating with the addition of heat sealed seams therefore fully covering the edges of paper and card, e.g. wipe clean menus.
Imposition	Large plates are used to print a number of double-sided pages together. Imposition is the process of laying out pages so that they appear in the right order when collated.
Scoring	A manual or automated process which breaks the surface of a material on the external edge of a fold to allow bending.
Gathering and collation	This process assembles the publication in the correct order. Automated machines feed one page or section at a time onto a belt from hoppers at high speed. The same machines can be set up to use collation marks to make automatic checks.
Binding	Binding is the process which joins the pages of a publication together. The designer needs to consider: • aesthetic requirements • the costs involved for each process • the quantity of material to be bound.

Table 3.21 Binding methods

Method	Description	Applications
Saddle-wire stitched	The simplest method of binding by stapling the pages together through the fold	Documents for presentation
Side-wire stitched	Staples are passed through the side of the document close to the spine. Used when the document is too thick for saddle-wire stitching	Documents for presentation
Pcrfcct binding	Pages are held together and fixed to the cover by means of a flexible adhesive. This method produces a higher-quality presentation and the spine can also be printed on	High-quality documents for presentation, magazines, less expensive books
Hard-bound or case-bound	Usually combines sewing and glueing to create the most durable method of commercial binding. Stiff board is used on the cover and back to protect the pages	Books
Spiral or comb-binding	Pages are punched through with a series of holes along the spine. A spiralling steel or plastic band is inserted through the holes to hold the sheets together	Documents for presentation

Packing and distribution

Appropriate packing is necessary to contain, protect and identify the finished product and to make it easier to handle. Methods include shrink-wrapping, use of corrugated boxes, and storage on pallets.

EXAMINATION QUESTION

Example question and answer

 *a) Name **two** stages in the production of a magazine, other than binding, which take place after printing.* **(2 marks)**

Acceptable answer
1 **Gathering/collation**
2 **Cutting.**

b) 'Perfect binding' is the process chosen to produce the magazine. Describe the main features of this process. **(3 marks)**

Acceptable answer
The collated signatures have **spines cut off and roughened**. A **strong adhesive is used to attach covers**. Strength is derived from the glue holding the edges of the pages, so **this process is not always very durable**.

Testing materials

You need to

know about comparative testing of materials, components and processes for quality, performance, safety, ease of manufacture, aftercare, maintenance and fitness for purpose.

- ☐ **standard performance tests**
- ☐ **testing at critical control points in manufacture**
- ☐ **the purpose of British and International Standards**
- ☐ **the use of ICT as a testing aid.**

KEY TERMS

Check you
understand these terms

Quality and safety testing, Tensile strength, Hardness, Toughness, Ductility, Sampling, Virtual products

Further information can be found in *Advanced Design and Technology for Edexcel, Product Design: Graphics with Materials Technology,* **Unit 3A, section 4.**

KEY POINTS

Standard performance tests

Quality and safety testing techniques have been developed over the years to compare the properties of materials in order to predict how they will perform under a range of conditions. Many of these tests can be carried out under workshop conditions. There are two categories of tests.

- destructive testing (testing until failure)
- testing by deformation (non-destructive testing).

In order to make a fair comparison, tests should be carried out under safe, controlled conditions using equipment and materials conforming to BSI standards.

Testing at critical control points in manufacture

Quality control procedures are covered in Unit 1. **Sampling** is used to test products at planned intervals. Results of inspections are gathered and analysed. It is often possible to use this data to predict when a particular machine needs adjustment or repair because accuracy in the components will gradually drift and the problem can be addressed before components run out of tolerance. This system of sampling and inspection can also identify batches of faulty materials and inaccurate machine operators.

Quality control in print runs

Paper reacts to changes in the environment, such as temperature and changes in humidity, which may cause problems during a print run. Paper is kept in storage in order for it to adapt to the relative humidity of the print room. During the print run, regular quality control checks are made to ensure the quality of the printed materials.

The purpose of British and international standards

Quality and safety standards are covered in Unit 1 and you should refer to this material to refresh your memory.

Table 3.22 Standard destructive tests and comparative testing in the workshop

Property	Definition	Example
Tensile strength	The ability of a material to resist stretching or pulling forces.	A standard shaped test piece of the material is stretched until it fails. The force required is measured using a tensometer.
Hardness	The resistance of a material to abrasive wear and indentation.	A hard ball-bearing (tungsten carbide) is forced into the material. The size or depth of the impression is measured.
Toughness	The ability of a material to withstand sudden impact and shock loading without fracture.	A notch is cut from a standard size of material which is 'hit' with a sudden force. The amount of force required to break the sample is measured.
Ductility	The ability of a material to deform through bending, twisting or stretching.	A standard sized sample of material is bent or stretched. The length of the sample is measured until it fails.

Table 3.23 Potential problems and quality control measures during the printing process

Problem	Description	Quality control
Set off	Where the ink from one sheet smudges on to the underside of the following sheet	Use of sufficient anti-set off spray, use of sufficiently quick-drying inks or use of better quality paper stock
Colour variation	This occurs where the printer does not maintain consistent colour throughout the run	Use of colour bars and regular densitometer readings
Hickies	These are small areas of unwanted solid colour surrounded by an unprinted 'halo' area, and are caused by specks of dirt, paper debris or ink skin on the printing plate or blanket cylinders	Regular washing of the blanket cylinder
Bad register	This is where colours protrude beyond the edge of the four colour separations making the image look out of focus	Use and regular inspection of registration marks to line up the four colour separations exactly

The use of ICT as a testing aid

There are disadvantages to destructive testing of materials and products.

- Expensive equipment and facilities are often required.
- High costs may be incurred where expensive products, such as cars, are tested.
- It is impossible to test some products including large engineering projects such as bridges and ships.

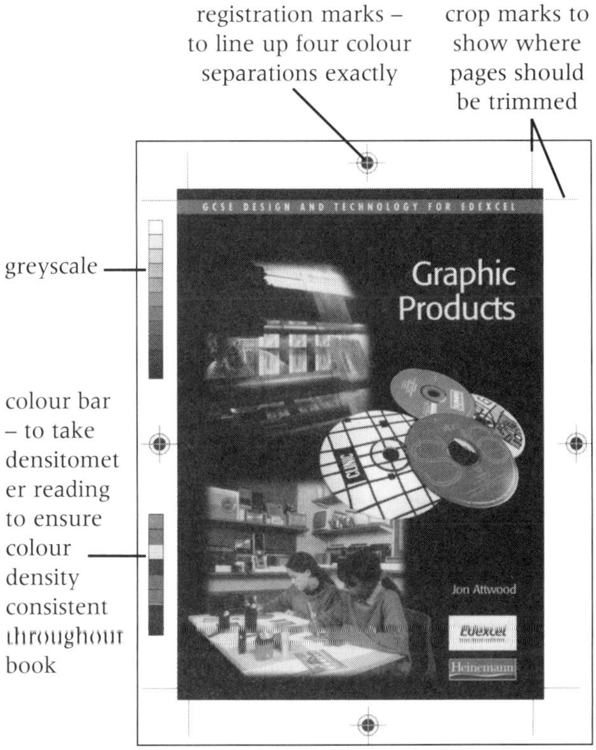

ICT can be used to test products.

- Virtual reality programs allow designers to generate virtual designs which allow the user to interact with the objects or environments on the screen. Architects can construct virtual buildings which allow the client or anyone else to 'walk' through the structure, viewing it from different angles or in different weather conditions. **Virtual products** can be created which allow the customer to view the object from different angles.
- Specialist software can be used to test two- and three-dimensional representations of products on screen. Products can be subjected to forces which simulate real life situations. From these computer models it is possible, for example, to predict how a car will behave in different crash situations.
- Probes and sensors can be used to test products during manufacture, such as the optical ink sensors used in the print industry.

Fig. 3.18 Printed front cover of a book showing printer's marks

registration marks – to line up four colour separations exactly

crop marks to show where pages should be trimmed

greyscale

colour bar – to take densitometer reading to ensure colour density consistent throughout book

Examiner's Tip

When you turn over the paper at the start of the examination, make sure that you read the question thoroughly so that you really understand what the examiner is asking you to do. Don't just skim through the questions.

EXAMINATION QUESTIONS

Example questions and answers

Q1 *a) Describe the aims of quality control.*
(2 marks)

Acceptable answer
Quality control seeks to **ensure high standards during production through regular, pre-planned checks** with the aim of **creating a system with zero faults.**

*b) Name **one** method of non-destructive testing.*
(1 mark)

Acceptable answer
Ultrasound

*c) Describe **two** different ways in which ICT can be used to model and test a new building.* **(2 marks)**

Acceptable answer
1 Using specialist software, **the building can be subjected to forces which simulate real life** situations. From these computer models, it is possible, for example, **to predict how the building will behave in high winds.**
2 **Virtual reality programs allow designers to generate virtual designs** which **allow the user to interact with the objects or environments** on the screen.

PRACTICE EXAMINATION STYLE QUESTION

1 It is important to produce products with finishes which appeal to the end user or which enhance the characteristics of the product.
  a) Explain the meaning of the term 'self-finishing' which is often used in connection with some plastics. **(1 mark)**
  b) Outline **two** processes which could be used to cut or 'eat' away the surface of glass to produce decorative designs. **(2 marks)**
  c) Outline **one** advantage of acrylic varnishes over polyurethane varnish. **(1 mark)**
  d) Outline **one** use for vinyl graphics. **(1 mark)**

2 Wood is a commonly used material, which varies greatly in structure, aesthetic characteristics and mechanical properties.
  a) Explain **two** of the following terms.
     • heartwood
     • sapwood
     • fibres. **(2 marks)**
  b) Explain **three** factors which may affect the characteristics and/or structure of timber. **(3 marks)**

3 Using notes and/or sketches, describe **one** of the following manufacturing processes.
  • injection moulding
  • blow moulding
  • vacuum forming. **(5 marks)**

4 Explain how computers can be used in the design process. **(5 marks)**

5 Describe how printed publications such as magazines are finished and bound following the printing process. **(5 marks)**

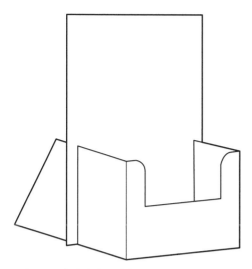 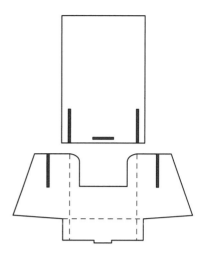

Fig. 3.19 A point of sale leaflet holder

6 Figure 3.19 shows a drawing of a point of sale leaflet holder.

a) Produce a freehand orthographic drawing (third angle) to show three views of the **assembled** point of sale display.

b) The example shows a point of sale display which is constructed from two pieces of card. Using notes and sketches, show how this point of sale display could be redesigned so that it could be assembled from **one** piece of card, as a single net. **(5 marks)**

Total for this question paper: **30 marks**

Design and technology in society (G302)

This option will be assessed in section B during the $1\frac{1}{2}$ hour, Unit 3 examination. If you have chosen this option you should spend half of your time (45 minutes) answering all of the questions for this section. It is important to use appropriate specialist and technical language in the exam, along with accurate spelling, punctuation and grammar. Where appropriate you should also use clear, annotated sketches to explain your answer. *You do not have to study this chapter if you are taking the CAD/CAM option.*

The physical and social consequences of design and technology for society

You need to

understand the effects of design and technological changes on society.
- ☐ mass production and the consumer society
- ☐ the 'new' industrial age of high-technology production
- ☐ the global marketplace
- ☐ issues related to local/global production.

understand the influences on the development of products.
- ☐ aesthetics
- ☐ design and culture
- ☐ new materials, processes and technology.

KEY TERMS
Check you understand these terms

Consumer society, Global marketplace, Global manufacturing, Arts and Crafts, Memphis, Bauhaus, Art Deco, The New Design, New materials, Smart materials, Eco-design

 Further information can be found in *Advanced Design and Technology for Edexcel, Product Design: Graphics with Materials Technology,* **Unit 3B1, section 1.**

KEY POINTS

Mass production and the consumer society

The Industrial Revolution and mass production changed the way in which design and technology influenced society. A gradual, evolutionary pattern of development in technology and society was replaced by rapid technological and social change, which has led to positive and negative consequences.

- Some advantages of modern technology – more consumer choice; more affordable products; higher living standards
- Some disadvantages of modern technology – environmental damage due to pollution; social problems caused by globalisation; influence of computer games on children

Mass production

The history of design began with the Industrial Revolution and the invention of the steam engine in the mid-1700s. Coal mining, iron and steel and machine production took on a new importance and set the scene for the development of industrial mass production. Until the Industrial Revolution and the advent of powered, automated machinery, production was limited to the quantities of products which could be produced by craftspeople by hand. Until the invention of modern printing techniques, for example, texts had to be laboriously copied by hand.

Mass production simplified the production process by dividing it into simple, repetitive tasks.

- Many traditional trades could not compete, leading to unemployment.
- Unskilled jobs led to lower wages.
- Poverty led to social tensions, strikes and uprisings.
- The movement of labour from the countryside to the cities led to many social problems.
- Unregulated development led to environmental problems such as pollution.

The concerns of the workers led to the birth of the modern trade union which fought to combat these problems.

Assembly lines

Assembly lines transported the work to the workers within the factory and vastly accelerated the production process. Products became cheaper and more widely available to more sections of society.

Design tradition and design for mass production

Early, mass-produced products tended to imitate traditionally produced styles. It was not until the second half of the nineteenth century that designers began to reflect the new social conditions and new production processes. The heavy, over-ornate styles were replaced by products which reflected the needs of the market. Designers began to recognise the market potential of the new class of people created by the Industrial Revolution. Simple, inexpensive consumer goods began to be produced for the expanding working classes.

Design in the USA

The lack of competition and drive to mass-produce products meant that designers concentrated upon the functional and technical aspects of products, often at the expense of styling.

The development of the consumer society

It was not until the twentieth century that fashion and styling became important as a dominant feature of product design. A rise in incomes and change in attitudes to consumption led to the growth of the **consumer society** as society demanded more products. People no longer bought products just for their function.

Table 3.24 The effects of some political, social and technological developments on consumer society

Developments	Effects
World conflicts	Fuelled demand for new products and new technologies
Introduction of the national grid (1920s)	Stimulated demand for new 'labour-saving' electrical appliances
Increasing standard of living	Higher demand for luxury goods and travel
Growth in media industry	Growth of advertising, packaging and design industries which fuelled consumer demand
Development of new materials and technologies for space exploration	Allowed new products to be produced, e.g. streamlining in the automotive industry which reflected advances in aerodynamics research and the desire to appear modern

Designers began to develop new features in their products.

- Packaging became a much more important part of the product.
- Products began to be designed with limited lifespans (planned obsolescence) to be replaced with restyled or improved variants.
- Styling became significantly more important as competition between products increased.

The 'new' industrial age of high-technology production

The latter stages of the twentieth century have seen an evermore rapid pace in technological development with the introduction of new materials and new processes.

- Computer technology: the development of the silicon chip in the 1960s had a profound effect on society.
- New materials, such as aluminium, stainless steel, heat resistant glass and modern polymers, have made new products possible.
- New technology, such as miniaturisation which allows the functions of different devices to be combined into a single product, has led to a consumer trend of being attracted to the latest technological products.
- Fashion: as new technologies become increasingly affordable and accessible, styling becomes a more important factor in attracting consumers.

Examiner's Tip

Familiarise yourself with a range of high-tech products so that you can talk about them in the exam. You need to be able to discuss the development of these products by referring to the older products that they have replaced.

Case study: the Swatch watch

Originally developed in the 1980s, Swatch watches were targeted at the lower end of the market. The company produced affordable watches which were heavily styled and aimed to reflect contemporary fashions. Swatch watches today have switched their emphasis by

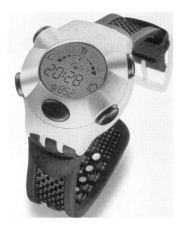

Fig. 3.20 A modern Swatch watch

concentrating on integrating new technology. Watches have been produced which can be used as electronic ski-passes or travel tickets. More recently the company has started to develop models which can be used to access Internet services or act as a mobile phone.

The global marketplace

In order to remain competitive, companies who operate in the **global marketplace** (operate in different countries) need to ensure that their products appeal to a wide range of people from different cultures. Some companies employ designers in different countries while others are careful to conduct thorough market research in unfamiliar niche markets. Products may be remodelled to reflect differences in fashion, taste, legal requirements and other cultural differences. Remodelling may involve:

- changing from right- to left-hand drive in vehicles
- changing a product name to take account of linguistic differences
- changing packaging to reflect regional tastes
- increasing the amount of recyclable materials used in the product
- a decision as to whether to fit a plug or not/different voltages
- the fitting of different visual displays
- using devices to suppress noise levels.

Global manufacturing

Global manufacturing is associated with multinational companies who rely on overseas manufacturing capacity.

- Global manufacturing has only become possible through developments in international communications technologies and is attractive to multinational companies because it allows them to take advantage of much lower labour and materials costs.
- Products can be designed and developed in one country, manufactured in another and shipped all over the world.
- The flexibility of modern industry means that it is easy to switch production between countries.

The trend towards global manufacturing often involves designing products, such as books or computer games covers, in one country and printing them in another. Design studios, equipped with state of the art computer technology and broadband, can receive briefs in any format, speeding up the turnaround from concept to the finished design. Systems are on-line 24 hours a day to allow continuous contact between clients, the design team and the film planning, plate making, printing and finishing departments.

> ### Examiner's Tip
>
> You should familiarise yourself with a range of global manufacturers so that you can use them to illustrate your answers in the exam.

Table 3.25 The advantages and disadvantages of global manufacturing

Advantages of global manufacturing for NICs* and LEDCs**	Disadvantages of global manufacturing for NICs and LEDCs
Higher employment levels and living standards. Improved the level of expertise of the local workforce. Source of foreign currency improving the balance of payments. Widening of the economic base. Transfer of technology possible. *NICs: Newly Industrialised Countries such as Singapore and Taiwan **LEDCs: Less Economically Developed Countries such as many nations in Africa or Asia ***MEDCs: More Economically Developed Countries such as most of western Europe and North America	Possible environmental damage to unspoilt areas. Jobs require only low-level skills. Managerial posts are filled by people from MEDCs.*** Profits are exported back to MEDCs. Poor legislation or enforcement allows multinationals to cut corners on health, safety and pollution. Multinationals can exert political pressure. Raw materials are often exported with no value added. Manufactured goods are exported and do not benefit local community. Decisions are made in a foreign country and on a global basis. Reduced need for the local workforce due to automation.

Influences on the development of products

Important changes have emerged as a result of improving standards of living and changes to industrial organisation, including:

- the emergence of the 'professional designer'
- the growth in importance of fashion and style.

The modern designer needs to consider that:

- form has become as important as function for many products
- designs must be 'market led' or 'market driven' reflecting the needs and tastes of the consumer
- customers buy products which reflect their aspirations
- products need 'personality' to make them stand out from competing products.

1906 – Strowger Calling Dial, Stroger USA

1931 – Siemens telephone, designed by Jean Heiberg

1970s – Standard GPO British telephone

2001 – Nokia 9210; a modern mobile phone able to access the Internet and email

Fig 3.21 The development of the telephone

Fig 3.22 Philippe Starck's lemon squeezer

Fig 3.23 A traditional lemon squeezer

Product reliability and aesthetics

Designers consider the aesthetic qualities of a design carefully. If an otherwise well-designed, high-performance product is painted the 'wrong' colour, for example, few people will buy it. Designers need to think carefully before making aesthetic decisions about shape and form, line, balance, colour, decoration, surface pattern, scale, styling and texture.

As second and third generation products are developed, designs evolve into very reliable products. Different manufacturers use identical components within their products and can afford to provide long guarantees with confidence. Products are increasingly differentiated by aesthetic qualities or 'styling'.

Form and function

Form and function can place conflicting pressures upon the development of a design. The most successful designs both 'do the job well' and 'look good'. The history of design has seen many debates over the relative importance of form in relation to function, for example:

- the **Arts and Crafts** movement of the nineteenth century reacted against the highly decorated forms of mass-produced Victorian products

- Postmodernist movements such as the **Memphis** group reacted against the pure functionalism of modernism.

Modern products, such as packaging can be said to have three basic functions.

- The practical and technical function: does the packaging contain, protect and preserve the product?
- The aesthetic function: does the packaging have visual appeal to attract the consumer?
- The symbolic function or the image it gives the user: does the packaging project a desirable brand identity?

Products usually evolve gradually because it is easier to avoid mistakes and control development costs.

Examiner's Tip

Remember that you will need to revise the whole specification. It is quite possible for a topic to be repeated for a second year and it is quite possible that a topic could be omitted for a couple of years.

Design and culture

The designer needs to work within the constraints of:

- the design brief (or specification)
- available materials
- production technologies

- the expectations of the consumer in terms of appearance or style.

The most successful designers are able to establish 'new' styles which are often adopted and transferred to different products. The Dyson vacuum cleaner, for example, adapted existing cyclone technology to domestic use. The styling of these new cleaners was boldly different, using bright colours and transparent plastics. As these products became popular, new products such as washing machines were developed which reflected the 'Dyson style'.

Examiner's Tip

You need to learn about the history of important design movements from different periods. It is unlikely that the following outlines will provide you with enough material to answer the questions fully. You should read around the subject in preparation for the examination.

Arts and Crafts

The Arts and Crafts movement was founded in 1890 by the English artist, designer and writer William Morris.

- The movement was founded as a reaction against the effects of industrialisation and mass production of the Victorian era.
- The concepts of art, craftsmanship and quality were emphasised during production which used natural materials and traditional techniques.
- Decoration was uncomplicated and based upon simple, organic forms from nature.
- The movement was involved in all areas of design from textiles to typefaces.
- Many modern European designers have been influenced by the Arts and Crafts movement.

Modernism and the Bauhaus

Walter Gropius founded the **Bauhaus** school early in the twentieth century (1919 and 1933). Laslo Maholoy-Nagy created simple geometric typestyles. Famous artists such as Paul Klee taught at the school. The Nazis closed the school in 1933 which encouraged the spread of Bauhaus ideology around the world.

- Function determined form in many Bauhaus products.
- Artistic education and crafts training were considered equally important.
- Modern materials and processes were widely used.
- Products were designed to be suitable for mass production.
- Bauhaus was, and is, very influential in inspiring the 'International Style' in architecture.

Art Deco

From 1925 onwards, the **Art Deco** style became extremely popular and influential. It was named after an international exhibition in Paris in 1925 in which all exhibits were required to be novel in their design. It was influenced by modern paintings and a popular interest in African and Egyptian art.

- The style is characterised by many visual elements such as bright colours, images of the Sun, geometric shapes and zigzag patterns derived from Egypt.
- There was an emphasis on the use of expensive materials such as ebony, ivory and bronze.
- It influenced the design of many products and made use of new materials including aluminium, plywood and Bakelite (an early thermoset plastic).

The 1940s and 1950s

In the 1950s, the development of the supermarket meant that food packaging became a marketing tool. Packaging had to be instantly recognisable to the consumer. 'Italian style' products became all the rage. The 1950s saw the development of new plastics such as foam, nylon and polyester, arising out of wartime research.

- New materials, technologies and processes inspired new, mass-produced, low-cost products.
- Images of new developments in science and technology, such as the splitting of the atom, were popular.
- New technologies inspired new graphic forms such as television graphics, information graphics and corporate identity systems.

Youth culture

The 1960s and 1970s were a period of rapid political, social and economic change.

- Young people became a new and important market.
- Youth culture inspired new styles such as 1960s 'psychedelic' art.
- The growth of the media led to the development of marketing and advertising.
- New scientific advances, such as those driven by the space programme, introduced new materials
- New futuristic products were inspired by science fiction television programmes and films.
- Improved production techniques enabled designers to tailor products to small niche markets.
- Pop music and the 'hippie' movement influenced graphic design, fashion and interior design.
- Artists such as Andy Warhol were influenced by graphic styles and in turn influenced new graphic designers.
- Packaging became bolder, using vivid colours and strong visual images.
- New materials such as cellophane, aluminium and plastics enabled the development of new types of packaging such as disposable, ring-pull cans, Tetrapak™ cartons and moulded plastic containers which were lighter and cheaper to transport than fragile glass.

Memphis

Memphis was the name of a group of designers who established themselves in
Milan in Italy in 1981. Ettore Sottsass was an architect who moved into product design and became the principal figure of the movement.

- The Memphis designers were interested in mass production, advertising and the practical objects of daily life.
- Designs were colourful, witty and stylistic, influenced by comic strips, films and punk music.
- Products were designed with unusual combinations of materials such as melamine, glass, steel, industrial sheet metal and aluminium. Many products looked like children's toys.
- The 1980s saw the status of design grow. Design took over a key role in the development of individual lifestyles.

Design after Memphis

The New Design of the recent era was led by designers such as Ron Arad, Jasper Conran and Tom Dixon.

- Many designers moved away from functionalism and aimed to reflect the influences of daily life.
- Designers in Germany and the UK simplified forms and began working with materials such as concrete and steel.
- Designers made use of unusual combinations of colour and modern materials.
- Designers became more environmentally aware, designing products using recycled or recyclable materials.
- Marketing in the 1980s and 1990s developed into a much more significant force within product development. Companies have become much more successful at creating new markets and promoting lifestyle brand images. The domination of a particular 'style', unique to a particular time and culture, has disappeared allowing designers a much wider choice of inspiration.

New materials, processes and technologies

The stimulus to develop **new materials**, processes and technologies may result from:

- new legislation, for example the banning of dangerous materials
- scientific research, for example the space programme.

The development of new materials, processes and technologies is a constant influence on the design of products. Throughout modern design history, newly discovered materials have provided designers with the opportunity to develop products which become desirable because of their 'modern' or 'high tech' appearance. New processes and technologies have also transformed society because of their functional possibilities. Consider the changes brought about by the silicon chip.

Examiner's Tip

New technologies are emerging all the time and you should keep yourself informed – through the media – to watch out for new developments.

In recent years a range of so-called 'smart' materials has been developed. **Smart materials** react to changes in the environment and have led to the development of new types of sensors, actuators and structural components (Table 3.26).

Modern production techniques

Modern materials required the development of new production techniques.

Developments in plastics

The 1950s saw the development of new plastics such as acrylic, PVC and polypropylene, which were perceived as modern, exciting materials. The suitability of plastics for high-volume production

resulted in a proliferation of products such as furniture. In the 1970s the oil crisis and a change in fashion led to a drop in demand for plastics which became associated with cheap, poor-quality

Table 3.27 Examples of modern production techniques

Process	Description and advantages
Powder metallurgy	A range of processes including a form of injection moulding used to form pure metal and alloyed components. Increasingly used for precision car components. Small, accurate components for products such as watches. The advantages of this process are that it is accurate and cost effective
Self-chilling aluminium cans	Twisting the can breaks an internal barrier which allows water, trapped in a sealed layer of gel, to vaporise. The vapour is absorbed by a clay-drying agent, sealed in the base of the can. This process transfers the heat from the drink into the clay absorber. The advantages of this process are that it removes the need for any refrigeration; and novelty value attracts customers.

Table 3.26 Smart materials

Material	Description	Uses
Piezo-electric actuators	Small, slim electronic components which produce a sound in response to an electrical input.	Used in novelty greeting cards
'Polymorph'	A polymer which becomes soft and pliable in hot water (62°) and hardens when cool.	Used for rapid prototyping of graphic products
Light emitting plastics (LEPs)	Thin, flat, robust, flexible, energy-efficient, plastic displays, made by sandwiching a thin layer of polymer between two electrodes. When a low voltage is applied, polymers with different properties can emit red, blue and green light.	Likely to be used in hoarding advertisements, safety signage, mobile phones, CD players, TV and computer monitors
Smart ceramic materials	Absorbs and re-emits light energy to 'glow in the dark'.	Watch dials, emergency signs, torches
Thermochromatic materials	Microscopic liquid crystal capsules which can be combined with polymers. Change colour in response to changes in temperature.	Kettles, children's feeding spoons, battery test strips

Table 3.28 Examples of new biopolymers (environmentally friendly plastics)

Biopolymers	Description	Advantages
Enpol	Comparable strength to polythene	Fully biodegradable; two and a half times less material required to achieve comparable performance with conventional plastics
d2w™	A degradable polythene packaging already used by some supermarkets for their carrier bags	Fully biodegradable; can be recycled in the same way as non-degradable plastics
Ecofoam	Made from chips of foamed starch polymer	Ecofoam is water-soluble, reusable and free from static; it can replace polystyrene packaging materials

and non-ecological products. Plastics' popularity may improve in the future with the development of new eco-friendly biopolymers.

Computers and design

The single most significant technology to influence product development has been the ICT revolution. Computer technology has transformed the way designers work.

- It has enabled the development of small, multifunctional devices such as wrist watches which include compass, telephone and navigation utilities.
- CAD/CAM has revolutionised the development of technical and industrial products through the use of, for example virtual and rapid prototyping.
- The use of CAD graphics has led to new approaches to typography, layout and image making.
- The 'Mac-to-plate' process has revolutionised the digital press, and digital printing is increasingly used in fabric printing.
- The growth in home computing has stimulated awareness in the design of graphic products.
- The design of web pages has provided a new medium for designers.

Miniaturisation

Smaller products require fewer materials, less energy and less space. Advances in digital and microchip technologies have enabled designers to produce ever-smaller products. Micro technologies have been superseded by nano technologies which can construct working devices on a

Fig. 3.24 A microscopic gear shown next to a fly's leg

microscopic level. Components such as gears have been produced which are smaller than the diameter of a human hair. Suggested applications of micro and nano technologies include:

- tiny robots which are designed to clear human blood vessels
- the world's smallest silicon gyroscope with no moving parts.

Design and the environment

Designers have become more aware of how their work can affect the natural world and our quality of life. Increasingly, product specifications will include design requirements which help to protect the environment. This may include:

- the use of renewable materials
- reducing the amount of materials used

- the use of recycled materials
- designing for recycling
- using processes which reduce energy consumption
- using processes which do not produce harmful waste products.

Eco-design takes these issues as a priority, ensuring that all design and manufacturing activities will have the minimum of impact on the environment. Recent products include:

- the wind up Freeplay flashlight
- pencils made from recycled plastic cups
- electric- and solar-powered vehicles with longer lifespans, reduced weight and emissions. Modern cars are designed so that maintenance is simplified and old components can be recycled.

EXAMINATION QUESTIONS

Example questions and answers

 Q1 a) *The globalisation of the marketplace means that products must be suitable for consumers in different cultures and countries. Describe two issues which the designer might have to consider when designing products which will be marketed internationally.*

(2 marks)

Acceptable answer

1 Most automotive manufacturers supply vehicles around the world and need to ensure that their designs are **easily adapted to suit legal requirements** of different countries including right and left hand drive.
2 Design and marketing needs to take account of **linguistic differences** to avoid brand names which have negative connotations in some countries.

b) *Outline the advantages to 'newly industrialised countries' (NICs) and 'less economically developed countries' (LEDCs) of allowing foreign manufacturing companies to site factories within their borders.* **(5 marks)**

Acceptable answer

The jobs created will lead to **higher employment levels and living standards**. The new industries will require new skills which will **improve the level of expertise of the local workforce**. Taxes and export duties will provide the government with a **new source of foreign currency improving the balance of payments**. If the industry is new to the area it will help to **widen the economic base**. In addition the introduction of new technology may result in a useful **transfer of technology** into other domestic industries.

Professional designers at work

You need to

☐ **understand the relationship between designers of one-off, batch-produced and high-volume/continuous products and clients, manufacturers, users and society**

☐ **understand professional practice relating to design management, technology, marketing, business and ICT**

☐ **understand the work of professional designers and professional bodies.**

 KEY TERMS
Check you understand these terms

Design and production teams, Concurrent manufacturing, Product data management (PDM), Profit, Value for money, Moral and ethical values

 Further information can be found in *Advanced Design and Technology for Edexcel, Product Design: Graphics with Materials Technology*, Unit 3B1, section 2.

KEY POINTS

The relationship between designers and clients, manufacturers, users and society

The role of the designer

Very few designers work alone. In large companies, designers usually work as part of a **design and production team,** which shares the responsibilities described as follows.

Artistic and aesthetic role

Often the most significant selling point of a product is the way it looks and the image it projects. Designers often try to inject 'personality' into brand image and products. Designers need to take into account current and future user and market needs, moral, cultural, social and environmental issues, the competition from other products as well as more basic qualities such as shape, form, colour, pattern and style. Automotive manufacturers, for example, spend millions purely on colour research.

Functional and technical role

Designers need to make decisions about function, purpose, materials, systems, construction and finishing. It is important that designers are up to date with the latest technological developments in these areas.

Economic and marketing role

Designers need to be aware of market conditions and should have a clear understanding of production processes and costs so that innovative and attractive products are developed on budget and at the right price.

Organisational and management role

Concurrent manufacturing is becoming more common and brings together all the different departments to work simultaneously on product development. **Product data management** (**PDM**) enables fast and easy communication between design, production, suppliers and clients, and results in a faster time to market of products that meet customer needs.

The role of design and production teams

It is the responsibility of designers and production teams to develop products which match the quality and price requirements of the target market. In order to achieve this, they need to undertake some or all of the following activities.

Identification of needs and opportunities

- Market research
- Research into materials, processes and technology
- Develop a design brief and specification

Design (including CAD)

- Generate and develop ideas
- Test and model design proposals against the specification.

Production planning

- Produce working drawings and manufacturing specifications
- Organise main production stages
- Plan production schedule
- Plan resource requirements and cost production
- Plan quality control procedures.

Case study: British Airways' 'Go' airline

British Airways commissioned HHCL to help launch its new airline 'Go' which was designed to compete with other increasingly successful low-cost airlines.

Identifying the need and opportunity

The client/agency project team was briefed to identify the meaning of the brand to the

Fig. 3.25 The Go brand image

consumer and to develop a complete corporate image. Market research discovered that modern travellers wanted something in between the quality national airlines and low-cost airlines. The 'Go' brand was developed.

Design development

The design agency, Wolff Ollins, was briefed to develop a strong, simple, clever corporate image that would appeal to the target market. The result was the simple and uniquely recognisable 'coloured circles' design. Everything from the corporate stationery to the plane's livery was re-branded.

The success of the product

A simple and manageable advertising campaign was then planned which resulted in a smooth and successful product launch. The campaign utilised everything from television to sandwich bags to ensure that the target market recognised and understood the brand. The product was so successful that its rival, Easyjet, bought out the company.

> ### *Examiner's Tip*
>
> You will find it helpful to be able to refer to your own case studies which look at the development of new products or graphic identities and concentrate upon the role of the designer and production teams.

Professional practice relating to design management, technology, marketing, business and ICT

Design and marketing

Good design is not enough to make a successful product: many good products have failed to sell or even reach the market. Marketing involves:

- developing a product marketing plan aimed at the target market group
- providing well-designed, reliable, high-quality products at a price customers can afford

- establishing the right image ('lifestyle marketing')
- advertising and promotion (retailers, newspapers, magazines, TV, radio, film, Internet).

Target market groups (TMGs)

Markets are divided into segments which classify potential customers according to indicators such as age, disposable income, lifestyle and product end-use.

Marketing plan

A successful marketing plan uses market research to find out:

- consumer needs and consumer demand
- the age, income, size and location of the TMG
- the product type customers want
- the price range they are prepared to pay
- trends affecting the market
- competitors' products and marketing style
- deadlines for the product launch (such as Christmas).

Efficient design, manufacture and profit

Successfully managed product development and production planning will reduce costs and increase profits.

- Careful design management is important as, on average, 80 per cent of costs are incurred from the design stage.
- The difference between the selling price of a product and the costs (design, manufacturing, distributing and marketing) is **profit**. Efficient manufacture is essential to make a profit. This may be channelled into research and development of new or improved products.
- Production levels have to be planned so that supply will match demand. Unused production capacity is a waste of resources while insufficient production capacity will result in dissatisfied customers.
- Efficiency is measured as a percentage.

Design for manufacture

Well-designed products will take account of the manufacturing processes. Many companies will analyse design proposals with the aim of making any modifications which will reduce manufacturing costs. These modifications may include:

- simpler designs with fewer components
- changing materials to lighter or more cost-effective alternatives
- choosing materials and processes which reduce waste
- choosing materials and processes which require less energy
- changing the shape of components to make them more suitable for moulding
- altering machining processes to reduce waste or to save time.

Case study: Coca-Cola

In the light of the growing popularity of PET bottles, Coca-Cola Enterprises Ltd made a decision to re-examine the design of the '206' aluminium can. As part of the specification the new can had to:

- be suitable for the manufacturing process
- be suitable for the filling process
- be as strong as the 206 can
- retain stackability for distribution and display
- be suitable for vending machines
- be adopted by all European manufacturers to ensure standardisation.

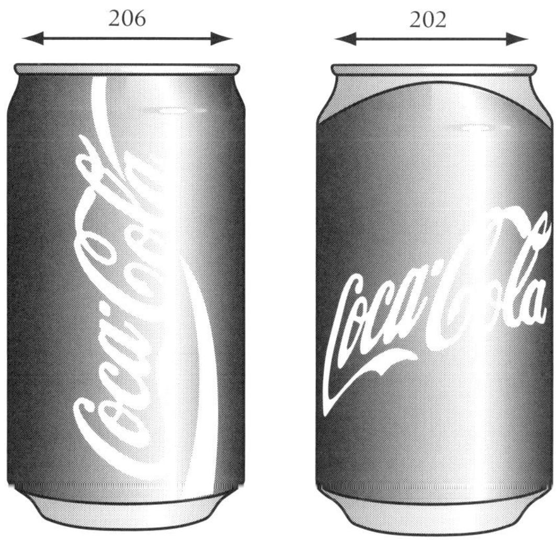

Minor changes to a product can lead to significant savings. The introduction of the '202' aluminium can, with a reduced-end diameter, reduced costs by a mere one-tenth of a penny. However, considering that Coca-Cola Enterprises Ltd sell around two billion cans a year you can work out that these savings become significant. The new lighter design resulted in additional benefits, reducing transport costs and the raw materials required as well as simplifying the production process. The company was careful to ensure that the new specification was agreed by all manufacturers across Europe.

The development of PET bottles has also led to significant savings. The two-litre bottle now uses about half the amount of PET plastic than its predecessors did, while shrink-wrapping six-bottle packs removes the need for cardboard trays.

Aesthetics, quality and value for money

Designing always involves a compromise between function, appearance (aesthetics), materials and cost. Quality and cost can vary in different products but must match customer expectations, in terms of aesthetics and function, so that they feel that they are getting **value for money**.

Fig. 3.26 The new '202' Coca-Cola can is a good example of 'lightweighting'

Examiner's Tips

- Make sure you can refer to products which illustrate your answer. The clockwork radio, for example, was developed by Trevor Baylis to give poor African communities access to information such as important health advice. Production was sited in South Africa providing welcome employment to many disabled people. However, production has been moved to China in order to reduce costs.
- Remember to read around the subject of professional designers at work. Pick a selection of significant designers, working in different fields, which appeal to you. Find out about their design philosophies and look at their work so that you can use the information to illustrate your answers in the examination.

Value issues related to design

The designer has to be aware that his or her **moral and ethical values** might conflict with those of the client, customer or society in general. These include:

- environmental issues (recycling, pollution)
- social issues (affordability, effects on quality of life)
- cultural issues (choices of colour, brand names)
- economic issues (effects of production and marketing on local economies).

The work of professional designers and professional bodies

Product Design

Ron Arad:
- Born in 1951
- Founded One-off Ltd, furniture company
- Designed the Rover Chair (1981)
- Is interested in industrial decay which is reflected in his one-off furniture products which are constructed from reclaimed industrial materials and components, such as sheet steel and concrete

Tom Dixon:
- Born in 1959
- Founded SPACE, a shop selling furniture including the Eurolounge range
- Appointed head of design at Habitat in 1998
- Designed the 'S' chair (1987) produced in volume by the Italian company Capelini
- Inspired by the Punk movement, Dixon worked with reclaimed and industrial materials, such as sheet metal and concrete to produce innovative furniture

James Dyson:
- Born in 1947
- One of the UK's best-known inventors/designers
- Founded the Dyson company in 1992
- Launched the Dual Cyclone vacuum cleaner in 1993
- Dyson is synonymous with vacuum cleaners which combine industrial cyclone technologies with boldly styled design. He is also responsible for many other inventions from wheelbarrows to marine vehicles and, more recently, washing machines. He is keen to blur the distinction between designers and engineers

Michael Graves:
- Born in 1934
- Architect and product designer
- Graves' early work was inspired by classicism and cubism
- He is a postmodernist and has designed in the Memphis style for Alessi

Jasper Morrison
- Born in 1959
- Designed the Universal range for the Italian company Cappellini
- A furniture designer committed to simple, practical and well-known products, Morrison is well-known for his storage units and minimalist furniture using unfinished plywood

Philippe Starck:
- Born in 1949
- Described as a 'super designer'
- In the 1980s Starck designed the interior of the Parisian café Café Costes, which brought Starck to prominence
- Starck designed all the fittings for Café Costes, including a three-legged chair
- Likes to design relatively inexpensive products for mass production including the iconic 'Juicy Salif Lemon Press', designed for Alessi
- Other work includes furniture, televisions, lights, water taps and toothbrushes
- His work fuses a range of influences and enjoys using unconventional combinations of materials

Architecture and product design

Ettore Sottsass:
- Born in 1917
- One of Italy's best-known designers
- Formed the Memphis design group in 1981
- Sottsass is best known for producing witty and colourful designs influenced by his interest in 1960s Pop Art and Aztec art
- He combined plastic laminates and wood veneers to produce products which contrasted with the modernist style and which was compared with children's toy design

Graphic Design

Nevil Brody:
- Born in 1957
- One of the UK's best-known graphic designers
- Founded FontWorks UK, an innovative typeface design company (1990)
- Neville Brody designed record covers before becoming a magazine art editor
- His work for *The Face* magazine was highly influential and Brody often ignored the conventions of layout grids and typesetting, influenced by Dada, Russian Constructivism, the Bauhaus and De Stijl

Peter Saville:
- Born in 1955
- Founding partner of Factory Records
- Has created the visual identity of brands such as New Order, Joy Division, Ultravox, OMD, Wham!, George Michael, Pulp and Suede. His album covers are well known and use computer technology to combine and transform 'borrowed' images with symbolism

Corporate identity

Michael Wolff and Wally Olins:
- Wolff Olins's company founded in 1965
- Created a new corporate image for British Telecom
- Wolff Olins pioneered the development of innovative corporate identity programmes for companies such as ICI, P&O, Prudential and British Telecom. Changes within BT resulting from privatisation and increased international activity along with a negative domestic public image signaled the need for a new corporate makeover. A completely new corporate identity was developed by Wolff Olins in response, which included completely new logos, stationery bills, telephone books, vans, shops, offices, company sign systems, telephone boxes, staff uniforms and internal newsletters.

Animation

Nick Park:
- Born in 1958
- Co-Director of Aardman Animation, an animation company
- Created Morph – an early 1970s TV character; Wallace and Gromit – TV characters featuring in a short TV series; Chicken Run – first Aardman animated feature film
- Films start life as storyboards which are turned into 2D, 3D or computer-generated animations. Aardman specialise in 3D stop-frame animation which relied upon detailed, scaled sets and moveable chracacters constructed from a jointed armature, a resin body and modelling clay. Lighting and sound are added to increase the sense of realism
- Successful merchandising (spin-off products) has helped to make the company particularly successful

The Crafts Council

The Crafts Council was created in 1975 from the Crafts Advisory Committee. It promotes contemporary crafts in the UK and provides services to craftspeople and the general public including educational activities, a reference library, a register of designer/makers and a picture gallery.

The Design Council

The Design Council was established in 1960 following the Council for Industrial Design. The aim of the Design Council is 'to inspire the best use of design by the UK, in the world context, to improve prosperity and well being'. The Council does this through encouraging business, education and government to work together productively and to communicate more effectively. It provides resources for schools and colleges as well as offering design and marketing advice to professionals.

The Engineering Council (EC)

The Engineering Council was created in 2002 as the main professional body for engineers, technologists and technicians. It also promotes engineering and technology education through the Neighbourhood Engineer Scheme and Women into Science and Technology (WISE).

EXAMINATION QUESTION

Example question and answer

 Q1 *The role of the designer and the production team can be summarised under the following headings.*

- *artistic and aesthetic*
- *functional and technical*
- *economic and marketing*
- *organisational and management.*

State the importance of these roles and explain what they might involve. **(12 marks)**

Acceptable answer
Artistic and aesthetic role

In most cases **a product will not sell unless it looks attractive**. It is the role of the professional designer to determine the look of a product. In order to create an aesthetically successful product, the designer **must consider qualities such as shape, form, colour, pattern and style**. In addition, the designer **must take account of wider issues such as value issues, competition from other products and future user and market needs**.

Functional and technical role

It is vital that products are **capable of performing the task for which they were designed**. Designers need to make **decisions about function, purpose, materials, systems, construction and finishing**. In

order to design successful products, designers **need to be aware of the latest technological developments** in these areas.

Economic and marketing role

The designer must be **aware of economic and market conditions so that the product represents value for money to the consumer**. This means that the designer should have a clear **understanding of production processes and costs so that price can be kept to a minimum**. In addition the designer must be **aware of current trends and styles so that the product will appeal to the target market**.

Organisational and management role

Delays cost money and the complex process of product development must be organised and managed effectively for products to reach profitability. Within a **concurrent manufacturing environment, departments work simultaneously on product development and require careful co-ordination. Concurrent manufacturing** systems will often take advantage of **product data management (PDM), which is used for fast and easy communication between design, production, suppliers and clients** and results in a faster time to market of products that meet customer needs.

Anthropometrics and ergonomics

You need to

☐ **understand the basic principles and applications of anthropometrics and ergonomics**
☐ **know about UK and International Standards.**

 KEY TERMS
Check you
understand these terms

Anthropometric data, Standard sizes and dimensions, Ergonomics, British Standards Institution (BSI), International Organisation for Standardisation (ISO)

> **Further information can be found in** *Advanced Design and Technology for Edexcel, Product Design: Graphics with Materials Technology*, **Unit 3B1, section 3.**

KEY POINTS

The basic principles and applications of anthropometrics and ergonomics

Anthropometrics

Anthropometrics is the study of human physical dimensions. These include height, width, length of reach, force exerted. Commonly, **anthropometric data** constitutes measurements taken from 90 per cent of the population, that is between the 5th and 95th percentile range ignoring the top and bottom 5 per cent. Designers use this information to design products suitable for this range of people. Data, providing **standard sizes and dimensions**, can be taken from published tables but it is sometimes necessary to take your own measurements when designing for a person with special needs, for example.

Ergonomics

Ergonomics is the science of designing products for human use. Ergonomics uses and applies anthropometric data to ensure that products and environments are straightforward, safe and comfortable to use.

Interacting with products

Almost all products need to be designed with ergonomics in mind.

- Jewellery needs to be designed to fit the people who wear it.
- Furniture needs to be designed carefully to ensure comfort and safety. When chairs, such as computer chairs, are used for long periods additional features are incorporated into the design such as adjustable seating positions, foot rests, rollers and contoured cushioning.
- Some products need to be tailored to very specific markets such as talking calculators for the blind.

When designing products designers need to consider areas such as shape, form, ease of use, size, weight, colour, noise, materials, maintenance, safety, texture and feel.

Interacting with users

The way in which a person uses a product is also an important ergonomic consideration.

- The size of the hand and the force of the grip are important factors in the design of handles for cutlery, tools and doors.
- Carrying handles must be sufficiently wide to allow a large hand to hold them.

Interacting with equipment

Control switches on equipment and machines have to be designed so that they can be operated easily and safely.

- Emergency switches need to be accessible but protected from accidental operation.
- Instrument displays need to be clear and unaffected by reflected light.
- Push button and catch-operated release mechanisms should allow ease of maintenance on products such as vacuum cleaners.
- Weight is an important consideration, especially when designing portable or specialist sporting equipment.

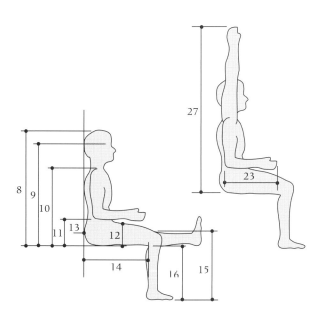

Fig. 3.27 Anthropometric data can be taken from tables and diagrams published for designers

Interacting with environments

Environments include buildings, landscaped gardens, workspaces and vehicle interiors. When designing environments designers need to consider areas such as movement, light, smell, noise, temperature, space, visibility, facilities, maintenance, safety, furniture and fittings.

- In vehicles, the seating and driving positions are adjustable. The driver is able to see and operate all the control, display gauges and meters. Foot pedals are of an appropriate size allowing the driver to exert sufficient force. Some systems are power assisted for ease of use.
- Checkouts in shops are arranged so that the lifting is minimised. Barcode readers are both fixed and portable for efficient operation. Prices are displayed for both the operator and the customer.
- Power station control rooms and aeroplane cockpits allow operators to monitor data easily, using gauges and displays. The layout of these must be clear so that they can be located and identified quickly when needed.

British and International Standards

British Standards Institution (BSI)

Formed in 1901, the **British Standards Institution** is now the world's leading standards and quality services organisation. The BSI works with manufacturing and service industries to develop UK, European and International standards. The BSI is:

- independent of government, industry and trade associations
- non-profit making
- recognised globally, operating in more than 90 countries

Fig. 3.28 Quality control marks on product packaging. Left to right: the kitemark logo, the 'e' mark, the 'CE' logo

- serves both the private and public sectors.

The BSI along with European and International Standards organisations establishes national and international standards, testing procedures and quality assurance processes. Most standards are established at the request of industry or to implement legislation. Many standards are voluntary but some are established by these organisations to support legislation. Products are allowed to display the appropriate logo such as the BSI 'Kitemark' as long as:

- they meet these standards and testing procedures
- quality systems are in place to ensure that all future products will conform to the same standards.

There is a range of British Standards that apply specifically to packaging. They are classified under the following headings.

- Marking and labelling on product packaging – including special requirements for food and toy labelling.
- Performance requirements for packaging materials and appropriate tests to determine risks of asphyxiation, resistance to harmful or unwanted substances, odour contamination and so on.
- Glossary and checklist – which define and illustrate technical terms and conditions.

International Organisation for Standardisation (ISO)

Other international organisations include:

- **International Organisation for Standardisation (ISO)** – the umbrella organisation responsible for the harmonisation of standards at an international level·
- International Electrotechnical Commission (IEC)
- European Committee for Standardisation (CEN) which implements the voluntary technical harmonisation of standards in Europe
- European Committee for Electrotechnical Standardisation (CENELEC)
- European Telecommunications Standards Institute (ETSI).

Setting standards

Most standards are set at the request of industry or government to implement legislation. Standards organisations establish:

- safety and product specifications
- testing procedures
- quality assurance techniques.

Products which meet the appropriate standards can carry the logos such as the Kitemark but companies need to demonstrate that quality control systems are in place to ensure that products will continue to meet these standards.

The advantages are:

- consumers benefit from being able to identify safe and quality products
- accurate product information is available to consumers, allowing more informed choice
- in many areas it is the responsibility of the retailer to ensure quality and safety
- the consumer is supported by national organisations which exist to enforce legal standards
- manufacturers benefit from clearly defined standards
- manufacturers benefit from increased sales.

The disadvantages are that it is more expensive to produce products to exacting standards.

Ergonomic considerations for designs and models

Designing products involves certain important considerations.

- It is not sufficient to design for yourself or for the 'average' person as this may exclude most of the population.
- Seemingly insignificant errors in design can lead to problems such as back pain over time.
- Good aesthetics can mask bad design.

Examiner's Tip

Look at the number of marks available in each section. It will give you a good idea of the number of points that the examiner is expecting you to cover to gain full marks.

EXAMINATION QUESTIONS

Example questions and answers

Q1 a) Name **one** national or international standards organisation. **(1 mark)**

Acceptable answer
British Standards Institution (BSI) or **International Organisation for Standardisation (ISO)**

b) Outline the role of these national and international standards organisations. **(5 marks)**

Acceptable answer
Most standards are set at the **request of industry or government**. Standards organisations establish **safety and product specifications, testing procedures** or **quality assurance techniques**. Products which meet the appropriate standards can carry the **logos such as the Kitemark** but companies need to demonstrate that **quality control systems** are in place to ensure that products will continue to meet these standards.

PRACTICE EXAMINATION STYLE QUESTION

1 a) Compare the personalities, history, philosophies and design styles of two of the following design movements.
   - Arts and Crafts
   - modernism and the Bauhaus
   - Art Deco
   - design of the 1950s and 1960s
   - the New Design. **(10 marks)**

   b) Good design is not enough to make a successful product: many good products have failed to sell or even reach the market. Marketing is just as important as design to the success of a product. Explain the main features of marketing. **(5 marks)**

2 a) Explain the terms:
   - anthropometrics
   - ergonomics. **(2 marks)**

   b) Explain how anthropometric data and ergonomics might be used by the designer in **one** of the contexts listed as follows:
   - products
   - equipment
   - environments. **(5 marks)**

   c) Explain how design and manufacturing standards are created by national and international standards organisations. **(4 marks)**

   d) Describe how the establishment of standards benefits both the consumer and manufacturer. **(4 marks)**

Total for this question paper: **30 marks**

3 B2 CAD/CAM (G303)

This option will be assessed in section B during the 1½ hour, Unit 3 examination. If you have chosen this option you should spend half of your time (45 minutes) answering all of the questions in this section. It is important to use appropriate specialist and technical language in the exam, along with accurate spelling, punctuation and grammar. Where appropriate you should also use clear, annotated sketches to explain your answer. *You do not have to study this chapter if you are taking the Design and Technology in Society option.*

The impact of CAD/CAM on industry

You need to

☐ **understand changes in production methods**
☐ **understand global manufacturing**
☐ **understand employment issues**
☐ **understand the trend from the use of manual CNC programming to the use of software programs that generate CNC codes from drawings**
☐ **understand the use of software applications that process production data and control a network of different machines from a central system.**

KEY TERMS

Check you
understand these terms

CAD, CAM, CIM, EDM, OCR, Photo realistic images, Virtual products, RPT, Global manufacturing, Remote manufacturing, CNC, G&M codes, FMS, TQM

📖 **Further information can be found in** *Advanced Design and Technology for Edexcel, Product Design: Graphics with Materials Technology*, **Unit 3B2, section 1.**

KEY POINTS

Changes in production methods

CAD/CAM and product development

CAD (computer-aided design) is used to create, develop, communicate and record design information. **CAM (computer-aided manufacture)** is used to translate design information into manufacturing information including production/process planning.

CIM (computer-integrated manufacture) is a means of integrating CAD and CAM.

Most products need to undergo a continual process of development through improvements in design or improvements in production methods. The stimulus for change is 'pushed' by the development of new technologies or 'pulled' by the changing demands of the market. Companies need to develop competitive products and services and ICT has become an increasingly important part of the process. Production systems are designed to ensure that the correct personnel, hardware, software, equipment, processes and systems are used to ensure that the client or customer receives the optimum product or service.

The pressures for change

New products are developed for many reasons.

- The emergence of new technologies allows designers to develop new, improved or cheaper products.
- Fluctuating market demand encourages companies to invest in the development of new, improved products.
- The development of new materials such as smart materials provides new design opportunities.
- Differences in national legal and cultural requirements lead to the development of design variants.
- Changes in the requirements for product lifespan can lead to longer- or shorter-lived products.
- Political and social changes will lead to changes in the demand for products.

Electronic document management (EDM)

EDM is a means of organising the vast amount of paperwork generated by the modern company. This is achieved by switching from a reliance upon paper-based documentation and correspondence to an ICT-based system, which is much swifter, more efficient and flexible, and more cost effective.

- Computer-generated documentation and correspondence can be stored, retrieved and transmitted electronically without any loss in quality or condition.
- Documentation and correspondence can be organised more effectively allowing searches to gain instant access to a wide range of information.
- The speed of EDM systems means that customers and clients enjoy an instant response to their enquiries.
- Paper-based documentation and correspondence can be scanned into the system, often using optical character recognition (**OCR**) software to translate the information into an editable form.

Architects, for example, produce a large quantity of plans which are difficult to manage because of their size. Bureau services allow these companies to convert these into digital files which allows the architects to archive all their work.

Changes in design and production methods

CAD applications allow the modern designer to:

- develop design concepts and ideas rapidly, down to the smallest detail
- integrate components in an assembly, all drawn to standard conventions
- use CAD applications to establish design dependencies so that changes to values in one part of the design cause changes in all of the dependent values. This is known as parametric designing
- produce **photo realistic images**: the designer can select materials, lighting conditions and lens settings
- produce **virtual products**: three-dimensional images of products can be viewed and manipulated on-screen. Specialist rendering software is used to heighten the sense of realism
- develop design concepts, model and test ideas. Accurate models can be produced quickly using technologies such as rapid prototyping (**RPT**) allowing designers to reduce potential communication problems and to find costly, potential errors or technical and tooling problems
- use DTP to allow designers to carry out a wide range of complex tasks, replacing time-consuming, manual processes. DTP also allows designers to output their publications onto film or even directly to plate
- use powerful, specialist tools. 'PowerSHAPE' allows designers to take CAD designs and prepare them for manufacture by adding features such as fillets and drafts.

The impact of CAD/CAM on design companies

Most industries in this sector work to tight deadlines and need to be able to respond instantly to changes in design requirements and technical problems which arise. Smaller companies must respond to a range of client and customer demands but cannot afford the large investments required to pay for skilled personnel and specialist equipment. Services provided by freelance (self-employed) experts and specialist bureau are used to fill the gaps.

Global manufacturing

The developments described so far, combined with the wider availability of cost effective transport, have made it possible for people in different areas of the world to work together effectively. Increasing international competition has encouraged companies to respond by looking beyond national borders to find specialist goods and services or to reduce costs. Large engineering projects commonly draw parts and utilise services from many different countries and many large manufacturers are able to transfer production to take advantage of lower wage costs and other incentives. This is known as **global manufacturing**.

Remote manufacturing

The ability to communicate instantly, using videoconferencing, with people all over the world combined with new technologies allowing reliable electronic data exchange means that designs can be manufactured anywhere in the world. This is known as **remote manufacturing**.

- Videoconferencing and other communication technologies make sure that designs can be developed in discussion with the manufacturer, ensuring they meet the constraints of the manufacturing process.
- The finished design can be sent electronically directly to the manufacturing centre where it is machined using CNC equipment. The process can be monitored by the design team using video links.
- The whole process is very quick. The finished components can be checked and dispatched the same day.
- The whole process allows designers to take advantage of CNC manufacturing technology without having to make the heavy investment necessary to purchase all the machinery.

Employment issues

CAD/CAM technologies and the growth in new working practices have led to changes in the patterns of employment. Increased automation has led to a reduced labour force. New technologies have created a demand for new skills.

Employment trends with design industries

Traditionally, designs were hand drawn by teams of skilled draughtspeople who worked together in large drawing offices. The development of CAD and related technologies has led to significant changes in working practices.

- Designers need to be highly skilled and more flexible in their approach.
- Designers are no longer tied to a location.
- Skills need to be updated regularly as new generations of software are developed.
- Smaller manufacturers may not be able to employ adequate numbers of these skilled workers and so turn to specialised bureau services to provide CAD/CAM services.

Employment trends within manufacturing industries

Traditionally, the skilled and semi-skilled workforce grouped itself into narrowly specialised trades. Demarcation placed rigid barriers between workplace activities which led to an inflexible workforce. New CAD/CAM technologies have created a demand for new skills and models of workforce organisation.

- Workers need a broader range of skills.
- Ongoing training is a feature of these new professions.
- All employees need to be more flexible in their approach, be prepared to take on new responsibilities and to operate as part of a team, cell or work centre. Workers and resources are directed to where they are needed to reduce bottlenecks and production times.

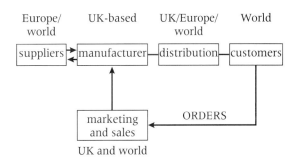

Fig. 3.29 The worldwide distribution of a UK manufacturing company

- Job security has weakened as manufacturing companies are more prepared to relocate to take advantage of fluctuating markets and changing economic conditions.
- These new demands have often led to skill shortages.

Future development of CAD/CAM technologies

Systems which rely on ICT, including CAD and CAM, must evolve to remain competitive. There is always pressure to increase productivity and to reduce the 'lead time' from product development to market. This requires continuous research and development into data manipulation and communication systems. Developments in the use of DTP, electronic data transfer and mobile communications are examples of evolving technologies which have helped to increase productivity. Innovation can be categorised into three areas.

- Critical technologies: the 'building blocks' from which products develop. Innovation arises from the development of new sensing and control systems, materials handling, storage and retrieval systems and the development of robotics technology.
- Enabling technologies: critical technologies are used to develop new products such as CNC machinery.
- Strategic technologies: these are concerned with planning systems which incorporate critical and enabling technologies. Decisions have to be made concerning capital investment in new products and factory layout.

Computer numerically controlled (CNC) machines

CNC machines are controlled by **G&M codes**, which are a list of number values and coordinates. Each number or code is assigned to a particular operation. These used to be typed in manually by machine-operators. Nowadays most CAD software is able to generate these G&M codes, automatically, from the design drawings. The advantages of CNC machines are shown in Table 3.32 (later in this Unit).

Computer-integrated manufacture (CIM)

Traditional, linear approaches to manufacturing ('over the wall') are straightforward but can have major drawbacks: design errors and manufacturing problems take longer to identify and 'lead times' (the time taken to develop a product so it is ready for sale) are much longer.

Concurrent engineering

CIM systems enable concurrent engineering where multidisciplinary teams start working together from the start of product development. Errors and problems are recognised much more quickly and lead times are reduced. You may need to refresh your memory of CIM by referring to Unit 1.

Flexible manufacturing systems (FMS)

Thorough, responsive planning and organisation are essential in the modern business in order to respond quickly to changes in demand and customer requirements. The features of a **FMS** include:

- multi-purpose, automated ICT and CNC equipment
- centralised control of a network of systems and machines
- robot technology
- relational databases making data accessible
- computer aided process control (CAPP) used to plan manufacturing operations

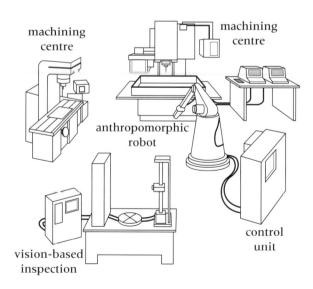

Fig. 3.30 A flexible manufacturing cell

- computer aided production management (CAPM) uses data to manage manufacturing operations.

It is much easier to make last-minute changes and to organise the most efficient use of resources without compromising on quality.

Total quality management (TQM)

The improved management of design and production data allows quality to be monitored closely through all stages of product development. **Total quality management (TQM)** seeks to develop a culture where all employees are responsible for ensuring quality and are committed to continuous improvement (CI).

The use of software applications that process production data and control networks

The advantages of centralising and integrating control systems has been discussed above. CIM and FMS systems, for example, rely on sophisticated software to control and co-ordinate a complex range of processes and CNC machinery. Figure 3.31 illustrates the range of centrally controlled operations within a CIM system.

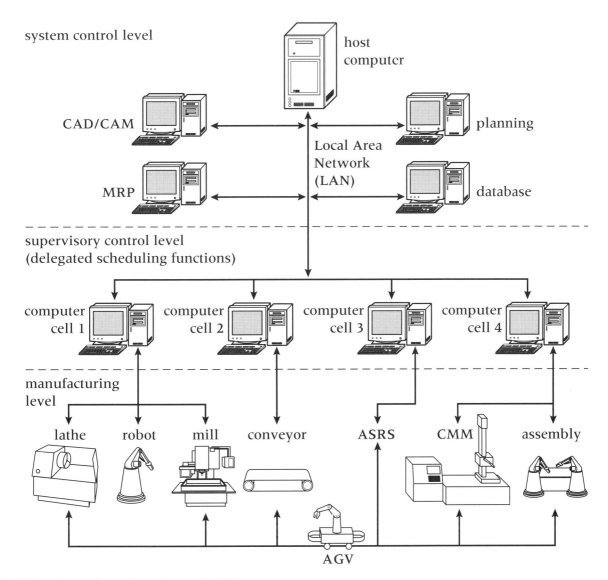

Fig. 3.31 A schematic diagram of a centrally controlled CIM system

EXAMINATION QUESTIONS

Example questions and answers

 Q1 *a) Give **three** advantages of computer-integrated manufacture (CIM).* **(3 marks)**

Acceptable answer

1 CIM allows a **number of people to work on a project** at the same time (concurrent engineering).
2 CIM **increases the effectiveness of quality control using automated sensing systems**.
3 CIM **increases flexibility** by allowing **changes to designs or production processes** to be made **quickly**.

b) Describe the consequences for the workforce of increased reliance on CAD/CAM technologies.

(4 marks)

Acceptable answer

Workers need a **broader range of skills** which require an **ongoing training programme so that they can keep up to date with developing technologies**. These new demands have often led to **skill shortages**. Employees cannot rely on a job for life as **job security has weakened** as manufacturing **companies are more prepared to relocate** to take advantage of fluctuating markets and changing economic conditions.

Computer-aided design

You need to

- ☐ **understand the use of CAD to aid the design process**
- ☐ **know common input devices**
- ☐ **know common output devices.**

 KEY TERMS
Check you
understand these terms

Parametric, PCBs, Virtual products, Total design concepts, Multimedia, Input devices, Output devices

Further information can be found in *Advanced Design and Technology for Edexcel, Product Design: Graphics with Materials Technology*, **Unit 3B2, section 2.**

KEY POINTS

The use of CAD to aid the design process

Components of a CAD System

A computer-aided design (CAD) system is the combination of software and hardware used to create, develop, test, communicate and record design information.

Hardware

CAD programs require powerful processors (CPUs) and lots of memory (RAM). CAD systems used to require specially designed (dedicated) systems and mainframe/minicomputers computers but, due to advances in the power of personal (micro) computers (PCs), it is possible to use this software on conventional networks (LANS, Intranets and WANS) or on stand-alone computers.

Software

Hardware is useless without software. Operating Systems (OS) such as Windows allow several

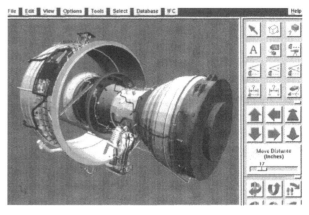

Fig. 3.32 A complex product designed using CAD software

tasks or programs to run at the same time, and provide a graphical user interface (GUI) which offers a more user-friendly method of communication through the use of menus, buttons and icons or through keyboard 'shortcuts'. Modern software also allows users to customise their workspace. Applications such as CAD programs work within the OS environment.

Table 3.29 Design software

Software	Description; Use; Advantages
CAD drawing software Examples: Techsoft 2d Design PTC ProDesktop AutoCAD TurboCAD	Generally refers to 2D and 3D technical drawing applications which are used to create and modify accurate, dimensioned working drawings. • Many are **parametric** programs which automatically adjust the whole drawing to accommodate changes made by the designer. • Some programs allow the structure to be tested on-screen. • Dimensions are generated automatically and can be easily adjusted. • Drawings can be organised in layers to allow for ease of editing. • Instructions can be embedded in the design such as attributing line colours for different operations, e.g. scoring/cutting or changing tools. • Drawings can be rendered to test aesthetics. • Working drawings and parts lists can be generated automatically for designers, machine operators and stock control. • Libraries of pre-drawn 'primitives' (2D shapes or 3D forms) or pre-drawn components can be used to save time. • Commonly used functions such as sweep techniques are incorporated as commands in drop-down menus or as buttons. • G&M codes can be generated automatically and sent to a CNC machine. • Multimedia and virtual reality technologies allow the user to interact with the program. • Advantages are: speed; accuracy; repeatability; ease of modification; ease of storage; ease of transport; ease of testing; range of tools • Used for complex engineering drawings and architectural plans; packaging nets and lay planning; circuit board layouts; 2D/3D modelling and prototyping; virtual products
DTP Draw, paint and photo applications Examples: CorelDraw Adobe Photoshop Macromedia Freehand	These applications are used to create and manipulate visual images. Designs can be created from scratch or conventional images can be scanned into the program and manipulated using a wide range of tools. Photographs can also be introduced directly using a digital camera. • Initial drawings are sent to client for approval. • Once approval is granted, the drawing is scanned and imported into the application. • The image is traced on-screen to create a digital outline. • The image can now be manipulated and colour can be added. • A hard copy is printed. • Images can be stored as vector drawings or bitmaps. • Used for web graphics; logos; magazine illustration; advertising images; photograph retouching • Advantages are: designs can be modified easily; wide choice of typefaces and clipart; manual processes such as zoom, cut and paste can be reproduced electronically; a wide range of tools is available for use to create interesting effects automatically; the image can be built up in layers which can be modified individually; most applications now include features to help in the creation of web graphics

Refer to Unit 3A to refresh your memory of desktop publishing.

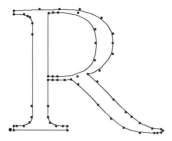

Fig. 3.33a Vector graphics: stored as a line drawing with colour fills. Can be manipulated in many ways without losing image quality. Small sized files

Fig. 3.33b Raster graphics: (bitmaps) stored as a large collection of different coloured pixels (tiny squares). Limited manipulation possible but enlarging leads to loss of image quality. Large file sizes

Software standards

To ensure compatibility, it is important that designers and engineers can work to common standards. Designers need to work to standards such as ANSI, ISO or BSI for technical engineering drawings. Some standards have been established by recognised standards organisations, but many CAD/CAM standards have tended to be established over time by the most successful companies in any particular field. These include:

- Hayes command set for modems
- Hewlett Packard Printer Control Language (PCL) for laser printers
- Postscript (PS) page description language for laser printers
- Data Exchange File (DXF) for CAD files created by AutoDesk.

Managing CAD data

CAD data can be stored in many forms including hard discs, magnetic tape, CD(R)-ROM and network servers. Large files can be compressed using WinZip or similar programs. There are many file formats including DXF, WMF, PICT and VRML.

Constructing accurate drawings and complex products

Engineers use CAD in a variety of ways to design and test a product's function, form, structure and aesthetics. Materials, surface finishes and dimensions can be specified within the drawing. Modern CIM systems are also able to share design data among different departments, suppliers and systems. Applications include:

- promotional images to sell the product
- sales presentations and company reports
- marketing materials and brochures for company websites
- system flow diagrams
- PCB track design
- accurate and complex drawings which contain all the information necessary to make the product
- drawings used to test the product.

2D and 3D drawings

Traditionally, 2D drawings were used to communicate designs. They are still important but the advantages of 3D software now mean that most products are developed in 3D. Most 3D CAD applications will generate 2D drawings automatically.

CAD drawings must communicate all the information required to manufacture the design. Complex products can be represented clearly and accurately using a wide range of features offered by a professional CAD system. There are two types of drawings.

- *detail drawings*: representations of individual parts
- *assembly drawings*: a representation of all parts which go together to form a product.

In order to communicate all the information required, designers may use a range of drawing conventions.

- Sectional views allow the designer to slice the product open along a 'cutting plane' to show hidden features. Cross-hatching shows cut surfaces. CAD programs can generate these views automatically.

- Exploded views show the product partially disassembled (exploded) and are used to show assembly details and internal features.

Dimensioning and annotation

It is essential to provide accurate dimensions and additional details to support CAD generated drawings. In industries which take advantage of global manufacturing opportunities it is essential that everyone uses the same conventions and works to the same standards. CAD programs generate dimensions automatically and can be set to use ISO standards to ensure the correct practices are used. General principles of dimensioning include:

- the minimum number of dimensions should be used
- dimensions should incorporate appropriate tolerances
- dimensions should not interfere with the drawing wherever possible
- dimension lines should not cross.

CAD modelling

It is far more cost effective to make mistakes and modifications at the early stages of product development than later in the process. CAD allows products to be modelled digitally so that virtual prototypes can be modified and tested on-screen reducing the expense of producing actual prototypes. Commonly used functions such as sweep techniques are incorporated as commands in drop-down menus or as buttons. The software requires powerful computers and processors to carry out the complex mathematical calculations.

- *Wireframe models* are 'transparent' representations of the product constructed from lines. Surfaces are not shown and cannot therefore be rendered. They are useful for showing external features and details but can be difficult to understand.
- *Surface models* are 'translucent' representations which share some of the advantages of wireframe models but which are easier to understand
- *Solid models* are 'solid', opaque representations of the product. These are the clearest representations and they also contain most data about the product.

Fig. 3.34 Crash Bandicoot – A three-dimensional computer-generated character from a computer game

Rendering

Rendering is the process of applying colour, pattern, texture, light and shade to a computer model. Realism is improved by hiding unwanted elements such as construction lines and adding backgrounds. Solid, rendered models are opaque so hidden details remain hidden. CAD and specialist rendering software use a range of methods to render on-screen objects including:

- flat shading
- graduated shading
- phong shading (slower process which generates highlights to improve realism)
- texture mapping (slow, memory intensive process which applies 2D textures around 3D forms. Textures apply 2D properties such as colour and brightness and 3D properties such as transparency and reflectivity).

Creating and modifying designs and layouts

Computer to plate and digital technologies

Traditional methods of producing printing plates involve the creation of negative or positive films from camera-ready artwork. The film is then used to expose photosensitive printing plates, which then have to be developed. 'Computer to plate' techniques use laser technology to produce printing plates directly from digital files. This shortens the whole process, reduces costs and improves the quality and definition of the end product by cutting out the intermediate stages of production. Modern digital printers are now able to print high-quality images onto a range of materials and products. These printers can be used to produce high-quality mock-ups for new product lines or to personalise marketing materials such as mouse mats.

Using computers to design PCBs

Printed circuit boards (**PCBs**) are used to link components to form an electronic circuit. They can be very complex, linking thousands of components, and are often double-sided. Designers rely on computer technology to test virtual circuits and to plan the route of the copper tracks on the PCB. The design data is then passed to the production engineers who use it to set up the CNC machines used to automatically insert the components. There are three stages.

1 The schematic circuit is drawn as a diagram using symbols.
2 The circuit is simulated to test for faults.
3 The track layout is auto-routed.

Creating virtual products and total design concepts

Virtual reality programs enable designers to generate virtual designs which allow the user to interact with the objects or environments on the screen. Architects can construct virtual buildings, which allow the client to 'walk' through the building, viewing it from different angles or in different weather conditions. **Virtual products** can be created which allow the customer to view the object from different angles.

It will be much easier to develop and communicate design proposals and **total design concepts** in the future with the help of ICT. Two-dimensional and three-dimensional CAD images, animations, text, sound and global communications technology can be combined together to create a detailed and comprehensive **multimedia** working environment. Designers will be able to work

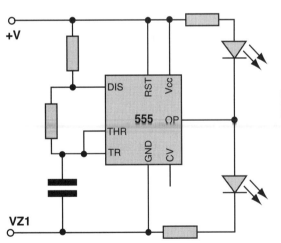

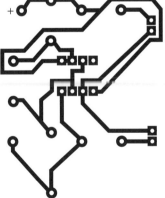

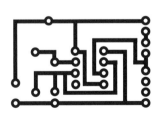

Stage 1
Software can be used to simulate different circuits. Components are shown as symbols in a schematic diagram. The circuits can then be tested on screen and the software will identify problems such as overloaded components

Stage 2
When the designers are happy with the circuit they can use auto routeing software to generate tracks for PCB

Stage 3
The auto routeing software will arrange the tracks to make efficient use of space and will output the masks needed to produce the PCB

Fig. 3.35 A simple circuit designed using simulation and auto routeing software

together with the help of 'expert' systems linked to large databases of production data. Features of these systems will include:

- communications systems integrating videoconferencing, intelligent whiteboards and intranets
- rapid data transfer systems, such as broadband, allowing engineers and designers to work together on the product simultaneously
- multimedia presentations for clients and customers using VRML to show virtual products
- efficient management of communications which automatically routes electronic documents to people who need them.

Common input devices

Input devices describe hardware which is used to control or enter data into a computer. Command-driven interfaces have been largely replaced by graphic user interfaces (GUIs). These GUIs use pull down menus and icons to generate commands and manipulate the design on-screen. Input devices tend to produce analogue signals which need to be converted into digital signals by a digital signal processor (DSP). Input devices allow:

- ease of control by clicking on icons
- information to be communicated
- data entry such as dimension
- selection and manipulation of the design.

Table 3.30 Input devices

Hardware	Description	Use	Advantages
Mouse	Mechanical or optical versions often incorporating a scroll wheel. Used to move cursor and to select software functions but not very accurate. Wireless mice also available.	Everyday computer use	Inexpensive; easy to use
Tracker-ball	An 'upside down mouse' with large ball and buttons. Rolling the ball moves the cursor.	Graphic programs, such as VR, where images are constantly being moved	Remains stationary; more precise than mouse
Digitiser	Large reactive electronic table and 'puck'. Pre-programmed buttons operate commonly used operations. Puck is moved over table surface and is used to send coordinates to screen or to select functions.	Technical drawings	Very accurate; drawings and sketches can be transferred directly to screen
Graphics tablet	Pressure sensitive tablet and stylus (pen), available in a range of sizes. Program functions can be selected from pre-programmed areas of tablet. Pen is moved over surface of tablet to create an image which is transmitted to the screen.	Art/design; artwork	Senses stylus pressure allowing variation in line quality; closest to drawing by hand
Photo CD	CD ROMs can be used to store large amounts of data required by large, high-resolution image files. Computers with CD drives can be used to manipulate images and to send to printer.	Personal photos; design images	Easily transportable; copies can be printed, saves using space on hard disc

▶

Table 3.30 Input devices *(continued)*

Hardware	Description	Use	Advantages
2D scanners	These allow the designer to input analogue data and photographs, creating digital, raster images which can be manipulated using different software applications. Resolution is measured in dots per inch (DPI). Scanning produces large file sizes especially when using colour. Can be used in conjunction with OCR software. A wide range of scanners is available including handheld, flatbed, sheet-fed, drum, overhead and transparency scanners.	Inputting line artwork to be developed into vector graphics; OCR; to digitise photographs or transparencies	Digitised images can be stored and transmitted more efficiently; a wide range of software allows images to be manipulated on-screen; images can be incorporated into publications or web pages
3D scanners	Objects can be scanned in three dimensions and the digital data used to create 3D computer models. There are two types of scanners: contact scanners (which use a probe to supply geometric data) and non-contact scanners (e.g. laser, ultrasonic and magnetic scanners which use triangulation to locate points). Most scanners are available in manual and automatic forms.	To transfer solid concept models into digital form; to make copies of existing forms	Allow designers to produce relatively accurate computer models of solid objects; increase flexibility of design development
Digital video Digital cameras	Digital video cameras can be used to record moving images. Digital cameras do not use conventional film but store images in digital format which can be down loaded directly into the computer.	Personal use; CD ROMs; Internet Used to create original digital images	Low operating costs; speed of data conversion; reliance on film/hard copy removed; digitised images can be stored and transmitted more efficiently; a wide range of software allows images to be manipulated on-screen; images can be incorporated into publications or web pages

Common output devices

Output devices describe hardware connected to a computer which convert data or designs into a useful form. CNC technology needs an interface between CAD and CAM to translate the drawing data into a useable form. The connection is made using cables or, in some cases, via wireless infrared or radio technology.

Table 3.31 Output devices

Hardware	Description	Use	Advantages
Dye sublimation printers	Expensive, high quality but slow process. The four colours of ink (dye) are stored on a film, which is transferred onto paper using a heated print head which turns the ink into a gas. The amount of ink released can be adjusted by varying the temperature of the print head.	Used where the highest-quality prints are needed	Very high-quality; precise dense colour without dots or dithering; smoothly gradated tones
Monitors	Monochrome, greyscale and colour.	Visual output	Larger, higher resolution monitors (measured by dpi) display more information
Thermo autochrome (TA) printing	Requires special TA paper, which is coated with three layers of coloured pigment, each activated by a different temperature. Three passes are required, each at a different temperature, and at each stage the colour is fixed with UV light.	High-quality digital prints	Very high-quality
Digital printing	Digital printing technologies link modern, digital printing presses and computers which can print directly without the need to make printing plates. Based on fast, high-quality laser technologies, these printers come with a full range of image handling capabilities much like some of the tools found in DTP software such as image cleanup, enlargement and reduction.	Affordable technology for small and large printing companies and reprographic departments in larger companies	Fast (250ppm), high-quality output, flexible, centrally controlled; production details can be specified and attached to print files; documents can be seen on-screen as they will be printed; simple to manage multiple print jobs – jobs can be rearranged to avoid unnecessary changes in paper; jobs can be stored easily for repeat orders; more effective response to fluctuating market demands
XY plotters	Plotters use pens for precise accurate lines on larger drawings.	Large technical drawings such as: architectural plans, engineering drawings, final designs	Clean accurate line drawings; quick; automatically changes between different coloured pens; suitable for large drawings

You also need to know about plotter-cutters (Unit 1), computer printers (Unit 3A) and CNC equipment (later in this Unit).

EXAMINATION QUESTIONS

Example questions and answers

 Q1 a) Name **one** input device which is commonly used with CAD applications. **(1 mark)**

Acceptable answer
Digitiser

b) Many CAD programs are described as 'parametric'. Explain what this means. **(2 marks)**

Acceptable answer
When using a fully parametric CAD application, the designer or engineer can **make a change to one part of the design** such as changing a dimension and **the software will automatically adjust the rest of the design to accommodate the modification.**

c) Describe **three** specialist features of CAD programs (not including parametric features) which help designers and manufacturers. **(6 marks)**

Acceptable answer
1 **Manufacturing instructions can be embedded in the design** such as attributing line colours for different operations. **This speeds up the manufacturing process as it avoids the need to start and stop CNC machinery to change settings manually.**
2 **Working drawings and parts lists can be generated automatically** which **speeds up the process and improves the quality of information available to manufacturers.**
3 Much **time can be saved** by utilising the **libraries of pre-drawn 'primitives' or pre-drawn components**.

Computer-aided manufacture

You need to

- ☐ **understand the applications of common CNC machines**
- ☐ **understand the use of CAM in one-off, batch and high-volume/continuous production**
- ☐ **understand the advantages and disadvantages of CAM.**

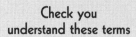

KEY TERMS
Check you understand these terms

RPT, LOM, Cutting tools, Tool paths, Speeds, Feeds

Further information can be found in *Advanced Design and Technology for Edexcel, Product Design: Graphics with Materials Technology*, **Unit 3B2, section 3.**

KEY POINTS

The applications, advantages and disadvantages of common CNC machines

Rapid prototyping

CAD/CAM technologies allow the designer to test ideas very quickly through rapid prototyping (**RPT**). Physical models can be generated directly and automatically from on-screen designs using CNC equipment. Stereolithography is a 'tool-less' process which uses laser technology to solidify liquid polymers to form complex 3D shapes (see Fig 3.36). Layered object modelling (**LOM**) produces models from CAD drawings, made from layers of self-adhesive card which are built up on a pegged jig.

- Accurate models can be generated very quickly from CAD drawings.
- RPT improves ability of designers to communicate designs to colleagues and clients.
- Potential errors such as tooling problems can be identified more readily.

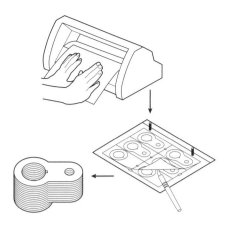

Fig. 3.36 Layered object modelling

Features of CNC machinery

Processing flexibility is the key feature of CIM and CNC machines. Features of CNC equipment include:

- the tool or material moves, or both
- tools can operate in 1–5 axes
- larger machines have a machine control unit (MCU) which manages operations
- movement is controlled by a series of servo-motors or stepper motors (actuators)
- feedback is provided by sensing devices (transducers) or encoders
- tool magazines are available to allow automatic tool changes.

Tools

- Most **cutting tools** are made from high-speed steel (HSS), tungsten carbide or ceramic materials.
- Tools are available in a wide range of profiles determined by their purpose.
- Tools are designed to direct waste material away from the work (e.g. flutes on milling cutter).
- Tools are usually held in collets.
- Some operations require coolant, such as oil, to protect tool and work.

Tool paths, cutting and plotting motions

- **Tool paths** describe the route the cutting tool takes.
- Motion can be described as 'point to point', 'straight cutting' or 'contouring'.
- **Speeds** are the rate at which the tool operates (e.g. rpm of a collet, spindle or chuck).
- **Feeds** are the rate at which the cutting tool and work piece move in relation to each other (e.g. the rate (mm/s) at which a lathe

Table 3.32 CNC machines

Hardware	Description	Use
CNC lathes	Automated versions of manual lathes; programmed to change tools automatically	Turning and boring wood, metal and plastic components
CNC routers, milling machines and engravers	3 to 5 axis versions	Wood, metal and plastic: 3D prototypes, moulds, cutting dies, printing plates, sign making
CNC cutting machines such as flame, laser, spark erosion cutting machines	A wide range of specialist machines	Cutting and binding printed material
Pressing, punching, bending and die-cutting machines	A wide range of specialist machines	Used to process sheet metals, plastics, paper and boards: flat carton packs; document wallets
Knitting, sewing, embroidery machines and looms	Computer controlled textile machines	Used to construct or enhance textile products
Printers	Wide range including inkjet, laser, dye sublimation, thermo autochrome and digital printers	Ranging from general purpose printing to specialist applications

tool moves 'into' the work piece).

- Feeds and speeds are determined by the cutting depth, material and quality of finish required. Harder materials, for example, generally require slower speeds and feeds.
- Roughing cuts remove larger amounts of material than finishing cuts.
- Rapid traversing allows the tool or work piece to move rapidly when no machining is taking place.

Scale of production

The scale or level of production will fall into one of three categories: one-off, batch, high-volume or continuous production. You may need to refresh your memory of this subject by referring to Unit 1.

Recent developments

Flexible manufacturing systems rely on ITC to provide 'quick response' systems which can customise products to meet the requirements of the client.

Outsourcing allows smaller manufacturers access to specialist ITC resources in order to provide a real FMS service to clients. CAD bureau services, for example, provide specialist skills and access to expensive resources which can be used by smaller companies that are unable to make the heavy investment necessary to offer these services in-house.

Distributed numerical control (DNC) 'part programs' can be downloaded into the memory of the MCUs as and when required from a central computer within a CIM system. This avoids tying up the computer which can continue to service and coordinate the rest of production. The stages in part programming are:

1 CAD program identifies required machining operations
2 appropriate tools are suggested or selected from a tool library
3 tool paths are calculated
4 machining is simulated on-screen
5 errors such as collisions are identified and displayed
6 a cutter file is produced which can be read by the CNC machine
7 the cutter file is transmitted to the CNC machine.

Table 3.33 The advantages and disadvantages of CAM

Advantages of CAM	Disadvantages of CAM
Speed: although CAM machines may seem slow sometimes, they work much faster than humans. *Accuracy*: even school-based CAM machinery will work to tolerances approaching +/– 1/100th of a millimetre. Higher precision and less human error lead to less waste. It is now possible to manufacture very complex designs. *Reliability*: the software will check and simulate the machining operation. *Repeatability*: it is easy to reproduce identical components. *Productivity*: more products can be produced because CAM machines can work continuously without the need for breaks. *Safety*: since the operator is not in direct contact with the tools or materials, accidents happen rarely. CAM machines can work with dangerous materials. *Flexibility*: highly suitable for batch production and JIT where systems need to switch production between jobs regularly. Many machines are multifunctional such as plotter-cutters. *Operating costs*: speed and automation of previously manual operations lead to low unit and operating costs. There is also less waste.	*Employment issues*: reduction in workforce as many manual tasks become automated. Some human operations become repetitive and undemanding as the machines do all the work. *Skills*: increased flexibility and new skills required from the workforce. *Investment*: CNC machines are expensive and require a large initial outlay.

EXAMINATION QUESTION

Example question and answer

 Q1 *a) A school has purchased a new minibus and has approached a local sign maker to produce the school name which will be applied to the side of the minibus. What type of CNC machinery is most likely to be used to produce the school name?* **(1 mark)**

Acceptable answer
(CNC) vinyl cutter/(CNC) plotter-cutter

b) The sign making company has invested heavily in CNC equipment. Signs and transport livery used to be produced by hand. Describe two negative consequences of making such a change in production methods. **(4 marks)**

Acceptable answer
Investing in CNC machinery may lead to a **reduction in the workforce** because many **manual tasks become automated**.

CNC machines are **very expensive** compared with the equipment needed to produce signs manually. It will take a **long time** before the company sees a **return on the large initial investment**.

PRACTICE EXAMINATION STYLE QUESTION

1 a) Describe, briefly, how designers might make use of **two** of the following devices. **(4 marks)**
   - mouse
   - tracker-ball
   - digitiser
   - graphics tablet
   - photo CD
   - 2D scanners
   - 3D scanners
   - digital video
   - digital camera.

   b) Describe how specific tools and features within CAD programs aid the designer or engineer. **(5 marks)**

   c) Describe the use of virtual products in the modern design and manufacturing organisation. **(3 marks)**

   d) Explain, briefly, the meaning of the following innovation technologies.
   - critical technologies
   - enabling technologies
   - strategic technologies. **(3 marks)**

2 a) Explain **two** of the following terms.
   - computer numerical control (CNC)
   - G&M codes
   - computer-integrated manufacture (CIM). **(4 marks)**

   b) Name **one** specific example of CNC machinery. **(1 mark)**

   c) Explain the advantages of using CNC machinery during manufacturing. **(5 marks)**

   d) Describe the use of remote manufacturing. **(5 marks)**

Total for this question paper: **30 marks**

Part 3
Advanced GCE (A2)

UNIT 4a

Further study of materials, components and systems (G401)

At this point in the course you should have developed a sound understanding of a range of properties, materials, construction methods and industrial processes, so you may wish to refresh your memory by revising material you have covered for Units 1 and 3A.

Unit 4 follows the same pattern as Unit 3. It is divided into two sections.

- Section A: Materials, components and systems (compulsory for all candidates)

- Section B: Consists of two options (of which you will study only **one**).

Section A will be assessed during the $1\frac{1}{2}$ hour, Unit 4 examination. You should spend half of your time, about 45 minutes, answering all of the questions for this section. It is important to use appropriate specialist and technical language in the exam along with accurate spelling, punctuation and grammar. Where appropriate, you are encouraged to include clear, annotated sketches to explain your answer.

Selection of materials

You need to

- ☐ **understand, devise and select appropriate methods of construction for graphics materials and products**
- ☐ **understand the relationship between characteristics, properties and materials choice.**

KEY TERMS

Check you understand these terms

Material limitations, Wear and deterioration, Maintenance, Life costs

Further information can be found in *Advanced Design and Technology for Edexcel, Product Design: Graphics with Materials Technology*, Unit 3A, section 1, and Unit 4A, section 1.

Examiner's Tip

In order to answer examination questions based on this section you should be able to:

- discuss the choice of materials and processes for existing products
- make your own recommendations for the manufacture of new products.

KEY POINTS

Choosing materials and processes

Designers need to develop an understanding of materials, processes and finishing techniques. They need to be able to make appropriate recommendations for the manufacture of their products. The selection of materials depends upon the relationship between quality, manufacturing process, scale of production, material limitations, wear and deterioration, maintenance and life cost.

You should be familiar with most of these terms. All designs are constrained by **material limitations** and designers have to work within these. Material limitations can be overcome by:

- enhancing the properties of the material by combining it with another (e.g. varnishing card)
- using more of the material to increase strength (such as using more layers of veneer to produce stronger wood laminates).

Materials are prone to **wear and deterioration** and therefore need to be designed to allow for **maintenance**. The designer can counteract the effects of wear and deterioration by:

- choosing materials with appropriate properties (for example, using polypropylene for folders with integral hinges)
- enhancing the properties of the material (for example, painting steel to inhibit rust).

The designer will normally have to make compromises in one or more areas. Expensive finishes may not be possible if the designer is constrained within tight budgets. For example, a graphic designer may not be able to select expensive high-quality papers or print finishes, and a product designer may not be able to specify expensive aluminium casing for a product because injection moulded plastic may be more cost effective and more suitable for high-volume production.

Levels (scale) of production

The choice of manufacturing process and scale of production will determine the selection of materials (Table 4.1).

The level of production is determined by the estimated level of demand and available

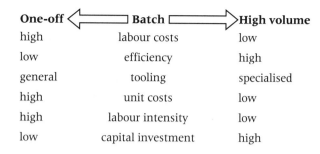

One-off	Batch	High volume
high	labour costs	low
low	efficiency	high
general	tooling	specialised
high	unit costs	low
high	labour intensity	low
low	capital investment	high

Fig. 4.1 Comparing costs and levels of production

manufacturing capacity. It affects costs and price. It also places differing demands on the designer and manufacturer.

Life costs

Life costs include the many hidden costs associated with products. Costs are calculated over the whole product life cycle, from the extraction of the raw materials to the disposal of the product. These hidden costs may include environmental costs and moral or social costs.

Environmental costs

All manufacturing has some effect on the environment and may generate additional costs such as:

- depletion of mature trees in managed forests
- soil erosion caused by deforestation of unmanaged forests
- damage to the physical environment through mining
- chemical pollution caused by the oil industry
- energy demands of major industries
- emissions from factories
- harmful industrial waste products which require treatment
- the disposal of products.

Table 4.1 Choosing processes appropriate to the scale of production

One-off	Batch	High volume/continuous
Sand casting, carving, CNC manufacture, laminating, digital printing	Sand casting, die casting, CNC manufacture, laminating, die cutting, lithography	Die casting, CNC manufacture, injection moulding, blow moulding

Case study: product design – kettles

The evolution of products reflects the development of new materials, processes and technologies.

- Victorian cast iron kettles conducted heat well but were heavy and handles were not insulated.
- Spun/soldered copper kettles were more efficient and lighter but handles still became hot.
- The development of new plastics and injection moulding techniques led to lighter, low-cost products with insulated handles and added features such as level indicators.
- Modern kettles reflect fashions using materials for aesthetic reasons.

Case study: product packaging

Functions of packaging

Packaging has become a very important part of modern products. It is designed to:

- contain without leakage or spillage
- protect from mechanical, environmental and biological damage

- inform and communicate the brand, product information and instructions
- sell by influencing buying decisions and attracting consumers.

Environmental issues

The growth in disposable packaging is a cause for concern for many environmental pressure groups and has prompted legislation to encourage manufacturers to adopt more responsible practices.

Table 4.2 Green packaging: the three Rs

Reduce	• Minimise materials used. • Avoid harmful materials by using CFC free materials. • Condense product, e.g. washing powder tablets. • Use biodegradable plastic (e.g. Biopol).
Recycle	• Use recycled materials. • Use recyclable materials. • Use recycled, biodegradable packing instead of polystyrene.
Reuse	• Use refillable containers. • Encourage customers to reuse shopping bags. • Design secondary functions into packaging.

Table 4.3 Materials used for packaging

Material	Examples	Advantages	Disadvantages
Card and paper	Solid board; recycled board; laminated card/board; corrugated card/board; polythene/foil/card laminates	Inexpensive; easily formed; wide range; can be flat packed for transportation; accepts wide range of printing processes; can combine recycled and high-grade materials; polythene/foil laminates resistant to liquids and grease; can be pulp formed	Laminates often impossible to recycle; less durable than other materials
Plastics	PET; HDPE	Some plastics are impenetrable to air, liquid and/or light; easily formed (e.g. vacuum forming, blow moulding, injection moulding); hygienic, lightweight, tough and durable; recyclable; impact resistant; translucent, transparent or coloured	Most do not biodegrade; injection moulding can be expensive to set up so high-volume, generic components are used
Metals	Aluminium; tin coated steel	Corrosion resistant; sterile atmosphere; impermeable to gases, liquid and light; recyclable; aluminium is lightweight	More expensive; lower-impact resistance in some cases

EXAMINATION QUESTION

Example question and answer

 Q1 *Identify the factors a designer might take into account when selecting the materials for a garden bench.* **(5 marks)**

Acceptable answer

Any material chosen for the bench must be **hard wearing and long lasting**. The **surface treatment and finish** must also be considered since all coatings on woods and metals must be **maintained** to protect the material from natural elements such as rain and sunshine. This will affect the overall integrity and **strength** of the material and therefore this would tend to favour the use of plastics.

The **scale of production** will be a major factor in the choice of material since some materials and processes are more appropriate for high-volume production (for example injection moulding) and others more akin to batch and one-off (for example forging, scrollwork and traditional woodworking joints).

The **sustainability** of the material is also important. Wood from managed forests and recycled metal and plastic should be used wherever possible. Disposal of the materials used and their potential to be recycled should be given full consideration as these matters are governed by European legislation.

New technologies and the creation of new materials

You need to

☐ **understand the creation and use by industry of modern and smart materials**
☐ **understand the impact of modern technology and biotechnology on the development of new materials and processes**
☐ **know how the properties of materials are modified.**

 KEY TERMS

Check you understand these terms

LCDs, Smart materials, Carbon fibre, Composite materials, Silicon, ICs, High-wattage lighting, Biotechnology, Genetic engineering, Micro-organism, Special effects, Holography, Mail merge, NCR

Further information can be found in *Advanced Design and Technology for Edexcel, Product Design: Graphics with Materials Technology*, Unit 3B1, section 1, and Unit 4A, section 2.

KEY POINTS

The creation and use by industry of modern and smart materials

Liquid crystal displays (LCDs)

LCDs are made from organic, carbon-based compounds, which exhibit liquid and solid characteristics in response to changes in voltage. They require much smaller currents then conventional seven-segment LED (light emitting diodes) displays. The numbers or letters appear on a silver-coloured display by applying a voltage to darken certain segments. LCD technology is now commonplace in a wide range of modern products from mobile phones to microwave ovens. Advanced LCDs make use of cholesteric liquid crystals. The advantage of this technology includes:

• smaller pixels resulting in higher resolution
• much sharper and brighter colours
• more stable, eliminating the screen flicker
• use around ten times less power reducing battery costs.

Smart and composite materials

Smart materials change their physical properties in reaction to an input. A

Table 4.4 Examples of smart materials

Material	Description	Uses
Thermochromic liquid crystals	A liquid which changes colour in response to changes in temperature. It can be put into microscopic capsules which can be printed onto paper or plastic to form a 'heat sensitive film'. An inexpensive and versatile method of indicating temperature changes requiring very little space.	Test panels on some batteries; some inexpensive plastic forehead thermometers; warning panels on computer chips to indicate overheating; also available in school kits to form simple displays; special printing effects for promotional items
Piezo-electric actuators and transducers	Small, slim, electronic components which can either produce a voltage when pressed or produce movement in response to an applied voltage.	Actuators used to play tunes in novelty greeting cards; input transducers which respond to sound or pressure used in burglar alarms
Carbon fibre	Carbon fibres are combined with a bonding agent and pigment in a mould. Heat and pressure are applied to produce components with enhanced properties. Excellent strength to weight ratio: tough glossy finish on surfaces in contact with mould; large, complex shapes possible; safety equipment must be used.	Car bodies; boat hulls; aerospace components; sporting equipment such as fishing rods, rackets and skis; body armour

composite material is formed when two or more materials are combined/bonded to produce a new material with enhanced properties.

New materials as used in the computer and electronics industry

Silicon is a semiconductor, which means it can behave as an insulator or conductor, depending on the temperature. It is used in the manufacture of silicon chips and other electronic components. It is also used in the glass, ceramic, cement and steel industries. About 28 per cent of the Earth's crust is silicon in the form of silicon oxides such as sand, quartz or rock.

The production of integrated circuits (ICs)

Computers rely on **ICs** and their central processing unit (CPU) is made from a single IC containing more than one million transistors. The evolution of computing depends upon the development of more powerful, faster ICs. Photolithography is the process used to transfer patterns onto the ICs and one 200mm wafer can contain 1000 million circuit elements. The main production stages are:

1 crystals of silicon are sliced into wafers
2 the wafers are coated with a photosensitive polymer
3 masks are produced to protect areas of the photosensitive layer
4 the photosensitive layer is exposed to light through masks and etched
5 the wafer is diced up to separate the individual ICs.

Smart labels

Manufacturers, suppliers and retailers are constantly looking for ways to improve the efficiency of their businesses. Electronic point of sale (EPOS) systems have been around for many years and have helped supermarkets to streamline stock control and speed up transactions. New technologies are under development which remove the need to scan codes manually. These technologies have the potential to create products to 'communicate' with EPOS systems, domestic appliances and other electronic devices such as mobile phones.

117

Table 4.5 Smart labelling techniques

Technology	Description	Uses
Electronic point of sale (EPOS) systems	EPOS has been used with great success for a number of years. Information is collected by scanning a product's unique barcode which reduces time between ordering and delivery; the price is checked automatically against a database; stock levels are adjusted and replacement products are ordered automatically.	Warehouses; supermarkets and shops; factories; libraries
Radio frequency identification (RFID)	RFID tags are 'intelligent barcodes' that can 'talk' to a networked system. This developing technology shares the benefits of EPOS systems but with added advantages. • instant totalling of purchases without having to unload and scan products, eliminating lengthy queues • enables business to track a product instantly throughout the supply chain • could be used to gather invaluable marketing information tracking the product after it has been sold • allows easy identification at the point of disposal for recycling.	Already used in the USA to track cattle; used to track airline baggage; under development to use as smart barcodes for major retailers

Use of high-wattage lighting for projecting images onto buildings

These **high-wattage lighting** systems use the same principles as conventional slide or overhead projectors to create temporary images on unconventional backdrops. They are used by the advertising industry and artists.

Ambient advertising

Ambient advertising is usually employed as a soft sell technique to promote a brand. This form of advertising uses the surroundings or environment of the target market, such as public transport, the nozzles of petrol pumps or sides of airships or blimps.

The impact of modern technology and biotechnology on the development of new materials and processes

Genetic engineering in relation to woods

Biotechnology is the study of technology applied to living organisms. Biotechnologists are able to alter genes of trees through **genetic engineering** in order to:

- provide quicker-growing trees allowing forests to regenerate more rapidly
- produce timber which naturally resists wear, rot or infestation, reducing the need to treat timber products with preservatives
- reduce lignin content of timber reducing the need to use the highly toxic chemicals which make paper production so damaging and costly to the environment
- change the natural colour of timber.

Many people are naturally cautious about the consequences of genetic engineering. The disposal of genetically engineered timbers which do not rot, for example, may cause environmental problems.

The use of micro-organisms to aid the disposal of environmentally friendly plastics

Most plastics do not decompose naturally as organic materials do. The finite nature of oil reserves and environmental concerns have increased the pressure on industry to develop biodegradable plastics from different sources. Biopol was developed from the fermentation of naturally occurring carbohydrates and sugar more than 60 years ago. More recently, developments in biotechnology have led to the creation of a new generation of plastics. Derived from natural hydrocarbons, these new plastics can be broken down by the action of naturally occurring **micro-organisms** (bacteria). Farmers are now using plastic film to warm and protect crops in winter and early spring. The sheet begins to decompose so that when the produce is harvested, the plastic sheeting can be ploughed back into the ground where it decomposes completely.

Special effects on television

Television production companies are beginning to use technologies developed by the film industry to create sophisticated **special effects**. Special effects are the techniques used in television and films to create the impossible. Two main types of visual effects used are blue screen and computer generated images.

Blue screen

In blue screen technology, the actors, scaled models and backgrounds are filmed separately. The colour blue is not recognised by the film so this colour is used for areas which need to be invisible. The process of compositing combines the scenes digitally or by projecting the two films simultaneously, frame by frame on to a third film.

Four pieces of film need to be produced – two originals and two mattes.

1 The background (plate)
2 The actor/model
3 The actor/model in black silhouette on a white background
4 The actor/model in white silhouette on a black background.

These pieces of film are layered over one another, for each frame, and combined to make a composite image.

Computer-generated image (CGI)

CGI combines computer-generated images with film sequences using layers. The scenes are filmed and scanned to produce high-resolution digital footage of 12.75 million dots per frame.

During post-production, the scenes can be manipulated using a range of techniques.

- Rotoscoping: elements within the scene can be outlined and lifted out so that they can be replaced by other images.
- 2D painting: used to remove unwanted elements or to add separately produced computer-generated images or elements to the scene.
- Compositing: the process of layering the separate images together to produce a final sequence.
- 3D tracking: involves the creation of a 3D digital scene which can be viewed from different angles.
- 3D modelling: figures and objects are computer generated as 3D models. Realistic animation is achieved through techniques such as motion capture. An actor is fitted with a suit with light reflective markers positioned on every joint. 3D cameras, filming from different angles, capture the actor's movements. Using the markers and computers the data is processed to produce an animated model. This can then be combined with the computer-generated characters.

Digital photography

(Photography is also discussed in Unit 3A, page 61.) Digital cameras work by converting light into electrical charges. There are two types of sensor.

- charge coupled device (CCD) for high-quality cameras
- complementary metal oxide semi-conductor (CMOS) for more basic models.

Light sensitive diodes called photosites convert light (photons) into an electrical charge (electrons). Brighter light generates a higher electrical charge. The electrical charge is converted from analogue to digital signals. For colour images, the light needs to be filtered into the three primary colours which can be achieved by the use of permanent filters positioned over each individual photosite. More green pixels are required to create an image that will be perceived as true colour by the human eye. In effect, four separate pixels determine the colour of a single pixel by forming a mosaic. 'Demosaicising algorithms' are used to convert the mosaic of separate colours into true colours. A true colour is formed for a pixel by averaging the colour value of the pixels that are closest to it. Digital images require a great deal of memory and need to be compressed.

- Repetition: this method relies on identifying the repetition of colour patterns within a digital image. This technique may only reduce the file by 50 per cent or less.
- Irrelevancy: any information which is undetectable by the human eye is discarded. Higher resolution equals less compression and vice versa.

Digital cameras store images internally, often using removable memory cards or sticks. They use adjustable apertures and shutter speeds in more expensive examples. This is to control the amount of light reaching the film.

Internet website design

All websites are constructed using HTML (hyper text mark-up language). Websites written in HTML function more efficiently although software applications can also be used for creating web pages. Text and images are combined in a similar way to DTP but can incorporate additional features such as animation, sound and scrolling pages. A number of linked pages create a site. Ease of navigation and consistency in design are features of well-designed websites. Pages and features are linked using hyperlinks (text) and hotspots (picture, graphic, designated area). They are identified by a change in the cursor (mouse pointer) icon as it passes over the active area. Hyperlinks and hotspots are created in the website design software and must be assigned to:

- another page on the site
- another section on the same pages
- another website on the Internet
- an email address.

It is necessary to compress images, using file formats such as JPEGs or GIFs, to reduce download times.

Colour printing in newspapers using the lithographic process

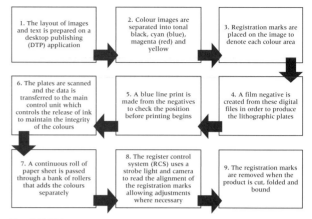

Fig. 4.2 Colour printing in newspapers

Holographic images

Holography is the science of recording three-dimensional, virtual images onto a photosensitive material. A laser beam is split into two using a beam splitter. The two beams are guided using mirrors and spread using lenses. The reference beam is directed and spread straight onto the photosensitive plate while the object beam is directed, spread and reflected off the object being 'photographed' before reaching the plate. The two beams interfere with one another as they pass through each other creating the conditions necessary to form the image. Holography is a constantly evolving medium which is generating many new applications including:

- credit card security images
- virtual instrumentation for pilots
- videoclip holograms.

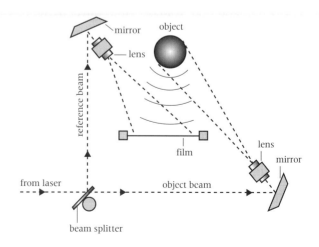

Fig. 4.3 How holographic images are produced

Mail-merge software, non-carbon reproduction (NCR), duplicate paper forms

Mail-merge software

Mail-merge software is available with most word processing packages. It is used to create personalised documents, letters and electronic mail from a standard template. There are two key files needed to perform a mail merge.

- data list – a database which contains standard information in fields
- document or letter template – containing fields corresponding to the template.

Special place holders are inserted in the document template corresponding to the fields in the database, for example 'Dear Sir/Madam' becomes 'Dear [name]'. When the document template is merged with the database, the generic entry [name] is replaced with the actual names of the recipients contained in that field for each copy of the document. This process can be repeated for all fields inserted into the document template.

Non-carbon reproduction (NCR)

NCR creates copies of documents without the need for traditional carbon paper which is messy and wasteful. Specially treated paper is used to create copies of the document which are bound together. The specially treated paper will respond to pressure, such as handwriting, creating a dye reaction to produce a copy of any marks made on the original. Carbonless copy papers are mainly used for continuous

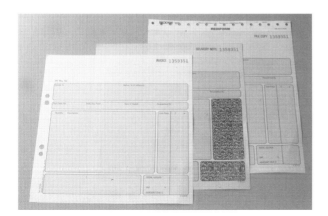

Fig 4.4 Several copies of an invoice made from non-carbon reproduction (NCR)

form sets, covered pay slips, delivery invoices and payment receipts.

The recycling of materials

Recycling is becoming an increasingly important issue as a result of consumer pressure and legislation. Millions of tonnes of waste are disposed of in landfill sites or incinerated causing environmental pollution. For recycling to be cost effective, materials must be of high value and easy to recover. Therefore more responsibility has been placed on suppliers and manufacturers to address recycling issues at the design stage or to take a more active role in the process of disposal, including:

- taking responsibility for the return and disposal or recycling of packaging
- establishing auditing systems which document component materials used in order to simplify identification and recycling
- reducing the complexity and variety of materials used in products
- car dismantling companies are encouraged to reuse components and chemicals
- non-recyclable parts need to be disposed of properly or passed to a certified disposal company.

Recovery and recycling of paper and board

Virgin fibres, high-quality fibres obtained from the timber industry, are used to produce strong, high-quality paper and board. Most papers and boards, however, contain at least some recycled fibres.

The properties and usefulness of cellulose fibres are affected each time they are processed or recycled.

- Strength: fibres lose strength each time they are recycled and can only be reused four to six times. Eventually they become unusable for the manufacture of paper.
- Quality: high-quality papers cannot use any recycled fibres because of impurities or lack of strength.
- Utility: it is not possible to recover all types of paper because they are laminated or varnished.

The main stages of the process of recycling are:

1 Collection by local authorities or commercial waste paper merchants
2 Sent to paper mill
3 Sorting of the fibres into different grades according to their length, strength and levels of impurities (the graded fibres are eventually turned into different products which reflect their properties)
4 The paper mill uses a hydrapulper filled with water to make the paper waste into a 'slush'
5 Large contaminants are removed
6 The paper slush is then filtered and screened through a number of cycles to make it more suitable for papermaking
7 Virgin pulp may be added if required

Waste paper, or 'recovered' paper, is the most important raw material for the UK paper and board industry. There are four broad grades of waste paper (Table 4.6).

New products

The growing awareness of environmental issues has had two effects.

• Government and industry bodies have encouraged industry to adopt more environmentally friendly practices.

• Companies have started to target the new 'green' market by promoting their concern for the environment
• Lyocell and 'Remarkable Pencils' are two examples of new environmentally friendly products.

Modification of properties of materials

Paper and boards

The properties of paper and boards can be modified with the use of surface treatments and laminates. Two examples are provided as follows.

Tetra Pak™ aseptic cartons

Aseptic packaging removes the need to use preservatives and/or refrigeration by creating a sterile environment for perishable products and a permanent barrier to contaminants such as micro-organisms. Traditionally tin cans and glass containers were used to create aseptic packaging.

The packaging is designed to maintain the flavour, texture and nutritional content of the product. Tetra Pak™ aseptic cartons are made of

Table 4.6 The four broad grades of waste paper

Paper grade	Characteristics	Sources	Recycled applications
Pulp substitute grades	Top-quality waste which requires minimal cleaning	Unprinted trimmings and off-cuts from printers and converters	Printing and writing papers
De-inking grades	Waste which requires removal of ink	Office waste, newspapers and magazines	Graphic and hygienic (tissue) papers; newsprint
Kraft grades	Long strong fibres that generally come from unbleached packaging materials	Paper sacks	New packaging including corrugated cases
Lower grades	Papers which are uneconomic to sort because they are mixed or because there is a high proportion of low-quality paper	'Junk-mail'	Middle layers of packaging papers and boards

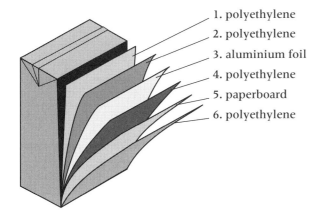

1. polyethylene
2. polyethylene
3. aluminium foil
4. polyethylene
5. paperboard
6. polyethylene

Fig. 4.5 Tetra Pak™ aseptic carton packaging laminate

three basic materials that result in a very efficient, safe and lightweight package. Each material provides a specific function.

- paper: (75 per cent) to provide strength and stiffness
- polyethylene: (20 per cent) to make packages liquid tight and to provide a barrier to micro-organisms
- aluminium foil: (5 per cent) to keep out air, light, and contaminating odours or flavours.

Combining these materials in a six-layer laminate produces a packaging material with enhanced properties and performance.

- high degree of safety, hygiene and nutrient retention
- excellent preservation of taste and freshness
- increased shelf-life removing the need for refrigeration or preservatives
- minimal materials
- lightweight compared with plastics, metals and glass.

Paper and board as a building material

Cardboard can be used as a very low-cost building material. Westborough School in Westcliff-on-Sea has been constructed using cardboard components. Paper and card building materials include:

- cardboard tubes are made from multiple layers of spirally wound paper plies, glued together with a starch or PVA glue. Higher-quality papers are used for the exterior surfaces

- most panels are multi layered consisting of solid board, honeycomb card for strength, a timber frame if necessary, plastic coated or aluminium foil layers for water resistance and fire-treated outer board layers
- papercrete is a form of concrete where paper is used as the aggregate.

Many problems had to be solved before these products could be used as building materials.

- Strength: tubes and panels need to be left for a period of drying out time before applying loads.
- Fire: fire treatments to the outer layers were applied to restrict flame spread.
- Water: water penetration is prevented with the use of water-resistant cardboard, external poly-coated layers, internal aluminium foil layers, over-cladding by a wood fibre and cement panel.

This construction technique has many exciting possibilities including:

- a low-cost and 'greener' alternative to traditional building materials
- temporary, kit form, disaster relief housing.

Fig. 4.6 Westborough School, Westcliffe-on-sea.

Metals

The properties of metals can be enhanced by combining them with one or more other metals or non-metals. The constituents are dissolved into the molten metal to form an alloy. Alloys exhibit enhanced properties such as better corrosion resistance. The International Standardisation Organisation (ISO) and similar bodies set standards for the composition of alloys.

Plastics

Plastics can be altered chemically through co-polymerisation and cross-linking. The properties of plastics can be further enhanced by the use of additives (Table 4.7).

Table 4.7 Additives

Additives	Description
Plasticisers	Added at the manufacturing stage in order to: • improve the material's ability to flow into the mould when being injection moulded • reduce softening temperatures • increase flexibility.
Fillers, fibres and foaments	Fillers, fibres and foaments are used in plastics to: • enhance properties such as strength and toughness • reduce the density of the plastic.
Stabilisers	Used to improve the lifespan of plastics, and the effects of exposure to ultra-violet light, such as discolouration.

Wood

Laminating

The properties of wood can be enhanced by bonding together veneers or laminates to form large sheets. Plywood is formed by bonding

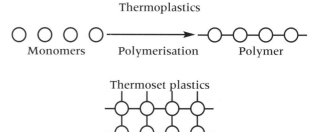

Fig. 4.7a The structure of thermoplastics and thermoset plastics

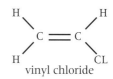

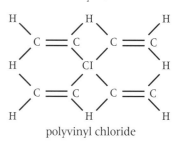

Fig. 4.7b Polymers are made up from monomers

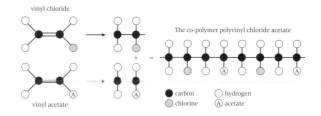

Fig. 4.7c Co-polymers contain two or more polymers

together layers of veneer at right angles to form large boards which are uniform, strong and stable. The properties of these manufactured boards can be further enhanced by facing them with high-quality veneers and by using waterproof adhesives. By laminating veneers over formers, complex shapes can be formed to produce curved components, such as chair legs, with enhanced mechanical properties.

EXAMINATION QUESTIONS

Example questions and answers

 Q1 *Explain **one** advantage of using biodegradable plastics.* **(2 marks)**

Acceptable answer

Since the biodegradable plastics will **ultimately break down in the ground** they do not need to be put into specific **landfill sites where they will take up large amounts of space**.

 Q2 *The property of metals can be modified. Describe the purpose and process of alloying.* **(3 marks)**

Acceptable answer

Alloying is a process of **combining two or more metals** in order to make a **new material with new or enhanced properties** in comparison with the original materials. An example of this would be **stainless steel which is formed by adding chromium to molten steel**, a process which creates a new **rust-resistant** material.

Values issues

You need to

- ☐ **understand the impact of values issues**
- ☐ **understand the responsibilities of 'developed' countries in relation to production and the environment.**

KEY TERMS

Check you understand these terms

Value issues, Life cycle assessment, Built-in obsolescence, Eco-labelling, Global pollution, Industrialisation, Deforestation

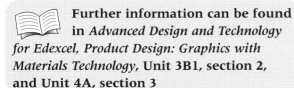 **Further information can be found in *Advanced Design and Technology for Edexcel, Product Design: Graphics with Materials Technology*, Unit 3B1, section 2, and Unit 4A, section 3**

KEY POINTS

Impact of values issues

All design and manufacturing decisions have wider consequences and industry has a responsibility to examine these. The process of design and manufacture involves many **value issues** and value judgements – designers or manufacturers have to decide whether the benefits of their work will outweigh the costs.

Decisions will fall into one or more of the following categories: technical, economic, aesthetic, social, environmental and moral. The pressure on the Earth's finite resources and fragile environment means that we need to promote sustainable design.

Life cycle assessment (LCA)

Life cycle assessment (LCA) is a technique used to quantify the true costs of product development and manufacture 'from the cradle to the grave'. Costs are calculated from the extraction and processing of raw materials, the production phase, the life cycle processes from distribution to use, and final disposal of the product.

Life cycle analysis method

There are two main steps in an LCA.

1 Life cycle inventory: this is an objective list of all the inputs and outputs of industrial processes that occur during the life cycle of a product, including:
   - environmental inputs and outputs of raw materials and energy resources
   - economic inputs and outputs of products, components or energy which are outputs from other processes.
2 Impact assessment: a general method of impact assessment includes three main steps.
   - classification and characterisation – all substances are sorted into classes according

125

to the effect they have upon the environment
- normalisation – the effects are compared to a known average.
- Evaluation of the normalised effect scores – the scores are weighted as some consequences are more significant than others.

Built-in obsolescence

Built-in or **planned obsolescence** is where products are deliberately designed with a limited life-span. There are four forms of obsolescence.

- Technological obsolescence: products become obsolete due to advances in technology, for example personal computers.
- Postponed obsolescence: companies delay the sale of existing technology so that current products have the chance to make a decent profit, for example mobile phones.
- Physical obsolescence: the design of a product determines its lifespan, for example disposable ink cartridges.
- Style obsolescence: changes in consumer tastes cause products to fall out of fashion, for example clothes.

Arguably a fifth and more cynical form of obsolescence occurs when products are changed or discontinued simply in order to justify a higher and more profitable price.

Sustainable product design

Five factors have been identified for perfect sustainable design.

1 Cyclic: products that are made from compostable organic materials or from recyclable minerals, for example products made from Biopol.
2 Solar: where renewable energy, alone, is used to manufacture and power products, for example products made using wind power and that operate using solar powered (photovoltaic) cells.
3 Safe: where all by-products released to air, water, land or space are food for other systems, for example products that do not emit unnecessary pollutants or chemicals during their manufacture.

4 Efficient: products which require 90 per cent less energy, materials and water in manufacture and use than equivalent products did in 1990, for example the reduction of materials in packaging.
5 Social: where product manufacture and use supports basic human rights and natural justice, for example Fairtrade products.

Minimising waste production

Waste is lost profit. There are some simple options to consider when deciding how to minimise waste production: they are referred to as the four Rs (Table 4.8).

Table 4.8 Minimising waste using the four Rs

Reduce	Optimising the amount of materials specified at the design stage has a positive impact on the environment and reduces costs. The Government's Envirowise programme suggests that manufacturers: • consider the materials and designs they use • examine ways of eliminating or reducing the packaging requirement of a product, e.g. changes in product design, improved cleanliness, better handling, just-in-time delivery, bulk delivery • optimise packaging use, i.e. match packaging to the level of protection needed.
Reuse	The reuse of products such as containers reduces the number of manufactured products required and the need for recycling. The cost of collection, washing and refilling should be less than that of producing a new container.
Recover	When a product is discarded and put into a landfill site, energy is lost. This energy could be recovered through incineration in specialised power stations.
Recycle	It is important for designers to consider design for recycling and the product's LCA. Components should be designed so that they can be identified and recovered easily for recycling.

Eco-labelling

Effective **eco-labelling** needs to be regulated to avoid confusion or misleading claims. It is important that labelling reflects the true costs of using LCA. Three types of eco-label can be distinguished.

1 Single issue/mandatory – required by law to identify a notable attribute.
2 Single issue/voluntary – used voluntarily to identify a notable attribute.
3 Multiple issue/voluntary – used voluntarily to indicate an overall assessment, for example the Fairtrade Mark.

There are several eco-labelling schemes, such as EC Ecolabel, which can cause confusion. Global standardisation is clearly needed for consumers to be able to make a clearly informed choice.

Responsibilities of developed countries to production and the environment

Global sustainable development

The environmental impact of economic development and over-consumption have highlighted two challenges.

- to live within the limits of the Earth's resources and capacity to regenerate itself
- to share these resources so that everyone's basic needs are met now and in the future.

At present society is failing on both counts. **Global pollution** (the disposal of damaging waste products into the environment) and depletion of natural resources are becoming worse, while the quality of life for those living in poor environments has not progressed. The rapid **industrialisation** (the evolution from an agricultural economy to a manufacturing economy) of developing countries has led to tremendous social pressures. This situation creates a contradiction.

- Developed countries need to consume less.
- Developing countries need to expand their economies by consuming and selling more.

The current dominance of private profit-driven corporations has been seen as a major factor in preventing developing countries from accessing sustainable technology. Developed countries have a responsibility to share technical consultancy, personnel training, mechanism building and education. The transfer of environmentally sound technologies is a key element of sustainable development.

UK responsibilities: forest products

The UK is a major consumer of tropical hardwoods. Fifty-two per cent of Brazil's mahogany production ends up in the UK (Friends of the Earth, 1992). Very little of the profit generated by this trade remains in these countries. This issue is a major concern for the UK public.

Deforestation

Global **deforestation** is currently taking place at a rate of approximately 17 million hectares each year – too fast for forests to regenerate. The main pressures come from the demand for land for agriculture, settlement and industry. The effects of deforestation are severe.

- environmental degradation of forest areas
- loss of biodiversity
- loss of cultural assets and knowledge
- loss of livelihood
- climate change.

The UK and other developed countries have a responsibility to encourage the development of sustainable production and trading systems in order to minimise the amount of deforestation and its effects upon the environment, including:

- discontinuing any imports from sources that involve deforestation
- using sustainable sources of timber, such as managed forests
- using certification systems to identify sustainably managed timber
- reducing consumption through education
- encouraging exporting countries to make the transition to sustainable forest management
- removing obstacles to change, such as reducing debt
- improving aid for poor communities involved in current deforestation methods.

The new global job shift

There is an increasing trend in large companies to move their operations to take advantage of the economic conditions in other countries. This trend, sometimes referred to as outsourcing, depends on developments in digital technology and efficient communications. The advantages to manufacturers of outsourcing include:

- lower wage economies
- lower costs
- access to expanding overseas markets.

These developments have been criticised by some people because they:

- create unemployment in the UK
- exploit workers in developing countries
- lead to a lack of opportunity for promotion, pay-rises, company benefits, and union membership
- new jobs are often unskilled and displace traditional trades
- profits do not remain in the country where they are generated.

EXAMINATION QUESTION

Example question and answer

 Q1 *Explain the causes of deforestation and its impact on the environment.* **(8 marks)**

Acceptable answer

Global deforestation is currently taking place at an alarming rate: too fast for forests to regenerate. The main pressures come from the **demand for timber** and the **demand for land for agriculture, settlement and industry**. The increased industrialisation of developing countries causes **air pollution which contributes to a reduction in forest health**. The effects of deforestation are severe. The loss of forests can cause **soil erosion,** **watershed destabilisation** and **microclimate change**. Deforestation also contributes to a **rapid reduction in ecosystems, species** and **genetic diversity**. Some scientists estimate that **1 per cent of all species are being lost each year**. Many **indigenous communities** are destroyed by deforestation and their **culture and knowledge** dies with them. Forest-dependent communities **lose the source of their livelihood** through deforestation, which **leads to population pressures and consequent social problems** as people move to the cities. Forests play a major role in recycling carbon from the atmosphere and deforestation has been cited as a **major cause of global warming**.

PRACTICE EXAMINATION STYLE QUESTION

1 The property of plastics can be modified. Explain **two** of the terms listed below.
   - co-polymerisation
   - cross -inking
   - plasticisers
   - foaments
   - stabilisers.   **(4 marks)**

2 Describe how the properties of commercial papers and boards can be modified with the use of surface treatments and laminates. You must refer to at least one specific example in your answer.   **(4 marks)**

3 Describe how colour newspapers are printed. **(5 marks)**

4 Explain the meaning of 'life costs' associated with the development, manufacture and disposal of products. **(4 marks)**

5 Explain **two** advantages to the environment of using genetically modified timbers. **(4 marks)**

6 New technologies are becoming increasingly important in all types of industry. Describe and give an example of the use of **two** of the following.
   • liquid crystal displays (LCDs)
   • thermochromic liquid crystals
   • Piezo-electric actuators and transducers
   • carbon fibre
   • electronic point of sale (EPOS) systems
   • radio frequency identification (RFID)
   • high-wattage projection. **(4 marks)**

7 Identify the factors a designer might take into account **when selecting the materials** for a counter-top, point of sale display which will be used to hold leaflets at supermarket checkouts. **(5 marks)**

Total for this question paper: **30 marks**

Design and technology in society (G402)

This option will be assessed in section B during the 1½ hour, Unit 4 examination. If you have chosen this option, you should spend half of your time (45 minutes) answering all the questions in this section. It is important to use appropriate specialist and technical language in the exam, along with accurate spelling, punctuation and grammar. Where appropriate you should also use clear, annotated sketches to explain your answer. *You do not have to study this chapter if you are taking the CAD/CAM option.*

Economics and production

You need to

☐ understand the economic factors of one-off, batch, high volume and continuous production
☐ know the sources, availability and costs of materials
☐ know the advantages of economies of scale of production
☐ understand the relationship between design, planning and production costs
☐ understand the material and manufacturing potential for a given design solution.

KEY TERMS

Check you understand these terms

Variable costs, Fixed costs, Productivity, Scale of production, Ore, Crude oil, Economies of scale, Internal/external failure costs

Further information can be found in *Advanced Design and Technology for Edexcel, Product Design: Graphics with Materials Technology*, **Unit 4B1, section 1.**

KEY POINTS

Economic factors of one-off, batch, high volume and continuous production

The production chain is the sequence of activities required to turn raw materials into finished products.

Table 4.9 The production chain

Primary sector	The extraction of natural resources as in agriculture, forestry, mining and quarrying. Less economically developed countries (LEDCs) often rely heavily upon the export of raw materials.
Secondary sector	The processing of primary raw materials and the manufacture of products. This sector employs a decreasing proportion of the workforce in the more economically developed countries (MEDCs) such as the USA.
Tertiary sector	The provision of services which include education, retailing, advertising, marketing, banking and finance. This is a growing sector in MEDCs and the largest employer.

Profit is the difference between total costs and income derived from sales. In order to remain profitable, calculations of price must allow for variable costs, fixed costs and a realistic profit. Profits are maximised by reducing costs. Costs are divided into:

- **variable costs**: (direct costs) costs which are incurred directly from production activity and which vary depending upon the number of products made, including materials, services, wages, energy and packaging
- **fixed costs**: (indirect costs or overhead costs) costs which have to be paid at regular intervals, even if production is stopped, including routine marketing, maintenance, rent and rates, depreciation of plant and equipment. Fixed costs will be divided between the various product lines, so that each product carries its share.

Productivity, labour costs and the scale of production

Productivity is a measurement of the efficiency with which raw materials (production inputs) are turned into products (manufactured outputs), commonly measured as output per worker, or labour costs per unit of production. Productivity is encouraged by:

- setting up an internal market within the company where departments buy and sell their services
- setting budgets for each department.

The **scale of production** (one-off, batch, high-volume or continuous) is important because it affects decisions relating to manufacture such as the location of factories and the choice of processes. One-off products are more expensive than batch or high-volume products due to the high costs of the specialised tools and processes involved, high labour costs and lower levels of productivity.

Sources, availability and costs of materials

Costs of materials

All manufacturers require a reliable supply of raw materials. The sources, availability and costs of materials depend on the type and quantity of materials required. Larger manufacturers, for example, need more materials and can negotiate lower prices. The price of materials increases as a result of limited supply, high demand, complex processing requirements and transportation costs.

Timber, manufactured board, paper and card

The UK imports almost 90 per cent of its timber, which is usually supplied in board form, ready for further processing.

Metals

Metals are extracted from **ores** which occur naturally in rocks and minerals. They form about a quarter of the weight of the Earth's crust. Aluminium and iron are the commonest ores and account for almost 95 per cent of the total tonnage of all metal production. By smelting ore close to its source, transport and labour costs are often reduced. Large users of metal, such as makers of tin plate for the canning industry, often buy direct from companies producing final sections. Smaller users, such as those involved in small-batch and one-off production, often buy from specialist metal stockholders.

Table 4.10 Sources of ore

Ore	Sources	Properties
Iron ore	Europe, North America and Australia	High availability, high metal content and relatively low cost
Aluminium ore (bauxite)	Southern hemisphere	Accessible and cheaper to process than steel
Copper ore	Chile, the USA and Canada	Rare and more expensive than iron ore or bauxite

Oil and plastics

Crude oil is untreated oil extracted from the Earth's crust. It is the world's major source of energy and thermoplastics and thermosetting plastics.

The main sources of oil are controlled by the Organisation of Petroleum Exporting Countries (OPEC), a cartel of countries from the Middle East, South America, Africa and Asia which sets output quotas in order to control crude oil prices. Other oil producing areas include the USA, the Russian Federation and the North Sea. High prices in the 1970s allowed marginal oil fields, such as the North Sea, to be developed.

Plastics are available in sheet and rod or as granules for injection moulding. Plastic resins are supplied in liquid form. Because plastics are widely available, cost effective and require less processing they have replaced many other materials. For example, PET has replaced glass for bottles.

Advantages of economies of scale of production

Economies of scale are the savings in costs brought about by producing products in larger numbers. Products manufactured in high-volume and continuous production enjoy lower costs and higher savings. These are brought about by:

- specialisation of labour leading to increased productivity
- the spread of fixed costs
- bulk buying of raw materials at lower unit costs
- lower borrowing costs to fund capital investment
- the concentration of industry which allows a specialist labour force to develop
- the development of local supply and support networks.

Mass production and the development of new products

Mass production has led to lower prices and wider consumer choice. The increased pressure to remain competitive forces companies to continually develop new products. The cost of developing new products is high due to the level of investment required and needs to be carried out alongside existing production. There is a constant need to reduce the time to market of new products. The most successful companies produce the right product at the right time, in the right quantity and at the right cost.

The relationship between design, planning and production costs

Total costs and the product's selling price must be set at an appropriate level in order to achieve profit. All costs in a manufacturing company are set in the design phase. Designing for manufacture (DFM) is directly related to designing for cost. The main aims of DFM are: minimisation of component and assembly costs; minimisation of product design cycles and to produce higher-quality products.

The cost of quality

Building quality into products incurs costs. However, these costs are usually more than outweighed by the costs of producing poor-quality products.

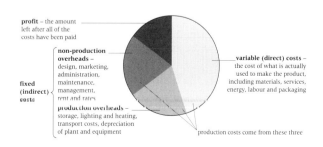

Fig. 4.8 The components of a product selling price (SP)

Table 4.11 The cost of quality

The costs of getting it wrong	The costs of checking it is right	The costs of making it right first time
Internal failure costs: Scrap products that cannot be repaired, used or sold; reworking or correcting faults; re-inspecting repaired or reworked products; products that do not meet specifications but are sold as 'seconds'; any activities caused by errors, poor organisation or the wrong materials. *External failure costs:* Repair and servicing; replacing products under guarantee; servicing customer complaints; the investigation of rejected products; product liability legislation and change of contract; the impact on the company reputation and image – relating to future potential sales.	These costs are related to checking: materials, processes, products and services against specifications; that the quality system is working well; the accuracy of equipment	Prevention costs are related to the design, implementation and maintenance of a quality system, including: setting quality requirements and developing specifications for materials, processes, finished products and services; quality planning and checking against agreed specifications; the creation of, and conformance to, a quality assurance (QA) system; the design, development or purchase of equipment to aid quality checking; developing training programmes for employees; the management of quality

Costing a product

Checks against a competitor's products are often used to establish the potential price range of a new product because setting the price too high will constrict sales and setting it too low will reduce profitability. Products have a value, a price and a cost.

- For manufacturers, the product value is always lower than the selling price.
- For consumers, the product value is higher than the selling price.

Profit

Profit is the amount left of the SP after all costs have been paid. Gross profit is calculated by deducting variable plus fixed costs from the sales revenue. Net profit is gross profit minus tax.

Net profit is used to pay: dividends to shareholders; bonuses to employees; for reinvestment in new machinery; for research and development (R&D) of new products and debts.

The break-even point

A 'break-even analysis' will show the minimum number of units which needs to be sold before all costs are covered and profitability is reached.

$$\text{Break-even point} = \frac{\text{Fixed costs}}{\text{Selling price} - \text{variable costs}}$$

Other factors influencing demand, supply and price include:

- what customers perceive as value for money
- what the competition is offering
- how essential the product is to consumers
- political influences
- changes in legislation
- economic conditions
- changes in fashion and trends.

The material and manufacturing potential for a given design solution

Once a design solution has been developed, decisions have to be made relating to pricing, materials, manufacturing processes, quality and quality control, the scale of production and size of production runs. The choice of manufacturing process depends upon the quantity of products required and the materials which will be used. The designer will have to adapt any designs to suit the chosen manufacturing process. It is important to plan quality control carefully before manufacturing commences. The production process is often represented as a flow chart showing where and how quality control procedures will be carried out. Sometimes it is necessary to make specialist equipment.

EXAMINATION QUESTIONS

Example questions and answers

 a) *Quality control involves time and money spent on inspection. Name **two** areas of any production process where checks should be made.* **(2 marks)**

Acceptable answer

1 **Inspecting raw materials** delivered to the factory.
2 **Checking the accuracy of equipment** during production.

b) *A manufacturer who does not carry out effective quality control procedures will risk producing faulty products. Describe, in general terms, **three** 'internal failure costs' and **three** 'external failure costs' associated with ineffective quality control and the production of faulty products.* **(6 marks)**

Acceptable answer
Internal failure costs:

Some products may have to be **scrapped** completely which will cause significant losses. It may be possible to **rework or correct** some of the faulty products but this will take time and money. It may be possible to sell some of the faulty products as **seconds** but the price will have to be reduced resulting in reduced profits or even losses.

External failure costs:

The manufacturer may have to bear the costs of **repair and servicing** of faulty products. If faulty goods are produced regularly, a reputable manufacturer will have to bear the cost of **servicing customer complaints**. More significantly, the manufacturer may lose the confidence of some consumers, which will affect the **company reputation and image**, threatening future potential sales.

Consumer interests

You need to

- [ ] **know the systems and organisations that provide guidance, discrimination and approval**
- [ ] **understand the purpose of UK, European and international standards relating to quality, safety and testing**
- [ ] **understand the relationship between standards, testing procedures, quality assurance, manufacturers and consumers**
- [ ] **understand the relevant legislation on the rights of the consumer when purchasing goods.**

 KEY TERMS
Check you understand these terms

Consumer 'watchdog' organisations, *Which?* magazine, ISO 9000, QMS, Statutory rights

Further information can be found in *Advanced Design and Technology for Edexcel, Product Design: Graphics with Materials Technology*, Unit 4B1, section 2.

KEY POINTS

Systems and organisations that provide guidance, discrimination and approval

There are many systems and organisations that provide guidance, discrimination and approval for consumers including:

- the Institute of Trading Standards Administration
- UK, European and international standards organisations
- **consumer 'watchdog' organisations**: commercial organisations or charities which evaluate and compare products on behalf of the consumer, such as *Which?* **magazine**.

Consumer 'watchdog' organisations

General publications, consumer 'watchdog' organisations, specialist magazines and television programmes provide independent consumer advice and information on new products.

- The Consumers Association publishes the magazine *Which?* and a website which provide reports about product testing and 'best buys', consumer news and links to electronic newspapers.
- The Citizens Advice Bureau (CAB) gives consumer advice and support.
- Product testing and reporting is also carried out by trade and professional organisations and journals.
- Motoring and government organisations, such as the Road Research Laboratory, also undertake objective reviewing and testing of vehicles.

The purpose of British, European and international standards

You will need to refer to Unit 3B1, section 3, to refresh your knowledge of this subject.

The relationship between standards, testing procedures, quality assurance, manufacturers and consumers

ISO 9000 is an internationally agreed set of standards for the development and operation of a quality management system (QMS). ISO 9001 and 9002 are the mandatory parts of the ISO 9000 series. They specify the clauses manufacturers have to comply with in order to achieve registration with the standard.

Quality management systems

Quality management systems (QMS) provide an overall approach to ensure that high-quality standards are maintained throughout an organisation. A QMS involves a structured approach to ensure that customers end up with a product or service that meets agreed standards. You should be familiar with the quaity management system summarised below.

1 Explore the intended use of the product, identify and evaluate existing products and consider the needs of the client.
2 Produce a design brief and specification.
3 Use research, questionnaires and product analysis.
4 Produce a range of appropriate solutions.
5 Refer back to the specification.
6 Refer to existing products. Use models to test aspects of the design.
7 Check with the client. Use models to check that the product meets the design brief and specification.
8 Plan manufacture and understand the need for safe working practices.
9 Manufacture the product to the specification.
10 Critically evaluate the product in relation to the specification and the client. Undertake detailed product testing and reach conclusions. Produce proposals for further development, modifications or improvements.

Applying standards

Risk assessment

As part of the Health and Safety at Work Act 1974 it is a statutory requirement for employers and other organisations to carry out risk assessments in order to eliminate or reduce the chances of accidents happening. There are six steps.

1 Identify the activity or process.
2 Identify potential hazards.
3 Estimate the level and nature of the risk (including people at risk).
4 Establish control measures to reduce risk and decide if the risk has been reduced as far as possible.
5 Eliminate the activity/process or prepare a risk assessment plan.
6 Record assessment and review risk assessment plan.

Ergonomics

Ergonomics makes use of anthropometric data, which exists in the form of charts, and provides measurements for the 90 per cent of the population that falls between the fifth and the ninety-fifth percentiles. Designers make use of this published data to produce better-designed products.

Relevant legislation on the rights of the consumer when purchasing goods

When you purchase a product or service in the UK, you immediately fall under the protection

Table 4.12 Consumers' statutory rights

General statutory rights	These statutory rights protect consumers' 'reasonable expectations' when buying products, irrespective of the supplier. In order to meet the requirements of the Sale of Goods Act, products must satisfy three conditions. • They must be 'of satisfactory quality' and free from defects. • They must be 'fit for purpose'. • They must be 'as described'. It is the retailer who is responsible, and the customer can expect a refund if the product fails to meet the above standards, as long as it is returned within a reasonable period.
Limits to statutory rights	There are no legal grounds for complaint if consumers: • were told about the fault • did not notice an obvious fault • damaged the product themselves • bought the item by mistake • changed their mind about the product. In order to build customer loyalty, many retailers often exchange products even if they are not faulty but are not under a legal obligation to do so.
Second-hand goods	You have the same rights when buying second-hand goods. You can claim your money back, or the cost of repairs, if goods sold to you are faulty provided the faults: • are not due to reasonable wear and tear • were not pointed out to you at the time of sale • were not obvious when you agreed to buy the goods.
Sale goods	You have the same rights when buying sale goods as when buying new ones. Notices that say 'no refunds on sale goods' are illegal.
If things go wrong	If there is something wrong with a product, a consumer should normally get a refund, provided the retailer is informed of the problem within a 'reasonable time'. • A consumer should contact the retailer as soon as the fault is discovered, and keep a record. • Sellers are legally responsible for the products they sell, not the manufacturers. • Losing the receipt does not mean a loss of statutory rights. • A consumer may be able to claim compensation if a faulty product causes damage. After a 'reasonable time' you may be able to claim compensation which could take account of the loss in value of the product or a repair or replacement.

of a wide range of legislation including the Trades Descriptions Act, which provides consumers with **statutory rights**, i.e. rights laid out in law (Table 4.12). You are entitled to have 'reasonable expectations' that manufacturers and advertisers will not mislead you and that their products will not harm you when used in accordance with instructions. You should also expect these products to function properly and to be of sufficient quality to last for a reasonable length of time. Your statutory rights are established by legislation such as:

- the Sale of Goods Act 1979
- the Supply of Goods and Services Act 1982
- the Sale and Supply of Goods to Consumers Regulations 2002.

The latest 2002 regulations became law in 2003. Consumers now enjoy protection across the EU. The regulations state that:

- every consumer has a right to a repair or replacement if goods are faulty
- for the first six months, it is the responsibility of the retailer to prove that the goods were **not** faulty
- after six months, the consumer has to prove that the goods were faulty (six-year limit).

Help in solving problems

Local authority Trading Standards officers enforce and advise on a wide range of legislation relating to consumer protection and deal with problems and complaints.

EXAMINATION QUESTIONS

Example questions and answers

 *a) Someone you know is planning to buy a new car. Name **one** independent source which publishes impartial information for consumers, and which would help them to make an informed choice.* **(1 mark)**

Acceptable answer
The **Consumers Association**/The **Road Research Laboratory**.

b) Your friend has statutory rights protected by consumer legislation (laws) such as the Trade Descriptions Act, the Sale of Goods Act and the Consumer Protection Act. Outline two of these statutory rights enjoyed by your friend and all consumers. **(2 marks)**

Acceptable answer
Products **must be fit for purpose** so that they can carry out the tasks for which they are designed. It is also illegal to make false claims for any products: they **must be as described**.

c) Your friend decides to buy a used car from a second hand car dealer. When the car breaks down your friend goes back to the second hand car dealer to ask for a refund. Under what conditions would your friend be legally entitled to a full refund, or the cost of repairs? **(3 marks)**

Acceptable answer
My friend would be entitled to claim back all the money, or be refunded the cost of repairs, if the car was faulty and provided that the faults were **not due to the reasonable wear and tear**, or if they **were not pointed out at the time of sale**, or if they were **not obvious at the time of sale**.

Advertising and marketing

You need to

- ☐ **understand advertising and the role of the design agency in communicating between manufacturers and consumers**

- ☐ **understand the role of the media in marketing products**
- ☐ **understand market research techniques**
- ☐ **understand the basic principles of marketing and associated concepts.**

KEY TERMS

Check you
understand these terms

Media, Advertising agencies, Marketing agencies, TMGs, Test selling, Market share, Consumer demand, Market pull, Brand loyalty, Lifestyle marketing, Competitive edge, Product proliferation, Price range, Promotional gifts

Further information can be found in *Advanced Design and Technology for Edexcel, Product Design: Graphics with Materials Technology,* **Unit 4B1, section 3**

KEY POINTS

Advertising and the role of the design agency

The **media** involves any means of communication such as TV, press and radio, and is often used by advertisers. Advertising relates to media communication designed to inform and influence existing or potential customers. Most companies employ the services of specialist **advertising agencies** which design and plan their campaigns. In marketing, research and planning are used to organise the development and sale of products and services. Although many larger companies have their own marketing departments, most companies use **marketing agencies** which provide specialist advice and marketing services.

Companies often make use of specialist design and advertising agencies such as Saatchi and Saatchi to promote their products. A 'hard sell' is a simple and direct message which promotes the unique features and advantages of the product (unique selling proposition – USP). A 'soft sell' advertising campaign promotes the personality or image of the product. Brand advertising focuses on creating a positive product image and creating positive emotional and psychological associations with the product. Jamie Oliver's association with the Sainsbury brand is said to have boosted the supermarket's profits by £153 million a year.

Advertising standards

Non-broadcast advertising is regulated by the Advertising Standards Authority (ASA) which checks to ensure that advertisers:

- are legal, decent, honest and truthful
- show responsibility to the consumer and to society
- follow business principles of 'fair' competition.

The role of the media in marketing products

Marketing through the media includes the press, direct mail, broadcast media, cinema advertising, outdoor advertising (billboards and sports grounds), and electronic marketing (direct email and the Internet).

The target group index (TGI)

The target group index (TGI) is a marketing research organisation which regularly surveys a representative sample of consumers. Subscribing to this survey allows a marketing organisation to match its target market with the media it uses most.

Market research techniques

Market research is expensive but relying on uninformed decisions is risky and can prove more costly if a product launch is badly planned. Market research is used to identify:

- the nature, size and preferences of current and potential **target market groups (TMGs)** and subgroups
- the buying behaviour of the target market group
- the competition: its strengths and weaknesses (known as competition analysis)
- the required characteristics of new products
- the effect price changes might have on demand
- changes in trends, fashions and consumer tastes (known as trend analysis) such as design, colour, demographics, employment, interest rates and inflation.

Table 4.13 Strengths and weaknesses of the major types of media

Media	Strengths	Weaknesses
Television (around 33% of UK advertising expenditure)	• High audiences, but spread over channels • Excellent for showing product in use	• Short time-span of commercials is limiting • High wastage – viewers not in target market
Newspapers and magazines (around 60% of UK advertising expenditure)	• Can target the market with detailed information • Can get direct response (reply coupon)	• Can have a low impact on consumers • Timing may not match marketing campaign
Radio (around 2–3% of UK advertising expenditure)	• Accurate geographical targeting • Low cost and speedy	• Low numbers compared to other media • Listen to it in the background to other tasks
Posters (around 4% of UK advertising expenditure)	• More than 100,000 billboards available • Relatively cheap	• Seen as low impact/ complicated to buy • Subject to damage and defacement

Market research comes from two types of sources.

• Primary sources provide original research, for example internal company data, questionnaires and surveys.
• Secondary sources provide published information, for example trade publications, commercial reports, government statistics, computer databases, the media and the Internet.

Quantitative research collects measurable data such as sales figures or consumer characteristics. The views of the whole target market group are based on the responses from a sample group. Qualitative research explores consumer behaviour by interviewing individuals about their thoughts, opinions and feelings. It can be used to plan further quantitative research.

Surveys

Typically, surveys are used to collect quantitative data about behaviour, attitudes and opinions of a sample in a target market group. The process can be summarised as follows.

1 initial exploratory research
2 set survey objectives and data requirements
3 plan administration of survey
4 design questionnaire
5 collect data
6 process data
7 interpret data and write report.

Questionnaires

Questionnaires should be carefully designed to provide useful and accurate information. The questions should be relevant, clear, inoffensive, brief, precise, impartial. Questions can be of two types.

• open (ended) – which allow unlimited responses and are difficult to analyse
• closed questions – which provide a choice of answers and are easier to analyse.

Product analysis

As you have learned from Unit 1 and your coursework, detailed product analysis can help designers to develop detailed specifications and successful ideas.

Test marketing (test selling)

A finished product is placed on sale and data collected to find out customer/retailer reactions.

This data is used to generate forecasts and plan production and marketing strategies. This is known as **test selling**.

Case study: the C5 car

The C5 was launched by Sir Clive Sinclair in 1985 as a new concept in transport. There was very little market research and no test marketing of the C5. When tested by the Consumers Association serious criticisms were reported.

- On the road, the C5 was the same height as the bumpers of other cars, which made visibility difficult, increased the chance of accidents and made it vulnerable to exhaust fumes, spray and dazzle from headlights.
- There was no reverse gear so drivers had to get out of the C5 to move it backwards.
- The top speed of the car was 15mph, which caused problems even where the speed limit was 30mph.

Production was stopped after only 14,000 had been produced (compared with an estimated demand of 100,000 per year). Many people put the failure of the C5 down to poor market research.

Case study: Coca-Cola

Coca-Cola is one of the world's most recognised trademarks. A large part of the brand's success can be attributed to the success of Coca-Cola's marketing and advertising. Most of Coca-Cola's advertising links the brand and product to positive images.

Examiner's Tip

You will find it helpful to be able to refer to your own case studies which look at the marketing of new and existing products or brands.

The market research process

- Planning: identify a clear reason and purpose (usually a design problem, need or opportunity), decide what data needs to be collected and how to collect it.

- Implementation: carry out the data collection as planned, from primary and secondary sources.
- Interpretation: a report is written to analyse and interpret the collected data. Recommendations are made for future planning.

The basic principles of marketing and associated concepts

Marketing involves anticipating and satisfying consumer needs. Prime marketing objectives include generating profit, developing sales, influencing customers' buying decisions, increasing **market share**, diversifying into new markets, and promotion of company image.

The sales of competing products can be expressed as a proportion of total sales. This is what is meant by market share. Sometimes companies set an objective to increase market share rather than to increase profits. This is especially common when new products are launched and companies are trying to encourage us to switch brands to the new product.

Marketing plan

The basic structure of a product-marketing plan includes:

- background and situation analysis
- information on markets, customers and competitors
- a plan for action and advertising strategies
- planning marketing costs
- time planning: the best time to market the product to an achievable timetable
- a plan for monitoring the marketing.

Target market groups (TMGs)

A market consists of all the customers of all the companies and organisations supplying a specific product. Often it is impossible to supply all potential customers because, for example, they are too scattered or because of strong competition in some areas. As a result target market groups are identified. These are market segments which have been identified by market research as the most likely potential customers. Companies will find out as much as they can about their TMGs so they can plan their marketing and advertising campaigns to appeal to these customers. The process of identifying TMGs and developing products for them is called target marketing.

Consumer demand and market pull

Consumer demand equates to the number of products sold or projected sales. This is also known as **market pull**. Customers in any market will demand or 'pull' products and services to satisfy their needs. Effective marketing can be used to consolidate **brand loyalty** where consumers make buying decisions based on name and reputation rather than on other factors such as price. Companies use marketing to stimulate demand in order to expand their market share.

Lifestyle marketing

People with similar demographic characteristics often lead similar lifestyles, and demonstrate similar tastes and buying patterns. Profiles are developed which describe the general characteristics of these population groups and **lifestyle marketing** is used to target these potential market groups by matching their needs with products. New products can then be developed to match their needs.

Brand loyalty

A brand is a marketing identity of a generic product that sets it apart from its competitors. Brands are developed over time and marketing strategies aim to associate the brand with attractive images, personalities and emotions. Successful marketing strategies generate strong brand loyalties and consumers are often prepared to pay a significant premium for these products.

Advantages of branding for the customer

Branding provides an expected and reliable level of quality. Strongly branded products can be used as benchmarks and can save time for the consumer when deciding which product to buy. Examples of successful brands include Coca-Cola, Microsoft and Diesel jeans. All these companies have managed to establish a distinct brand image. The consumer perceives these branded products, rightly or wrongly, as better than generic alternatives (e.g. supermarket own brands).

Competitive edge and product proliferation

Price is not the only factor which influences our buying decisions. Manufacturers are always seeking to achieve a **competitive edge** in order to increase sales. This involves incorporating unique qualities or features within products and can be achieved in many ways including:

- price reductions
- higher-quality products
- unique features
- enhanced company/brand image through successful advertising.

Successful products, such as Coca-Cola, have become very strong brands throughout the world. **Product proliferation** is achieved when a product becomes nationally/internationally recognised and is consumed across large sections of society.

Price range, pricing strategy and market share

How much consumers are prepared to pay for a product depends on how much they value it. The justification for a higher price may depend on the following.

- a product's extra features, characteristics or innovative design
- the perceived quality of the product
- rarity or shortage of supply
- strong brand image through advertising and promotion
- extra services such as credit facilities and home delivery.

Sometimes products are sold at a loss to establish or increase market share, to encourage product proliferation or to encourage sales of related products. Manufacturers and retailers establish the **price range** of products. It is expressed as an upper and lower limit and will reflect the unique qualities and features of these products, as well as local market conditions.

Promotional gifts

In some cases products are given away free. **Promotional gifts** may take the form of samples to encourage people to try a product or they may be products which are designed to strengthen brand awareness.

Distribution

Distribution makes a product available to the maximum numbers of target customers at the lowest cost. Without an effective distribution strategy, products will not reach the consumer.

EXAMINATION QUESTIONS

Example questions and answers

 Q1 *a) Companies invest much time and money into marketing activities. State **three** possible marketing objectives for a company launching a new marketing campaign.*

(3 marks)

Acceptable answer
1 Generating **profit**
2 Increasing **market share**
3 **Diversification** into new markets.

*b) Market research is an important source of information. Explain the following **three** stages involved in market research.*
1 Planning
2 Implementation
3 Interpretation.

(3 marks)

Acceptable answer
The planning stage is necessary to **identify the data which needs to be collected and to establish how it will be collected**. The implementation stage is **where the data is collected** as planned, from primary and secondary sources. During the interpretation stage, a report is written to **analyse and interpret the collected data, making recommendations** for future planning.

*c) Explain, using examples to illustrate your answer, the difference between **one** of the following pairs:*
1 *'Primary sources' and 'secondary sources' of market research data*
2 *'Quantitative research' and 'qualitative research' used in market research.* **(4 marks)**

Acceptable answer (one of the following)
Primary sources of data or information, such as **internal company data, questionnaires and surveys**, produce **original research**. Secondary sources are **existing publications**, such as **trade publications, commercial reports and government statistics**. This form of research is clearly much **less expensive** but **may not provide suitable data**.

Quantitative research collects **measurable data** such as **sales figures or consumer characteristics**. Qualitative research **explores consumer behaviour** by **interviewing individuals about their thoughts, opinions and feelings**.

Conservation and resources

You need to

☐ understand the environmental implications of the industrial age
☐ understand the management of waste, the disposal of products and pollution control.

KEY TERMS

Check you understand these terms

Conservation, Renewable resources, Non-renewable resources, Recycling, Environmentally friendly, Sustainable technology, Sustainable development, Biotechnology

> 📖 **Further information can be found** in *Advanced Design and Technology for Edexcel, Product Design: Graphics with Materials Technology*, **Unit 4B1, section 4.**

KEY POINTS

Environmental implications of the industrial age

Influencing the future

As economies develop, more of the world's resources are being lost and more environments are damaged. Economic activity and levels of consumption are often used as a measure of progress and twentieth-century industry and society have become increasingly wasteful (the 'purchase-attraction' society). In the long term, product designers need to ask how progress can be made in the future by producing fewer products and by making essential products more environmentally safe. The designer needs to consider issues such as:

- concentrating on the long-term use and usefulness of products
- developing products that remain the property of the manufacturer
- paying for the use of the product and its maintenance
- returning products to the manufacturer to be serviced, repaired, recycled and reused.

Conservation and resource management

Conservation is concerned with the protection of the natural and the man-made world for future use. This includes the sensible management of resources and a reduction in the rate of consumption of finite resources, such as coal, oil, natural gas, ores and minerals. Resources can be divided into:

- **renewable resources** – once consumed they can be replaced, for example timber
- **non-renewable resources** – once consumed they cannot be replaced, for example oil.

Efficient management of resources includes:

- using less wasteful mining and quarrying methods

- making more efficient use of energy in manufacturing
- reducing waste materials produced in manufacture
- **recycling** waste materials produced in manufacture
- designing products with components which can be reclaimed and reused or recycled.

Recycling is the process by which waste materials are sorted, reclaimed and reprocessed to produce new products.

In parts of the world, including south east Asia, some tropical hardwoods, such as jelutong, have been harvested faster than the trees can be replaced. In contrast, the Scandinavian timber industry, which provides the majority of paper used in the UK, is arguably one example of sustainable development. For each tree that is cut down within these 'managed forests', another is planted: a policy that has led to a net increase in the tree population. An additional benefit is the fact that young trees absorb more carbon dioxide and release more oxygen, helping to combat the greenhouse effect.

Renewable sources of energy, energy conservation and the use of efficient manufacturing processes

There has been an increasing reliance on non-renewable sources of raw materials and energy such as coal and oil. Consumer pressure, cost reduction and national/international legislation have forced product designers to consider:

- reducing the amount of materials used in a product
- reusing products and waste materials within a manufacturing process
- recycling waste in a different manufacturing process
- using efficient manufacturing processes that save energy and prevent waste
- designing for easy product maintenance
- designing the product so that the whole or parts of it can be reused or recycled.

Turning to renewable sources of energy is one means of conserving non-renewable resources.

Table 4.14 Renewable sources of energy

Source	Process	Advantages	Disadvantages
Wind	Power of wind turns turbines	• Developed commercially • Produces low-cost power	• High set-up cost • Contributes a small proportion of total energy needs • Wind farms sometimes seen as unsightly
Tides	Reversible turbine blades harness the tides in both directions	• Occurs throughout the day on a regular basis • Reliable and non-polluting • Potential for large-scale energy production	• Very high set-up cost • Could restrict the passage of ships • Could cause flooding of estuary borders, which might damage wildlife
Water	Running water turns turbines and generates hydro-electric power	• Clean and 80–90% efficient	• High set-up cost • Suitable sites are generally remote from markets • Contributes to a small proportion of total energy needs of an industrial society
Solar	Hot water and electricity generated via solar cells	• Huge amounts of energy available. Could generate 50% of hot water for a typical house • Relatively inexpensive to set up	• High cost of solar cells • Biggest demand in winter when heat from Sun is at its lowest
Geothermal	Deep holes in Earth's crust produce steam to generate electricity	• Provides domestic power and hot water	• Only really cost-effective where Earth's crust is thin, e.g. New Zealand, Iceland

The use of efficient manufacturing processes

Product manufacturers can contribute to sustainable development and cost reduction by using more efficient design and manufacturing processes.

Case study: Yellow Pages

Yellow Pages is used by almost 27 million households. A recent design overhaul led to savings totalling £1.5 million per edition and a large reduction in the quantity of materials used. The changes in design were popular with customers who found the book easier to use, which led to an increase in the number of advertisers buying space. The edition included:

• an emphasis on the Yellow Pages brand
• a new cover design, a smaller but clearer font and a more compact layout
• an index reduced from twenty-three pages to seven
• an emphasis on the local character of each edition, using customer friendly cartoon-style images.

New technology and environmentally friendly manufacturing processes

The government agency, Envirowise, helps manufacturing companies improve their environmental performance and competitiveness. **Environmentally friendly** processes reduce damage to the environment and the depletion of non-renewable resources. The main themes of the programme are waste minimisation, which reduces costs, and the use of cleaner technology, reducing the consumption of raw materials, water and energy.

Reducing waste in the paper and board industry

A large number of additives are used to improve machine performance and paper quality. These non-fibrous materials include cleaning chemicals for papers and machines, fillers to improve paper opacity, sizing agents, dyes, brightening agents and paper coating chemicals. The overuse of these additives is a result of:

- a lack of operating manuals
- specifying the wrong type and dose of chemicals
- using incorrect sizes of dosing pipes
- using incorrect pump speeds
- incorrect connections between chemical storage systems and papermaking machinery
- poor labelling on storage tanks, pumps and pipe-work.

Reducing these additives by 1 per cent could save the industry in the region of £4 million per year. The improved management of non-fibrous materials can:

- reduce raw materials costs
- reduce the generation of waste
- reduce waste disposal costs
- increase the amount of saleable paper produced
- reduce machine downtime
- reduce production losses by up to 5 per cent.

Cleaner technology using high-volume, low-pressure (HVLP) spray guns

In order to judge the true environmental impact of any product, it is important to study the whole life cycle of that product from 'cradle to grave'. Refer to Unit 4A to refresh your memory of Life Cycle Analysis (LCA).

Compared with conventional spray guns, HVLP guns atomise paint using a higher volume of air at a lower pressure. They reduce solvent use and meet the requirements of the 1990 Environmental Protection Act. The benefits of the use of modern HVLP spray guns include:

- an initial reduction in paint use of up to 21 per cent with obvious cost savings

- reduced use of solvents, compressed air and energy, further reducing costs
- a short payback period on the purchase price of the spray guns
- reduced environmental impact
- a better finish as over-spraying is reduced.

The importance of using sustainable technology

Sustainable technology and **sustainable development** are philosophies which emphasise an environmentally friendly approach to technological and economic development. Economic growth is welcomed, but people are encouraged to see the environment as an asset which should be shared and protected by all nations and future generations. According to the 1987 Brundtland Report, *Our Common Future* (World Commission on Environment and Development), sustainable development has been described as:

> *development that meets the needs of the present, without compromising the ability of future generations to meet their own needs.*

The key objectives of sustainable development include:

- giving priority to the essential needs of the world's poor
- meeting essential needs for jobs, energy, water and sanitation
- ensuring a sustainable level of population
- conserving and enhancing the resource base
- bringing together the environment and economics in decision making.

'Bio-Wise' is a government initiative that supports and advises companies and organisations on developing sustainable practices that make use of biotechnology.

Management of waste, the disposal of products and pollution control

There are three key approaches to reducing waste (the three Rs):

- reduce the amount of materials used in manufacture

a)

sheet

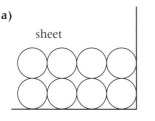

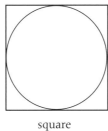

square

b)

sheet

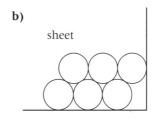

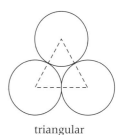

triangular

Fig. 4.9 Maximising the use of aluminium sheet in the production of aluminium can tops. Arrangement A produces 21.4 per cent waste while arrangement B produces only 9.3 per cent waste

- reuse materials in the same manufacturing process where possible
- recycle materials in a different manufacturing process if possible.

Reducing materials use

Small changes to manufacturing processes can lead to a significant reduction in waste and costs.

Table 4.15 The disposal of products and pollution control

Destination	Issues
Landfill 90%	Some materials, such as many plastics, will not decompose. Materials which do decompose release harmful chemicals and explosive gases which need to be managed. Landfill sites are unpleasant and use large areas of land.
Incineration 5%	Regarded as a more environmentally friendly method. However, burning some materials can release harmful gases which need to be filtered out. The process is more expensive than landfill but some incinerators can recoup costs by sorting and recycling materials and converting the heat generated into electricity.
Recycling 5%	Some countries recycle a large proportion of household waste. However, recycling can be a costly process and while it conserves resources, the process also consumes power and resources. Hence the need to 'design for recycling'.

Pollution is the environmentally harmful by-product of industrial activity. Concern about pollution has encouraged governments to legislate in order to protect the environment. In the UK, the 1990 Environmental Protection Act (EPA) introduced tight controls on the discharge of waste into water, land and air. Prosecution can lead to large fines and expensive clean-up costs.

Impact of biotechnology on manufacture

Biotechnology is the use of biological processes involving live organisms in industrial processes. Traditional applications include the use of yeast to make bread and enzymes added to improve the properties of laundry detergents. Consumer pressure, cost advantages and legislation have encouraged companies to develop and apply new, environmentally friendly biotechnologies. These include:

- reed beds and aerobic and anaerobic treatment of industrial effluent
- composting to treat domestic, industrial and agricultural organic waste
- 'bioremediation' techniques to clean up contaminated land
- the treatment of waste cutting fluids.

Biodegradable packaging material

Around 185,000 tonnes of polystyrene are used in the UK each year, most of which go straight to landfill. Biosystem ™, made from renewable corn starch, has been developed as an alternative to polystyrene foam which is used to package and protect consumer products. The advantages of Biosystem™ are:

- it is made from renewable raw materials
- it is biodegradable (can be decomposed by micro-organisms in landfill sites)

- it displays similar properties to polystyrene and polyethylene foams and competes with them on performance and cost.

Turning waste wood dust into garden compost

It is now possible to turn hazardous wood dust, a by-product of timber and manufacturing industries, into safe garden compost. This has been made possible by the discovery of microbes which feed on the lacquers, sealers and solvents used in these industries. Computers manage a controlled environment which optimises the action of these micro-organisms. This process reduces pressure on landfill sites and allows industry to generate a return on a previously useless by-product.

Biochips

The number of circuits which can be placed on a conventional integrated circuit (IC) is limited by:

- the width of the circuit tracks
- the occurrence of short circuits
- the heat produced by large numbers of components.

Biochips have been developed to replace silicon chips with semi conducting molecules in a protein framework. The proteins are grown to take up the complex 3D structures which can eventually lead to further miniaturisation in electronic products.

The advantages and disadvantages of recycling materials

The suitability of materials for recycling depends upon:

- the value of the materials when recycled
- the costs of processing.

Metal, glass and paper are the most cost effective materials to recycle and are treated differently according to their value.

- Non-ferrous metals are sorted into grades, due to their relatively high commercial value.
- Steel and cast iron are graded by size, due to their lower commercial value.

- Items made of glass, rubber and plastics are more difficult to sort and have a much lower value than metals.
- Plastics, paper and glass recycling are growing industries.
- Waste materials from the manufacturing process are the most valuable because their material content is known and they are easily available.
- Waste from old products is more difficult to process due to the varied nature of the chemical or physical make-up.

The advantages for the environment of recycling include:

- conservation of non-renewable resources and reduced dependency on raw materials
- reduced energy consumption
- less pollution, including greenhouse gas emissions.

Design for recycling

Due to existing and proposed European regulations, manufacturers are being encouraged to take more responsibility for the recycling of products. As an example some products are designed to disassemble themselves under controlled conditions. UK engineers have developed a mobile phone that falls apart when heated. The phone is made from shape memory polymers, plastics that revert to their original form when heated. Different components of the phone will change shape at different temperatures, allowing them to fall off at different times, when they pass along a conveyor belt. The reusable parts can then be recycled.

Recycling packaging

Facts and figures

- 1.7 million tonnes of plastic waste are produced per year in the UK.
- Less than 15 per cent is recycled.
- Around 85 per cent goes to landfill where it remains for a hundred years or more.
- An EC directive sets a target of at least 50 per cent of plastic packaging to be recycled.

Sorting plastics

Recycling is a complex and time-consuming process, but it has become more efficient with the increase of packaging designed for recycling with:

- easily removable labelling
- material identification symbols moulded into products (refer to Unit 1 Table 1.2 and Unit 3A Table 3.8).

Recycling is a growing concern for the packaging industry and local government. However, many local councils currently do not have adequate recycling facilities beyond those used for paper, aluminium and glass. As a result, tonnes of plastic packaging still end up in landfill. Plastics can be identified manually by using their identification symbols but it is more cost effective to use automated methods, for example

- as HDPE and LDPE floats, they are retrieved by placing the waste in a water tank
- PET and polyvinyl chloride PVC sink and are identified chemically using sensors.

Turning recycled plastics into new materials

PET is the main type of plastic used in recycling. PET bottles can be chopped, melted, extruded and blow moulded into similar products or they can be extruded into polyester fibres and yarns for clothing.

Biodegradable packaging

d2w™ is a new, fully degradable polythene packaging. A special additive is added to polythene which helps break down the material into water, carbon dioxide and environmentally safe biomass. d2w™ has the added advantage of being fully recyclable.

EXAMINATION QUESTIONS

Example questions and answers

 a) Discuss the aims and objectives of sustainable development. **(5 marks)**

Acceptable answer
Sustainable development **encourages environmentally friendly economic development**. The Earth, its environment and its resources should be treated as **an asset** for this generation which **requires careful management and investment for future generations**. Sustainable development is a global philosophy in which **priority is given to the essential needs of the world's poor**. It is important to **limit the world's population** to a level which can be supported by available resources. When governments or international organisations make decisions about development they are encouraged to **incorporate environmental costs into economic calculations**.

*b) Explain the term 'biotechnology' and give **two** examples of its use.* **(3 marks)**

Acceptable answer
Biotechnology is the **use of biological processes involving live organisms within industrial processes**. Biotechnology has been used successfully in the **composting processes used to treat domestic, industrial and agricultural organic waste**. Biological organisms have also been used **to treat waste cutting fluids from industrial machinery**.

PRACTICE EXAMINATION STYLE QUESTION

1 a) Crude oil is a non-renewable resource. Explain the term 'non-renewable'. **(1 mark)**

  b) Raw materials come from many different sources. Name the main producers of crude oil, and outline its importance as a source of other raw materials. **(3 marks)**

  c) Explain how industry can help to conserve fossil fuels and other non-renewable resources:
  - during the design stage
  - during manufacturing. **(5 marks)**

  d) Discuss the issues surrounding the disposal of waste products when they reach the end of their life. **(6 marks)**

2 a) Marketing relies on the media. Explain the terms:
  - marketing
  - media. **(2 marks)**

  b) Describe the role of the Advertising Standards Authority (ASA) in the advertising industry. **(3 marks)**

  c) Discuss the importance of branding and brand loyalty with reference to a product or products of your choice. **(5 marks)**

  d) Surveys and questionnaires are frequently used to gather valuable research. Outline the main stages of the process followed when creating and conducting a customer survey. **(5 marks)**

Total for this question paper: **30 marks**

CAD/CAM (G403)

This option will be assessed in section B during the 1½ hour, Unit 4 examination. If you have chosen this option you should spend half of your time (45 minutes) answering all the questions in this section. It is important to use appropriate specialist and technical language in the exam, along with accurate spelling, punctuation and grammar. Where appropriate you should also use clear, annotated sketches to explain your answer. *You do not have to study this chapter if you are taking the Design and Technology in Society option.*

Computer-aided design, manufacture and testing (CADMAT)

You need to

understand computer-aided design, manufacture and testing (CADMAT)
understand computer-integrated manufacture (CIM)
understand flexible manufacturing systems (FMS)
understand CADMAT, FMS and CIM applications within:
- ☐ **creative and technical design**
- ☐ **modelling and testing**
- ☐ **production planning**
- ☐ **the control of equipment, processes, quality and safety**
- ☐ **the control of complex manufacturing processes**
- ☐ **integrated and concurrent manufacturing.**

KEY TERMS

Check you
understand these terms

CADMAT, PDM, JIT, CIM, FMS, TQM and TQ, Concurrent manufacturing

Further information can be found in *Advanced Design and Technology for Edexcel, Product Design: Graphics with Materials Technology,* **Unit 4B2 section 1.**

KEY POINTS

Computer-aided design, manufacture and testing (CADMAT)

Manufacturers have always experienced pressures to maximise profit and reduce costs. Global manufacturing places additional pressures on manufacturers who have to:

- compete with low-cost imports
- satisfy customer demands for shorter production runs
- satisfy customer demands for improved delivery times.

Computer-aided design, manufacture and testing (**CADMAT**) is an extension of CAD/CAM and fully integrates the use of computers at every level and stage of manufacturing. Computers are used to manage

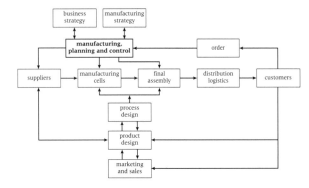

Fig. 4.10 A system flow chart describing integrated manufacturing

data and to help the decision making process in a variety of ways.

- gathering, storing, retrieval and organisation of data, information and knowledge
- computer model simulations to test new production methods or systems
- mathematical analysis of designs
- communication between project team and clients
- process and equipment control including the scheduling of routine maintenance
- monitoring safety and quality.

Fig 4.10 is a simplified model showing the complex relationships in the design and manufacturing process. Failure in one area can hold up the entire process and it is vitally important that up-to-date, 'real-time' data is immediately available so that the system can be managed effectively.

Project data management (PDM)

PDM provides a system to centralise and manage all data generated from the design and manufacturing process. Data is gathered from all areas and stored on a secure database. Different levels of access are established according to need and PDM also allows rapid communications between departments, manufacturers and retailers.

On-line order tracking

PDM allows customers to follow the progress of their purchases through on-line order tracking. Using the Internet, customers can check on their purchases by entering a unique access code on

the company website allowing them to track the progress of their order from the beginning of the transaction through to despatch.

The advantages of PDM include:

- fewer bottlenecks
- improved quality control
- more accurate product costing
- more effective production control
- making it easier to work at optimum capacity with minimum stock levels
- increased flexibility
- higher productivity and profits.

Just in time (JIT)

Companies are always seeking ways of reducing costs. Maintaining high stock levels incurs significant costs.

- Capital is tied up in raw materials, components, sub-assemblies and unsold products.
- Too much stock at the point of production can create safety issues and lead to deterioration.
- Storage of raw materials, components, sub-assemblies and unsold products costs money.

This is particularly significant for high-volume manufacturers. On the other hand, stock shortages in one section of the production line can halt production altogether. **JIT** is a management philosophy which seeks to minimise these costs. In the automotive industry some components are manufactured by suppliers literally hours before they are required at the factory. They are delivered to the production line so that each component arrives in the correct order. The result is that each product is manufactured to the specification of an individual customer.

Aims of JIT

- Raw materials, components and sub-assemblies are received from suppliers just before they are needed.
- Quick response to customer orders.
- Goods are supplied to a clearly defined level of quality and quantity.
- Waste (raw materials, time and resources) is minimised.

- Individual manufacturing units, throughout the organisation, follow the JIT philosophy as well as manufacturers, suppliers and customers.

Features of JIT

- Continuous operation.
- All employees are responsible for quality.
- Manufacturing is synchronised to avoid bottlenecks.
- 'Kaizen' – continuous improvement is encouraged to increase efficiency and reduce waste.
- Work is simplified using foolproof ('poka-yoke') tools, jigs and fixtures.
- The end product is the important focus and anything which does not contribute toward this should be removed.
- Factory layouts should be custom designed to minimise movement of materials and products.
- 'Jidoka' – automation seeks to use self-regulating machines reducing the need for direct human intervention and allowing decisions to be made centrally, based on electronically gathered data.

JIT and workplace organisation

- Operational set up times are reduced, increasing flexibility and capacity to produce smaller batches.

- A flexible, multi-skilled workforce is required which leads to greater productivity and job satisfaction.
- Production rates are flexible and can be levelled or varied, smoothing the flow of products through the factory.
- 'Kanban' control systems are used to control and schedule production rates. (Kanbans originally were cards which identified components, authorised and recorded operations and followed batches of components around the factory.)

Computer-integrated manufacture (CIM)

A **CIM** system uses ICT to integrate all aspects of a company's operations (production, business and manufacturing information) in order to create more efficient production lines. Tasks within a CIM system include product design, workflow planning, control of machining operations, control of materials ordering, stock control, and customer invoicing.

CIM and the print industry

The printing industry has had to respond to more demanding client requirements including:

- short, customised print runs
- faster delivery times

Table 4.16 CIM and the print industry

Digital pre-press solutions	High-volume printing	Adding value after printing
Documents can be seen on-screen as they will be printed. All production details including finishing can be specified and attached to print files. Digital printers come with a full range of image handling capabilities, much like some of the tools found in DTP software such as image cleanup, enlargement and reduction. Scanned images and whole print jobs can be stored easily for repeat orders. Some companies provide an Internet service. Shorter set up times lead to lower costs.	Fast (up to 250ppm); high-quality output; flexible and more productive so lower costs; centrally controlled so simple to manage multiple print jobs – jobs can be rearranged to avoid unnecessary changes in paper etc. Computer to plate (CTP); removes time-consuming and costly stages of production involved in the production of films	Finishing technologies have been forced to evolve in order to keep up with digital print technologies; digital finishing equipment has become more automated, faster, easier to programme and more accurate

- the ability to incorporate last-minute changes
- high-quality output
- cheaper products.

Digital print technologies within a CIM environment have made it possible for printers to meet these demanding requirements.

CIM and the packaging industry

The packaging industry has had to respond to more demanding client requirements including:

- pressure to develop more distinctive design concepts
- pressure to develop stronger corporate and brand images.

The packaging industry has taken advantage of ICT developments and CIM systems in many ways.

- Developing photo-realistic visualisations in place of costly one-off 3D models.
- VR technology can be used to place products in context (e.g. a product can be put on supermarket shelves).
- Volumes of packaging can be calculated more easily.
- Design drawings can be used to produce reliable manufacturing information for the production of accurate moulds and dies.
- Printed packaging enjoys the advantages of digital processes and CTP technologies described earlier.
- New printing technologies allow designers to print onto a wider range of materials such as plastic sheets and laminates.

Flexible manufacturing systems (FMS) and their wider application in industry

Characteristics of **FMS** include:

- the system responds quickly to changes in demand or supply
- multi purpose equipment and techniques are used to increase operational flexibility
- system effectiveness is constantly monitored and evaluated
- lead times from design to manufacture are reduced

- modifications to designs are incorporated rapidly
- minimum stock levels
- close relationships between suppliers, manufacturers and retailers (vertical partnerships)
- increased sales and stock turnover
- use of sophisticated computer-based management tools, such as manufacture resource planning (MRP), provides real-time processing data, to track work through the production cycle and to re-plan production in response to changes in demand.

Creative and technical design

Computer-aided engineering (CAE) supports and overlaps CAD/CAM technology. CAE takes advantage of ICT technology to gather, analyse and manage engineering data. For example, computers are used to simulate different conditions to test product performance. This is a convenient and relatively inexpensive technique which shortens the time needed for product development.

Modelling and testing

Modelling techniques have been covered in earlier units. Examples include:

- experimenting with different 3D forms and layout
- testing models using specialist software, for example manufacturing processes can be simulated to test suitability of the design for production
- virtual interactive models and environments are created using virtual reality modelling language (VRML).

Production planning

FMS and similar systems allow products to be produced in any order using any available machine. Careful and flexible planning is needed to make full use of the resources – 'time is literally money'. Any strategies which save time or increase responsiveness will increase profitability and generate a return on the high level of investment. Scheduling is part of the planning process and is supported by a wide range of software tools. Scheduling seeks to specify the scope and detail of work, production start date, production deadline, machinery and processes required and labour requirements.

There are two categories of scheduling.

- Finite capacity scheduling: bases planning on available production capacity.
- Infinite capacity scheduling: bases planning on customer deadlines assuming that sufficient capacity will always be available. A master production schedule (MPS) is used in infinite capacity scheduling systems to set short-term production targets based on known demand, forecasts and planned stock levels.

The advantages of time-based strategies over cost-based strategies

Pressures created by cost-based strategies can lead to low wages, narrow product focus, relocation to low-wage economies, and centralisation. Time/FMS/rapid response-based strategies are not as vulnerable to such pressures and are more inclined to site themselves close to customers.

Types of computer-aided scheduling functions

- Resource scheduling: is a finite scheduling function which focuses on the resources needed to turn raw materials into products. Data from sales orders, stock recording and cost accounting is entered into a database but the reliability of the system relies upon the accuracy of data input.
- Electronic scheduling boards: replace card-based boards, automating manual processes such as estimating production time, and provide notification of problems or conflicts.
- Order-based scheduling: prioritises the distribution of parts and components.
- Constraint-based schedulers: locate potential bottlenecks and ensure that these are well provided.
- Discrete event simulation: simulates the production line point by point to resolve bottlenecks and other production problems.

Control of equipment, processes, quality and safety

Control and feedback systems

Equipment can be controlled manually or by electrical, electronic, mechanical, pneumatic, computer or microprocessor systems. Control systems depend on feedback to maintain efficiency, accuracy, reliability, safety and minimal levels of waste. Control systems are found in:

- materials handling: for example ensuring materials arrive in the right place at the right time
- materials processing: for example equipment will automatically respond to changes in conditions; feeds and speeds will be adjusted automatically
- joining materials: for example heat sealing and bonding of plastics for PoS displays using electronic or computer control
- quality control: for example optical monitoring of ink quality adjusts feed rates
- safety systems: for example machines will not operate unless guards are in place or operators are not out of the way
- coordination of production: for example graphical display panels will show active cells of equipment and sound alerts when problems are identified.

Total quality (TQ)

Total quality systems, such as total quality control (TQC) and total quality management (**TQM**), link together quality assurance and quality control into a coherent improvement strategy. **TQ** programs are purpose driven, long-term processes which engage everyone in the design and manufacture process and involve comprehensive change.

ICT forms an important part of TQ processes, including interactive multimedia support for employee training and computer-aided statistical tools and methods for checking quality. For example, product barcodes can be used to trace manufacturing defects through a PDM system.

TQC and TQM tools

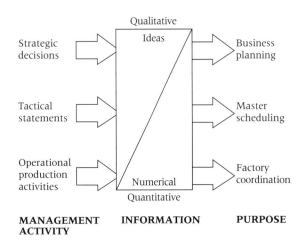

Fig. 4.11 The relationship between thinking tools and planned outcomes

There are three stages in the development of TQ.

1 Raising awareness
2 Empowerment
3 Alignment

Statistical process control (SPC) and the use of ITC

The study of statistics is concerned with the collection, analysis, interpretation and presentation of numerical data. The complexity of modern manufacturing organisations results in a large amount of data which necessitates the use of modern statistical techniques including Pareto charts, flow charts, cause and effect/fishbone/Ishikawa diagrams, bar graphs and histograms, check sheets and checklists.

Monitoring and inspecting quality

Despite QA procedures designed to eliminate faults before they happen, inspection programmes are still important. The costs associated with undetected faults escalate as the product moves through the production process and on to the customer.

- Manufacturing cells – each team or cell is responsible for product quality and has to meet specified quality indicators.
- Artificial vision – manual inspection methods are dependent on the effectiveness of the

individual. Automated quality control systems, such as digital image processing technologies used in the print industry, share many advantages including:
  – high-speed, real-time fault detection
  – automatic feedback and solutions
  – labour relieved to perform more productive tasks
  – lower operational costs
  – quality specifications can be adjusted.

Manufacturing to tolerances

- Tolerance is the 'margin of error' or degree of imperfection allowed in a product or component.
- Tolerance limits are expressed as a +/− figure.
- Tolerances can be checked manually through visual inspections or by using sophisticated probes and sensors including laser technologies.
- The data is gathered as on-process or post-process measurements and analysed.
- Tolerances can be set for any property including size, weight, colour, strength.

Control of complex manufacturing processes

Computer systems are used to:

- optimise factory layout of plant and equipment
- provide effective deployment of labour
- schedule processing operations
- monitor and control workflow
- manage and disseminate production data.

Managing workflow

Production plans and control systems manage the input of materials and components, work in progress, and output, to ensure orders meet deadlines to cost.

Monitoring workflow

Laser and barcode (data recognition tags) technology is used to record and monitor the progress of production, sending data to the supervising computer controlling the production line.

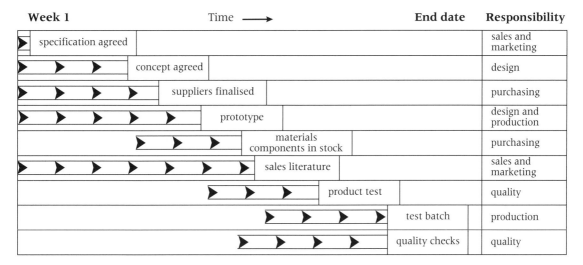

Week 1	Time ⟶	End date	Responsibility
▶ specification agreed			sales and marketing
▶ ▶ ▶ concept agreed			design
▶ ▶ ▶ ▶ suppliers finalised			purchasing
▶ ▶ ▶ ▶ ▶ prototype			design and production
▶ ▶ ▶ materials components in stock			purchasing
▶ ▶ ▶ ▶ ▶ ▶ sales literature			sales and marketing
▶ ▶ ▶ product test			quality
▶ ▶ ▶ ▶ test batch			production
▶ ▶ ▶ ▶ quality checks			quality

Fig. 4.12 A simplified milestone plan (Gantt chart) for a typical manufactured product

Controlling workflow

Project management software coordinates production cells within a Master Production Schedule (MPS). Workflow software ensures that individuals responsible for particular tasks are notified and provided with the information necessary to complete the tasks.

Integrated and concurrent manufacturing

Sequential manufacturing

Product development follows a linear path. Each stage of a product life cycle is dependent upon the completion of all preceding stages. This system has several disadvantages.

- In order to trace and correct faults, the product has to be sent back through each preceding stage.
- It is slow to respond to change or fluctuations in demand.
- There are longer lead times.
- There are quality problems due to separation and isolation of each department and costly redesign loops.

Concurrent manufacturing

Concurrent manufacturing (simultaneous manufacturing) is applicable to batch and volume manufacturing. Features and advantages of concurrent manufacturing include:

- operations run alongside each other
- team-based approach
- all departments are represented to ensure quality decision making
- shorter lead times
- manufacturers are forced to consider the whole product life cycle from conception to disposal
- suppliers and retailers involved early in the product development cycle
- good communications are essential, increasingly taking advantage of EDI systems
- the role of ITC becomes more important in design for manufacture (DFM)
- creation of customised 'expert systems' shared on company intranets
- the Internet is used to allow access to information across the world
- enables the use of JIT and quick response manufacturing
- production deadlines (milestones) become the responsibility of individual team members.

EXAMINATION QUESTIONS

Example questions and answers

Q1 *a) Explain how computers are used to organise data and help the decision making process in computer-aided design, manufacturing and testing (CADMAT).*
(4 marks)

Acceptable answer

CADMAT is an extension of CAD/CAM and **fully integrates the use of computers at every level and stage of manufacturing.** Computers are used to **gather, store, retrieve and organise data, information and knowledge.** Testing can be carried out using **computer model simulations to prototype new production methods or systems.** Designs can be assessed much more thoroughly using **mathematical analysis.** **CADMAT** systems allow **efficient communications** between project team and clients. Process and equipment control, such as the **scheduling of routine maintenance,** can be organised efficiently to avoid impacting production. Computer systems are used to **monitor safety and quality.**

b) CADMAT systems often incorporate project data management (PDM) software systems to manage data generated from the design and manufacturing process. PDM allows companies to establish on-line order tracking. Describe the features of on-line order tracking. **(2 marks)**

Acceptable answer

On-line order tracking allows customers to **follow the progress of their purchases** from the beginning of the transaction through to despatch. Customers can check on their purchases by entering a **unique access code on the company website** allowing them to track the progress of their order.

*c) Just in time (JIT) is a management philosophy which seeks to maximise efficiency and minimise costs. Explain the **two** most significant costs which are minimised by JIT systems.* **(2 marks)**

Acceptable answer

- **Capital costs** which are tied up in raw materials, components, sub-assembles and unsold products
- **Storage costs** of raw materials, components, sub-assembles and unsold products costs.

d) Describe some of the main aims and/or features of JIT and its effect on workplace organisation. **(7 marks)**

Acceptable answer

Raw materials, components and sub-assembles are only **delivered to the production line just before they are needed.** Every level of the manufacturing organisation, including **individual manufacturing units, suppliers and customers throughout the organisation, follow the JIT philosophy.** JIT systems are able to provide a **quick response to customer orders** and **goods are supplied to a clearly defined level of quality and quantity.** JIT is a **continuous operation which synchronises manufacturing to avoid bottlenecks.** A **flexible, multi-skilled workforce is required** which leads to greater productivity and job satisfaction.

Robotics

You need to

☐ **know the industrial application of robotics/control technology and the development of automated processes** ▼

Further information can be found in *Advanced Design and Technology for Edexcel, Product Design: Graphics with Materials Technology*, Unit 4B2 section 2.

☐ understand complex automated systems using artificial intelligence (AI) and new technology
☐ understand the use of block flow diagrams and flow process diagrams for representing simple and complex production systems including open/ closed loop control, feedback and degrees of freedom
☐ know the advantages and disadvantages of automation and its impact on employment, both local and global.

KEY TERMS
Check you understand these terms

Robotics, Artifical intelligence (AI), ASRS, AGVs, Expert systems, Machine vision systems, Neural networks, Voice recognition systems, NLP, Open- and closed-loop control systems, EDI, Fuzzy logic

KEY POINTS

The industrial application of robotics/control technology and the development of automated processes

Applications of robotics

The original driving forces behind the development of robotics technology were military and automotive applications. Typical roles and environments have been described as those which are dirty, dull, dangerous, demeaning, hot, heavy or hazardous.

Fig. 4.13 The Canadarm

Table 4.17 Robotic and control technologies

Technologies	Definition
Automation	The automatic operation and self-correcting control of machinery or production processes by devices that make decisions and take action without the interference of a human operator.
Robotics	A specific field of automation concerned with the design and construction of self-controlling machines or robots.
Mechatronics	Mechatronic devices integrate mechanical, electronic, optical and computer engineering to provide mechanical devices and control systems that have greater precision and flexibility.
Animatronics	Animatrons are animated sculptures used to entertain or inform as you might see at theme parks.
Artificial intelligence (AI)	Devices which have the capacity to learn from experience and which seek to imitate aspects of human thought processes.

Increasingly robots have been applied to dangerous and/or repetitive tasks throughout many industrial sectors such as assembly, painting, palletising, packing, welding, dispensing, cutting, laser processing, and material handling. Other emerging applications are in the advertising, promotional, leisure and entertainment industries such as animatronics. Robots are slowly finding their way into more warehouses for automatic stock control, laboratories, research and exploration sites, energy plants, hospitals and even hostile environments such as outer space.

Table 4.18 The parts of a robot

Controller	The controller is the 'brain' of the robot and allows it to be networked to other systems. Controllers are run by programs written by engineers. In the future AI robots will be able to adapt their programming in response to their environment.
Arm	The arm is the part of the robot that positions the end-effector and sensors. Each joint is said to give the robot 'one degree of freedom'. Most working robots today have six degrees of freedom.
Drive (actuators)	The drive is the 'engine' that drives the links (the sections between the joints) into their desired position. Air, liquid or electricity, powers most drives (actuators).
End-effector	The end-effector (end of arm tooling) is the 'hand' connected to the robot's arm. It could be a tool (or interchangeable tools) such as a gripper, vacuum pump, tweezers, scalpel, blowtorch or heat-sealing gun.
Sensor	Feedback is provided by sensors which send data back to the controller which will make adjustments in response to changes in the robot's environment.

Basics of robot design

For a machine to be classified as a robot, it usually has five parts (Table 4.18).

Work envelope

The work envelope is the range of space in which a robot can work: the maximum limits of movement of the end-effector in all directions. The work envelope is dependent upon the range of movement of the robot: jointed, cylindrical,

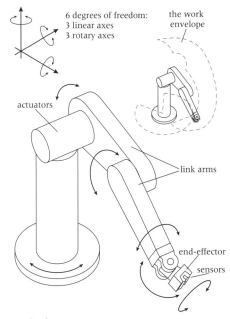

Fig. 4.14a A robotic arm

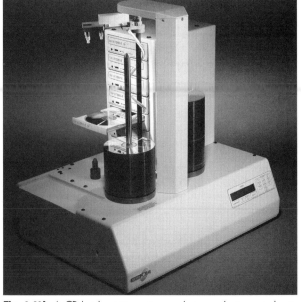

Fig. 4.14b A CD batch printing system employing a robotic arm to locate CDs

spherical or Cartesian (rectilinear). Robots may be fixed, move along overhead rails (gantry robots) or move along the floor (mobile robots).

The role of robots in batch and volume production

- Robots support continuous production which involves many repetitive tasks.
- Robots encourage flexibility because they can be reprogrammed to perform different tasks.
- They allow many processes to run concurrently, sequentially or in combination.
- A limited number of human operators are required.
- Safe and secure 'fail-safe' operating conditions use sensors to shut down operations in the event of a failure or emergency.

These robotic technologies are enabling technologies that allow innovative solutions to complex processing operations.

Control systems

Robots use sensors (transducers) to detect or measure properties. Computer or microprocessor control systems record and display this data, then regulate, check, verify or restrain actions of the robot or automated system.

The data generated by these transducers is processed within the robot control system, often using programmable logic controllers (PLCs), in order to perform tasks, or to be recorded, stored and sent to a display device which can be monitored by the operator.

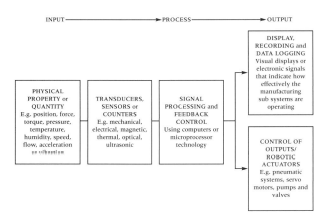

Fig. 4.15 A basic control system

Monitoring quality and safety

- Data from individual robots, machines and production cells is gathered locally and centrally. This data is analysed to identify problems before they affect production.
- The development of modern sensing techniques allows effective automated on-line inspection.
- Quality checks are conducted at each stage of manufacture before components are moved on to the next stage.
- 'Fail-safe' procedures are built into automated machinery to eliminate accidents or poor-quality components.

Types of robots include:

- simple robots which can be programmed to perform specific and repetitive tasks, for example numerically controlled robots which are programmed and operated much like CNC machines
- remote and sensor controlled robots which use data or commands generated outside their internal programming.

Automatic storage and retrieval systems (ASRS)

- **ASRS** are used in automated warehouses.
- They are commanded externally, either to transfer an object from a designated pickup point to a designated position in storage or vice versa.
- The required motions are internally programmed into the device.
- They are available in various sizes.
- The commands may come from a computer, which controls a larger operation, in which case the robot computer and the computer that commands it are said to form a control 'hierarchy'.

Mobile robots or automated guided vehicles (**AGVs**) are unmanned vehicles which carry 'loads' along a pre-programmed path and are typically used in component or pallet transfer. AGVs use different navigational systems and travel around under a combination of automatic control and remote control. Other uses of AGVs are in mail delivery, surveillance and police tasks, material transportation in factories, internal pipe inspection, military tasks such as bomb disposal, and underwater tasks such as inspecting pipelines and ship hulls and recovering torpedoes.

Robots for advertising and promotional purposes

Robots are used for advertising and promotional purposes because they are attention grabbers.

Their services have been employed at trade shows, parades, theme parks and museums, and to publicise special educational programmes such as anti-drugs campaigns and fire safety. Types of robots used include mobile robots, talking signs and animated figures (animatrons).

The features of mobile robots may include:

- rechargeable batteries
- speech via wireless microphone systems using an operator with a voice modifier and synchronised mouth movement/lights
- customisation to convey corporate image
- a digital messaging system, sirens or back-up alarm, or a combination of these attention-getting noisemakers
- a remote camera that allows moving graphic images to be relayed between the operator and the person that is engaged
- recorded messages on a cassette tape or digital chip activated manually or automatically by infra-red sensor that senses when a person is nearby (used by 'talking signs').

New uses for robots in manufacturing

Robots are increasingly used in the plastics manufacturing industry.

- Finishing plastic components using a six-axis robot with a trimming device for drilling, routing, blow moulded bubble removal, flash removal, de-gating or any other type of plastic removal application.
- Insert loading systems in which the robot will load metal threaded inserts, other plastic components and appliqués into the moulds.
- Part removal systems which remove parts from the moulding machines.
- Infrared plastic welding systems.
- Laser cutting systems.

The key benefits of robotics are:

- continuous operation – most robots can switch effortlessly between different pre-programmed operations without the need to stop production
- reproducibility – pre-programmed operations can be stored indefinitely until required
- consistent quality – the accuracy and reliability of robots and automatic sensors virtually eliminates human error
- safer work environment – the ability of robots to operate in hazardous environments combined with 'fail-safe' procedures leads to a reduction in risk to human operators
- reduction of labour costs – robotics requires heavy initial investment but automated systems have much lower operational costs.

Complex automated systems using artificial intelligence (AI) and new technology

AI seeks to imitate characteristics associated with human intelligence (such as learning, reasoning, problem-solving and language). In short AI seeks to create devices which can 'think'. In 1997, an IBM supercomputer called 'Deep Blue' defeated the world chess champion, Garry Kasparov.

AI activities broadly encompass: expert systems; computer/machine vision; natural language processing (NLP); artificial neural networks; and fuzzy logic.

Features of a thinking machine

- It must be able to perceive and understand.
- It must possess intelligence and knowledge including the ability to solve complex problems or make generalisations and construct relationships.
- It must be able to consider large amounts of information simultaneously and process them faster in order to make rational, logical or expert judgements.
- It has to pass the Turing test, which states that a computer would deserve to be called intelligent if it could deceive a human into believing that it was human.

Knowledge-based or expert systems

Expert systems are designed by knowledge engineers who study how experts make decisions. They identify the 'rules' that the expert has used and translate them into terms that a computer can understand. This is then stored as a knowledge base which can be used to solve real-life problems.

Application of AI in design and manufacture

AI is still a developing technology which is not widely used, decisions being made by product development teams. However, elements of AI are available to be used in:

- CAD, process planning and production scheduling
- problem diagnosis and solution in machinery and equipment
- modelling and simulation of production facilities.

Applying design or production rules

Electronics has used logic gate truth tables for years to represent structured 'decision making' processes. Some electronic systems can be represented graphically using logic gate symbols. Each type of logic gate will respond to specific inputs by generating a predictable output. The inputs and outputs are represented as a '1' or '0' which can be thought of as 'signal' or 'no signal'. A computer printer, for example, can be designed to stop printing if it has either run out of paper or run out of ink. If either or both the ink sensor and the paper sensor sends a signal, the printer will stop printing and indicate a problem. This system can be represented by a logic gate called an 'OR' gate which will send an output signal if it receives a signal from either or both of the inputs.

Developing artificial intelligence

Machine vision systems

Machine vision systems are a good example of developing technology. AI systems are combined with cameras and other optical sensors to:

- analyse visual images on the production line for quality, safety and process control
- run product distribution and bar coding systems in computerised warehouses which can make electronic links between suppliers and customers.

These intelligent 'vision' systems can 'see', 'make decisions', then 'communicate' those findings to other 'smart' factory devices, all in a fraction of a second. Systems have been developed to identify criminal suspects through high street CCTV systems.

Neural networks

Rather than relying on binary systems, **neural networks** seek to imitate the thought processes of the human brain (which is made up from interconnected neurones). Although computers are very good at performing sequential tasks, the human brain is much better at performing pattern-based tasks which require parallel processing such as identifying individual voices in a crowd. Neural networks can predict events, when they have a large database of examples to draw on, and are used for voice recognition and natural language processing (NLP).

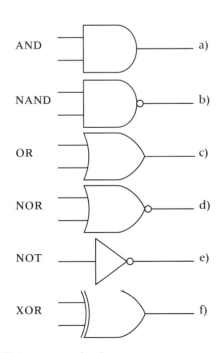

Fig. 4.16 Logic gates used to design systems

Voice recognition systems

Voice recognition systems technology will recognise the spoken word but does not understand it. It is used as an alternative computer input and can prove useful in hostile environments such as space, or when the use of a keyboard is impracticable because the operator is disabled. In the future, an operator will be able to talk directly to an expert system for guidance or instruction.

Natural language processing (NLP)

Communication with computers normally requires us to learn specialised languages. It is hoped that **NLP** will enable computers to understand human languages. Some rudimentary translation systems that translate from one human language to another are in existence, but they are not nearly as good as human translators.

The use of diagrams to represent simple and complex production systems

Systems and graphical system diagrams

- There are natural systems as well as man-made systems.
- Systems have limits.
- Systems can be broken down into sub systems.
- Systems are better understood when represented by symbols and diagrams which describe the flow of information and sequence of actions within a process.

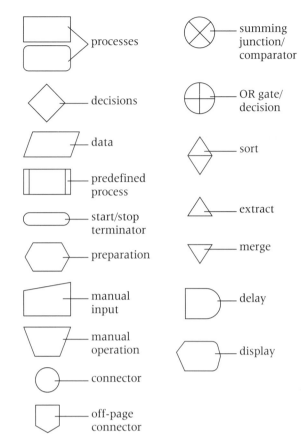

Fig. 4.17 Set of systems symbols

Open- and closed-loop control systems

- A system operating **open-loop control** has no feedback information on the state of the output.
- A system operating **closed-loop control** can have either positive or negative feedback.

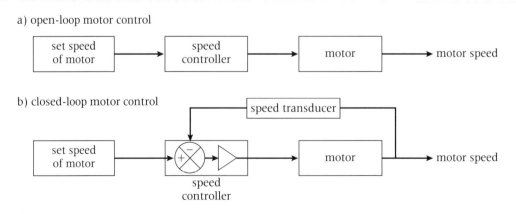

Fig. 4.18 Open- and closed-loop control of a motor

Positive and negative feedback

Positive feedback increases to match increasing outputs while negative feedback reduces inputs to a system to avoid instability. Kanbans are used in some manufacturing systems to control the flow of work on a production line.

Error signals

The difference between the input signal and the feedback signal is called the error signal. If this is higher than required, it will generate a positive error signal to decrease production levels. If production falls, this generates a negative error and production is increased.

Lag

The time delay before the system is able to respond to failures is known as lag and it is a common feature in closed-loop control systems. Electronic data interchange (**EDI**) and improved 'real-time' sales data from electronic point of sale (EPOS) information systems are used to inform the manufacturer of the need to adjust production to correct the 'fault'.

Automated systems using closed-loop control systems

When using a closed-loop system to operate a conveyor belt, feedback is provided by a transducer. This senses when the actual speed of the motor differs from the required speed and sends an error signal to the speed controller. The speed controller will compensate by adjusting the speed of the motor to prevent it overheating.

Sequential control

Robotic and automated processes often use sequential control programs in which a series of actions take place one after another.

Logical control of automated and robotic systems

Combinational logic or 'multiple variable' control requires a series of conditions to be met before an operation can take place.

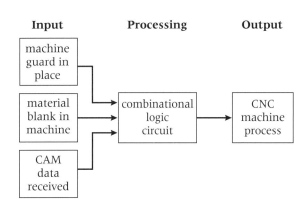

Fig. 4.19 Sensors and software need to be able to verify all three inputs before the CNC machine will operate

Fuzzy logic

Fuzzy logic is based upon the observation that good decisions can be made on the basis of non-precise and non-numerical information. Conventionally, computer systems operate on the basis of limited true or false conditions. Fuzzy logic systems can process vague or imprecise information into degrees of truthfulness or falsehood, for example '80 per cent true'. Fuzzy logic has proved to be particularly useful in expert systems, artificial intelligence applications, and database retrieval and engineering.

Fuzzy control

Fuzzy logic controllers (FLC) are the counterparts to conventional logic controllers such as PLCs. Expert knowledge can be expressed as 'fuzzy sets' in a very natural way using linguistic variables such as few, very, more or less, small, medium, extremely and almost all. A fuzzy set is a collection of objects or entities without clear boundaries.

Fuzzy control is useful when processes are very complex and non-linear, there is no simple mathematical model, or if the processing of (linguistically formulated) expert knowledge is to be performed.

Applications include:

• PCB design and manufacture
• product analysis
• sampling or testing

- e-commerce applications such as document management systems, data warehousing and marketing
- control systems in products such as washing machines which adjust the washing cycle for load size, fabric type, level of soiling.

The advantages and disadvantages of automation

The pressure for automated manufacturing

Manufacturers are under increasing pressure to devise and develop automated operations that are capable of performing consistently under continually changing or disturbed conditions on a global scale. This is a result of the demand for greater product variety, smaller batch sizes, frequent new product introductions and tighter delivery requirements. In addition, manufacturers have to be able to respond to

external or internal disturbances to a production process such as:

- sudden changes in demand for the product
- variations in raw material supply
- machine breakdowns.

The impact of automation on employment

Although automation replaces traditional jobs, there is a shortage of workers equipped with the qualifications and skills to work in modern manufacturing. Automated industries require new attitudes and skills including:

- a wider range of basic skills including literacy and numeracy
- ability to transfer their skills and knowledge in response to the rapid rate of change
- willingness to move jobs
- capability of multi-tasking so that they are competent in responding to different machines within a production cell.

Table 4.19 The advantages and disadvantages of automated manufacturing systems

Advantages	Disadvantages
• Reduced labour costs (including compensation costs arising from injury). • Shorter payback time on the capital compared with machines with human operators. • Precision and high speed improves production rates (which typically vary less than 3 per cent), cycle time, reliability and reduces downtime. • Design changes are easier to incorporate. • Faster time to market. • Tooling costs are reduced because complicated jigs and fixtures are not required. • Short set up time leads to less time required to change from product to product. • Machine tool uptime productivity improved by as much as 30 per cent by eliminating production problems such as bottlenecks. • Sensing, motion, process and system options allow for greater control, consistency and quality output in less time with less chance of scrap or damaged parts. • There is no indirect labour training of potentially large numbers of operators.	Automated systems are not always the most suitable solution and a human workforce can be more cost-effective. Too complex a manufacturing process slows down a robot's speed of action and therefore increases manufacturing time. Other significant cost factors include: • the high cost of buying, installing and commissioning • the cost of recruiting and training operators • the cost of keeping up with new technological advances.

EXAMINATION QUESTION

Example question and answer

 Q1 *a) Name **two** of the four components of the robotic arm illustrated below and outline their purpose/function.* **(4 marks)**

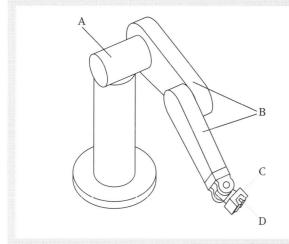

Fig. 4.20 A robotic arm

Acceptable answer – two of the following

a) **Drive/actuators**: components such as servo-motors or stepper motors are **used to control movement** in the arm.

b) **Link arm(s)**: the parts of the robot which **position the end-effector and sensors**.

c) **End-effector**: the **tool** at the end of the arm which **performs the programmed task**.

d) **Sensors**: devices which **provide feedback** to the controller allowing the robot arm to **monitor or react** to changes in the working environment or manufacturing process.

b) Industrial robots are very expensive. Describe the advantages of using robots in manufacturing which justify these costs. **(4 marks)**

Acceptable answer

Robots are used in manufacturing environments for a number of reasons. Most robots can **switch effortlessly** between different pre-programmed operations **without the need to stop production** which reduces lost production in downtime. These pre-programmed operations can be **stored indefinitely** until required and **identical components can be produced at any time**. The **consistent accuracy and reliability** of robots using automatic sensors virtually **eliminates human error**. The ability of robots to carry out **hazardous operations** combined with **'fail-safe' procedures** leads to a **safe working environment**. Although robots require a heavy initial investment, these automated systems have much **lower operational costs** and will eventually pay for themselves.

Uses of ICT in the manufacture of products

You need to

understand the impact and advantages/disadvantages of ICT within the total manufacturing process, including:

☐ electronic communications
☐ electronic information handling
☐ automated stock control
☐ production scheduling and production logistics
☐ flexible manufacturing systems
☐ production control
☐ product marketing, distribution and retailing.

 KEY TERMS
Check you understand these terms

Email, EDI, ISDN, LANs, WANs, Internet, Videoconferencing, CAMA, QRM, EPOS, Internet marketing

Further information can be found in *Advanced Design and Technology for Edexcel, Product Design: Graphics with Materials Technology*, Unit 4B2 section 3

KEY POINTS

Electronic communications

Email and modems

Electronic mail or **email** is the simplest form of electronic communication. It has a comparatively low level of reach (level of communication) and range (types of data transfer) when it is used for messaging or sending files to an individual or a work group. Email can be used over intranets, extranets or the Internet. The modem allows computers to communicate by converting their digital information into an analogue signal to travel through the public telephone network at a maximum rate of 56 kilobytes per second (kb/s). Advantages include savings in stationery and telephone costs, rapid transmission, all transmissions are recorded, and it facilitates work from remote locations.

Electronic data interchange (EDI)

EDI allows users to exchange business documents, such as invoices, delivery notes, orders and receipts, in a similar way to email. ICT is the tool that integrates computer systems and electronic links to create paperless trading. EDI is an essential tool in quick response and JIT systems.

Electronic data exchange (EDE)

CAD/CAM data interchange (CDI) is the process of exchanging design and manufacturing data. The system by which EDI and CDI are combined to provide automated transfer of data over a computer network is called electronic data exchange (EDE). There are various networks available for implementing EDE systems. The key to their usefulness in the field of graphics is their connection speed and the rate at which data can be transferred (throughput).

Integrated services data network (ISDN)

ISDN technology allows multiple digital channels to operate simultaneously through dedicated telephone lines. Advantages include improved data transfer speeds, improved connection speeds, and it dispenses with the need for a modem. The ISDN basic rate interface (BRI) provides two channels of 64 kb/s each or a total of 128 kb/s, and is intended for home-based users. The ISDN primary rate interface (PRI) provides 30 channels of 64 kb/s each or a total of 1920 kb/s, and is intended for business users. ISDN PRI can act as a gateway offering telephone services to users on LAN (local area networks) or can be used to accept large files which are then distributed.

Broadband

Broadband technology is not available everywhere but is growing in popularity and shares many of the benefits of ISDN. These advantages include:

- up to ten times faster than modem connections
- less expensive than ISDN
- easier to set up (uses existing telecommunications cables) and maintain than ISDN
- more effective support for multimedia and e-marketing features.

Local area networks (LANs)

As the name suggests, **LANs** are closed networks which are limited to sharing data, information, communications and resources within an organisation.

Wide area networks (WANs)

WANs allow data to be transferred globally using existing digital telephone systems. To ensure compatibility, WANs require dedicated equipment which can make them expensive.

Intranets and extranets

Intranets use web-based technology to set up local networks which can be password protected. Web browsers are used to navigate HTML pages and 'firewalls' protect the network from unauthorised, external access.

An extranet is used to share data with business partners and customers using the Internet. Levels of access to sensitive areas of the extranet are protected by passwords. Subscription services use this technology to protect 'expert knowledge' services, for example.

Global networks (the Internet)

The **Internet** is the international computer network linking together thousands of individual networks. The world wide web (www) is the familiar collection of inter-connected documents and files, such as websites, which are accessible through the Internet. These websites are held on Internet servers which process and communicate data via cable, radio and satellite. Features of the Internet and world wide web include:

- ISPs (Internet service providers), companies which provide access to the Internet
- web browsers, such as Netscape Navigator and MS Explorer, used to navigate the Internet
- search engines, such as Google, Alta Vista, Ask Jeeves, used to find information sources
- URL (universal resource locator), the unique address allocated to each website
- HTML (hypertext mark-up language), the language used to write web pages
- hyperlinks, the 'hotspots' such as buttons or underlined text, used to move between pages.

Advantages of using the Internet and the web include:

- a low-cost, easily accessible means of sharing ideas within interest groups
- an almost infinite source of information (which may or may not be useful or accurate)
- a medium for communicating with current and potential customers
- a means of researching what other designers or manufacturers are producing
- a readily accessible on-line reference source of commercial data.

Disadvantages of using the Internet and the web include:

- industrial espionage and 'hackers'
- computer viruses
- fraud.

Videoconferencing (VC)

Videoconferencing allows individuals in remote locations to hold 'virtual meetings'. **VC** is available in two forms.

1 Desktop videoconferencing (DTVC) designed for home user two-way communication.
2 Multi-point videoconferencing for business users who are able to conduct 'virtual conferences'.

VC has developed as a result of advances in processing power, electronic communications (including ISDN and broadband), and digital video technologies which allow people in different parts of the world to hold virtual meetings.

The advantages of videoconferencing

- On some VC systems, data such as CAD drawings can be transferred during the meeting.
- It removes the need to travel to meetings, such as marketing presentations, saving time, travel expenses and stress.
- The ease of use enables designers, manufacturers and executives to meet ensuring regular communication, immediate decisions and close control of the development process.
- Education and training can be carried out more efficiently. Expertise can be shared across the company without the need to travel.
- Problems can be solved much more effectively (remote diagnostics) since the relevant experts can meet immediately to address the problem reducing lost production time.

Remote manufacturing

The ability to communicate instantly, using videoconferencing, with people in any continent combined with new technologies allowing reliable electronic data exchange means that designs can be manufactured anywhere in the world.

- Videoconferencing and other communication technologies ensure that designs can be developed in discussion with the manufacturer to ensure they meet the constraints of the manufacturing process.

- The finished design can be sent electronically, directly to the manufacturing centre where it is machined using CNC equipment. The process can be monitored by the design team using video.
- The whole process is very quick and finished components can be checked and dispatched the same day.
- The whole process allows designers the opportunity to take advantage of CNC manufacturing technology without having to make the heavy investment necessary to purchase all the machinery.

New communications technology

Electronic whiteboards (interactive or smart boards)

An electronic whiteboard can be used in presentations, videoconferences, and training sessions and for recording data. Electronic whiteboards can provide the following features.

- an interactive writing surface
- a scanner and thermal printer for producing hard copy
- access to computer software, data and video images
- automatic recording functions
- remote control devices such as wireless touch sensitive tablets.

Information centres or PC kiosks

Interactive kiosks process, communicate and display graphic information and data stored on a computer or network. They can be accessed 24 hours a day from a touch-screen, keyboard or mouse-driven interface and provide services including:

- multimedia presentations of local information for the tourist trade
- video teleconferencing and public Internet access
- interactive services at museums, galleries and trade and product shows.

Electronic information handling
Features of agile manufacturing

Features of agile manufacturing include:

- flexible manufacturing systems (FMS) and quick response manufacturing (QRM)
- customer-driven rather than production-driven manufacture
- emphasis on quality
- close partnerships with customers and suppliers
- information rich
- ICT centred.

Computer-aided market analysis (CAMA)

Market research helps companies to predict demand, identify potential markets, target specific market groups (niche markets), identify market trends and tailor marketing strategies. **CAMA** is an ICT-driven strategy through which data is gathered from sources, including surveys and questionnaires, by manufacturers or specialist agencies. Relational databases are used to store, analyse and present this data as useful information.

- A qualitative analysis will provide information on customers and their opinions.
- A quantitative analysis will provide facts and figures such as sales figures or financial information.
- Regional trend analysis will provide performance information on a geographical basis.
- Market timing attempts to predict future market trends which will help investment decisions.
- Customer profiling using existing customers can help to identify future markets.

Benefits of CAMA include:

- large amounts of marketing data can be processed into useful information very quickly
- demand and trends can be calculated accurately leading to formation of sales targets and marketing strategies
- direct marketing initiatives, such as product launches, can be directed at specific target markets very precisely (market segmentation).

Computer-aided specification development

Complex products need complex specifications which take account of aesthetic requirements, functional requirements, ease of manufacture (design for manufacture – DFM) and ease of assembly (design for assembly – DFA).

Integrated ICT-based systems already exist where design features can be generated by CAD software and checked by a knowledge-based expert system for ease of manufacture and assembly.

Design specifications are generated with the help of computer technology. These specifications should contain all the information necessary to allow manufacturing to take place. Details can be drawn from a product data management (PDM) system. There are three classifications of information or knowledge held within an intelligent design system.

1 CAD data contains specific information about the physical characteristics of each component part being designed.
2 The design catalogue is a reference for data such as the costs and properties of standard materials and components.
3 The knowledge database contains 'rules' about design and manufacturing methods.

Automated stock control

Manufacturing systems such as JIT rely on sophisticated, automated and ICT-centred stock control systems. Bar codes or other methods of identification allow materials and components to be monitored in real time throughout the process, and waste is minimised. Automatic storage and retrieval systems (ASRS) and automated guided vehicles (AGVs) can be used for materials handling.

- Waste is minimised.
- The inventory is optimised but available on demand.
- Automated stock control systems enable the move from batch to continuous flow production.

- Waiting times caused by unbalanced production times are reduced through the use of scheduling techniques such as line balancing.

Production scheduling and production logistics

Because manufacturing systems such as FMS involve major capital investment, it is important to get the most out of the equipment. Traditional scheduling is generally quite rigid and production will stop in response to changes in production or mechanical breakdown. Computer-based scheduling and logistics systems ensure that production is 'smoothed' so that small variations in supply and demand are managed without causing problems. This is achieved by careful planning which spreads the product mix and the product quantities evenly over each day in a month. The advantages of computer-based production scheduling include:

- flexibility and responsiveness to changing conditions
- optimisation of work in progress
- reduction in the inventory
- production is balanced between the stations on the production line
- increase in productivity levels.

Flexible manufacturing systems and QRM

Quick response manufacturing (QRM)

Features of **QRM** include:

- reducing product lead times
- rapid production of small or large batches
- ability to automatically re-program manufacturing and business processes in response to market pressures
- stock levels are constantly evaluated and adjusted to reflect changing demand patterns
- individuals are able to review changes globally and are automatically alerted to changes
- information flow is carefully managed by PDM systems using highly integrated knowledge bases.

Production control

Quality monitoring (quality control)

Automated inspection systems gather and analyse data in order to provide feedback which is used to make automatic adjustments to the manufacturing process. Automated quality monitoring systems rely on a large range of sensor technologies including:

- mechanical methods – which use probes and sensors to collect physical data such as dimensions
- optical quality monitoring systems – which use scanning technology, optical devices, digital cameras and vision systems along with sensors to collect optical data which is automatically compared with the specification tolerances.

Using digital cameras for monitoring quality

Inspection has traditionally involved the inspection of random samples of finished components. These post-process inspection methods have led to a high level of waste and wasted time. Digital cameras connected to a computer or to a dedicated microprocessor allow on-line inspection. Advantages include:

- 100 per cent piece-by-piece inspection
- real-time quality control and fast response time
- collected data is automatically compared with specifications, evaluated and stored
- audible or visual signals can be used to alert operators to problems as they arise
- systems can incorporate automated responses
- no direct mechanical contact with the product
- cameras can be placed well away from machinery.

Product marketing, distribution and retailing

Electronic point of sale (EPOS)

EPOS systems use barcodes and laser-operated readers, which generate a large amount of information, to keep track of products throughout the supply chain. The software allows a two-way flow of data and information. When a product is sold at the checkout in the supermarket the fact is recorded and used to order replacement goods.

Advantages include:

- company financial performance can be monitored at all times due to the availability of detailed and up-to-the-minute records of transactions
- detailed sales histories can be used to predict future trends and fluctuations in demand
- companies can react quickly to changes in demand because the system will inform them instantly of unpredicted changes in consumer-buying patterns
- distribution chains can trace the progress of deliveries to ensure efficiency and allow transferral of products within company
- real time stock updates allow suppliers and retailers to maintain minimal stock levels saving money and resources; daily deliveries support continual product replenishment (CPR)
- allows a two-way flow of financial data, emails, price updates and information.

Internet marketing (e-commerce)

Many companies use the Internet, not only to promote their products and services, but as a means of promoting and selling their products and services (**Internet marketing**). In order to succeed, companies need to restructure their internal and external business processes, supply chains and relationships. Some companies trade exclusively on the Internet. Advantages include:

- cost effective access to a global marketplace for relatively small companies and large organisations alike, increasing the customer base and company profile
- all business can be conducted from one geographical site, reducing costs
- a large part of the transaction process can be automated resulting in faster processing of orders and transactions, reducing overheads and the need for sales staff
- enables the collection of detailed customer profiles
- reduces time to market

- product information is easily accessible and can be changed or updated easily. Virtual products provide access to detailed product information
- use of integrated ICT systems throughout the process leads to a very fast and efficient process.

EXAMINATION QUESTIONS

Example questions and answers

 a) *The Internet is a widely used resource. Explain the following terms with reference to the Internet.*
- *HTML*
- *hyperlinks*
- *web browsers.* **(3 marks)**

Acceptable answer

HTML: hypertext mark-up language is the language **used to create web pages**.

Hyperlinks: hyperlinks are the **underlined words or symbols** which enable you to **jump from one web page to another**.

Web browsers: Microsoft Explorer is an example of a web browser **program** which allows people to **navigate the Internet**.

b) *Discuss the advantages and disadvantages of using the Internet and world wide web for designers developing a new product.* **(8 marks)**

Acceptable answer

The Internet and world wide web provide the product designer with a valuable resource.

When developing a new graphic product, the Internet provides designers with a **low-cost, easily accessible means of sharing design ideas** with other colleagues and professionals. The Internet contains a vast amount of copyright free **information and design images**, which may be incorporated into designs, but users must be aware that this information **may or may not be useful or accurate**. As designers develop their ideas, the Internet provides a very useful means of **communicating with the client** using email or videoconferencing. Commercial websites can provide **valuable information about competing products**. When new products are launched, the Internet can be used as one **platform to promote** the new product by creating a website and through the use of e-marketing. However, connecting to the Internet opens the company to hostile attack from **hackers who may be looking for commercially sensitive information** on the company network. It also leaves the company open to attack from computer **viruses** which are often spread by email and which can cause **permanent damage to important data**.

PRACTICE EXAMINATION STYLE QUESTION

1 a) Outline the aims, features and effects of just in time (JIT) manufacturing. **(5 marks)**

b) Describe how automated control and feedback systems are used in modern industry. Refer to **all** the following in your answer.
- materials handling
- materials processing
- quality control
- safety systems
- coordination of production. **(5 marks)**

c) Artificial intelligence is a rapidly developing technology.
 i) Explain the term 'artificial intelligence'. **(1 mark)**

ii) Explain **two** of the following terms in relation to AI.
- expert systems
- computer/machine vision
- natural language processing (NLP)
- artificial neural networks
- fuzzy logic. **(4 marks)**

2 a) Referring to an industry of your choice, describe how computer-integrated manufacture (CIM) is used to enhance the manufacturing process. **(5 marks)**

b) Discuss the advantages and disadvantages associated with automated manufacturing systems. **(5 marks)**

c) Describe the benefits of videoconferencing technology compared with more conventional methods of communication. **(5 marks)**

Total for this question paper: **30 marks**

UNIT 6

Design and technology capability (G6)

Although no new learning is expected during Unit 6, it is essential that you can recall the content of previous units. As it is *synoptic*, this paper is taken at the end of the course and will examine all the areas covered during the two years of the course. You will be asked to develop a product which will incorporate two elements.

- a graphical element (such as brand identity, logos and packaging)
- a resistant material element (manufactured using materials such as wood, metal and plastic).

Some time before the examination, your school or college will be sent a Design Research Paper which will give you a *context* for the design. This is an 'open book' examination which means you can take your research with you into the examination. During the three-hour examination you will be expected to undertake a design problem from the initial analysis to a final evaluation. You should therefore give very careful consideration to the amount of information you take in with you. Too much information could do you more harm than good.

You should organise your research under the same headings which appear in the design specification criteria. However, research should be drawn from and focused upon the following areas.

- market research
- analysis of existing products
- research into materials, components and processes
- legal requirements and standards relating to quality and safety
- values issues, such as moral and environmental questions which might impact on the problem and solution.

Table 6.1 Mark allocation

Section heading	Marks available	Recommended time (mins)
Analyse the design problem and develop a product design specification.	15	30
Generate and evaluate a range of design ideas.	15	30
Develop, describe and justify a final solution, identifying appropriate materials and components.	15	30
Represent and illustrate your final solution.	20	40
Draw up a production plan.	15	30
Evaluate your final solution against the product design specification and suggest improvements.	10	20
Total	90	180

In the exam you will be provided with single-sided, pre-printed A3 sheets. You may find it useful to separate these but make sure that you work on the printed side only. At the end of the examination, double check that you have reassembled your sheets securely, in the correct order. You should not need to use any other exam sheets.

- The pasting of pre-prepared or photocopied sheets is *not* permitted.
- You are *not* allowed to use ICT facilities in the examination

The pre-printed sheets are headed up as follows, indicating both the marks available and the recommended amount of time.

You will be assessed on your ability to organise and present ideas and information clearly and logically within the three hours. More advice can be found in the Introduction to this book.

Examiner's Tip

Always make sure that you read the instructions on the pre-printed sheets carefully. It is possible that the allocation of marks may change, depending upon the nature of the design task. Examples of actual student responses can be found in the course textbook *Advanced Design and Technology for Edexcel, Product Design: Graphics with Materials Technology.*

Analyse the design problem and develop a specification

You need to

☐ use appropriate research techniques, primary sources and specialist information
☐ use appropriate analysis techniques to analyse the problem and identify the purpose/users/target market. From research and analysis, develop a design specification to form the basis for generating and evaluating ideas.

KEY TERMS

Check you understand these terms

Research, Analysis, Context, Design specification, Constraints, Attributes

Further information can be found in *Advanced Design and Technology for Edexcel, Product Design: Graphics with Materials Technology*, Unit 6.

KEY POINTS

Use appropriate research techniques, primary sources and specialist information

You may take all your **research** material into the exam, but this does not have to be handed in for assessment. Your research should address areas which may include:

- purpose and function
- trends and fashions
- target markets
- user requirements
- performance requirements
- work of other designers
- relevant materials, components and systems
- relevant processes and technology
- legal requirements
- external standards (safety and quality)
- cultural issues
- social issues
- moral issues
- environmental issues.

Research sources may include market research, asking experts and teachers, libraries, the Internet, CD ROMs, your course notes, and product analysis.

Along with your preparation and research materials, you should organise your own equipment for the exam. This might include:

- pen, pencils, sharpener, ruler and rubber
- fine liner
- coloured pens/pencils
- drawing equipment such as templates, set squares and compasses
- A3 isometric underlay for 3D sketching
- A3 grid underlay for orthographic drawings.

Analyse the design problem and develop a design specification (15 marks)

This section involves two distinct tasks: analysing the problem and producing a specification. It is important to produce good work here because you will refer back to your specification throughout the exam.

Analyse the design problem (6 marks)

Your **analysis** should help to clarify the problem. Your work should show that you

understand the problem clearly and that you are able to divide it into manageable chunks. As part of your analysis you should:

- clearly identify and expand the areas and issues relevant to the problem, which you have addressed in your research (refer to the areas just identified)
- make reference to your research material.

It is not necessary to write at length: short and concise points are sufficient. Methods such as brainstorming, thought showers, mind mapping and tables are proven methods of organising this form of information. You should clearly identify at least *six* appropriate areas for analysis, making sure that you expand on these to gain full marks. This will involve justifying your points, by explaining why they are important and how they will affect your designs.

Develop a product design specification, identifying appropriate constraints and attributes (9 marks)

The **design specification** headings are printed at the top of your answer sheet – use them. Your specification criteria/design requirements should be written as short, reasoned sentences (perhaps bullet points). You should describe at least nine constraints and attributes which should address all the headings (*at least five*) at the top of the exam sheet.

Constraints are design rules which provide limits for the design such as 'no more than 1kg in weight'. **Attributes** are qualities which need to be incorporated into the design such as 'portability'.

Your specification criteria should:

- be specific to the requirements of the set design problem
- be influenced by your research and analysis
- explain the design requirements of the product
- be measurable wherever possible.

Examiner's Tips

- You must concentrate a good proportion of your research on the construction details of products within the design **context**. You will need to find out about the specific materials and processes used. Remember that you will have to design something similar in the exam.
- Two things are essential to achieving a good mark in this unit:
  - thorough preparation before the exam: use the preparation sheet to prepare and practise
  - good time management during the exam: stick to the times given on the exam paper.
- The task outlined on the first page of the exam paper will often provide you with one or more constraints which needs to be included in your analysis and specification. Read the task carefully and highlight any constraints before you start.

The printed specification headings ask you to develop the following criteria.

- *purpose/function*: what the product and individual components are for and what they need to do
- *aesthetics*: how the product should look: its style, form and aesthetic characteristics
- *processes, technology and scale of production*: manufacturing processes and technology required to make the product at an appropriate level of production, either batch or mass production
- *cultural, social, moral and environmental issues*: which may influence your design ideas
- *market and user requirements*: market trends, user needs and preferences, ergonomic constraints
- *quality control*: the quality requirements of your product (and target market) and how you will achieve quality using quality control and quality standards

- *performance requirements of the product, materials, components and systems*: the properties and working characteristics which are required
- *legal requirements and external standards*: how the product will meet safety requirements, referencing external standards where appropriate (British Standards are not to be copied out).

Generate ideas, evaluate each idea and justify decisions made

You need to

☐ generate and record a range of design ideas using appropriate communication techniques

☐ evaluate each idea against the design specification to determine its feasibility. Justify the design selected for development.

KEY TERMS
Check you understand these terms

Annotation, Generate ideas, Evaluate, Justify

 Further information can be found in *Advanced Design and Technology for Edexcel, Product Design: Graphics with Materials Technology*, **Unit 6.**

KEY POINTS

Generate and evaluate a range of design ideas (15 marks)

Your ideas and **annotation** (notes and labels) must address the whole problem. If the problem has two or more parts, each of your 'ideas' needs to provide designs for all of these elements.

Generate and record a range of design ideas using appropriate communication techniques (10 marks)

You are expected to **generate a range of ideas** – a minimum of *three* original, realistic design ideas for *each* of the main aspects of the given design problem. You will be assessed on your use of:

- clear sketches and clear, detailed annotation
- your specification
- reference to scale of production and commercial processes (at least *two*)
- reference to specific materials (at least *two*).

Make sure that you are spending your time addressing the main problem. If you are generating designs for a series of signs, for example, do not spend all your time developing logos and graphics. You should concentrate on the construction details of the sign. While colour can help to communicate your ideas, do not spend too much time rendering (colouring) your drawings. Clarity and detail are more important. You must be able to work quickly – practise your freehand sketching as much as you can before the exam. *Above all, make sure that your designs meet the requirements of your product design specification.*

- Use labels to identify specific materials (refer to at least two). It may be appropriate to colour code parts of your design to identify different materials.
- Use notes to show how individual products or components will be manufactured (refer to at least *two*). Make sure you refer to specific industrial processes such as injection moulding.

Evaluate ideas against the design specification to determine their feasibility. Justify the design selected for development (5 marks)

All your ideas should be **evaluated** against the key points of your product design specification. This can be achieved through:

- annotation (notes), which refers clearly to individual specification points and/or
- tables which assess each idea against the main specification points.

You must make *five* valid, justified points as an absolute minimum.

You should clearly identify one idea to develop by drawing a border around it and adding a label. Your choice should be based upon your evaluations. **Justify** (explain briefly but clearly) why you believe it meets the requirements of the specification more successfully than the others.

Examiner's Tips

- You may separate your sheets carefully if you wish. This will allow you to refer more easily to your specification when you need to. You must, however, ensure that all of your work is reassembled in the correct order using a treasury tag at the end of the exam. It should not be necessary to add sheets.
- Make it clear to the examiner when you are evaluating your ideas against the specification. You could use a different colour pen, for example, but avoid red which will be used by your examiner.

Develop the chosen idea into an optimum solution; describe and justify a solution

You need to

☐ develop, record, model and refine the chosen design idea into an optimum solution
☐ describe and justify the solution.

KEY TERMS

Check you understand this term

Development

📖 **Further information can be found in *Advanced Design and Technology for Edexcel, Product Design: Graphics with Materials Technology*, Unit 6.**

KEY POINTS

Develop, describe and justify a final solution, identifying appropriate materials and components (15 marks)

Marks in this section are awarded against a number of criteria so read the following carefully. Make sure you address all the elements of the task and work to your specification.

Develop a final solution, identifying appropriate materials and components (8 marks)

You should use 2D and/or 3D sketches that **develop** – change, refine and improve – your chosen design idea. Your sketches should provide sufficient detail to explain how the product will look and function. You should not simply redraw your chosen idea. Your developed idea must:

- be based on one or more of your earlier ideas
- be workable
- show that you have adapted and changed the characteristics of your initial ideas
- refer to suitable and specific materials and components (refer to at least *two*)
- refer to the scale of production and suitable and specific commercial manufacturing processes (refer to at least *two*).

Examiner's Tip

The examiner needs to follow your train of thought. Include some arrows so that your ideas can be followed as they develop.

Describe and justify your final solution (7 marks)

You need to explain why and how the design you have developed is a good solution to the problem. Try to address all the headings provided at the top of the exam sheet. You should use technical language and short, reasoned sentences to describe and justify your design solution in relation to:

- function – explain and justify how your product will carry out the roles and tasks you have outlined in your specification
- appearance – explain and justify how the look, form and style of your product design meets the aesthetic requirements outlined in your specification
- performance – explain and justify how your product design meets the quality and safety requirements of the market and users outlined in your specification
- materials, components and systems – explain and justify how the properties and working characteristics of your chosen materials, components and/or systems meet the requirements of your specification
- processes – explain and justify how your chosen manufacturing processes are appropriate for your chosen materials and scale of production stated in your specification
- technological features – explain and justify how modern technology such as CAD/CAM and ICT could be used in the manufacture of your design.

Once again you will be making connections between what you set out to achieve (your product design specification) and how you hope to achieve it (your final design solution). It would be helpful to have your specification in front of you when you describe and justify your final solution.

Represent and illustrate the final solution

You need to

☐ **represent and illustrate the final solution, using clear and appropriate communication techniques.**

KEY TERMS

Check you understand this term

Final design solution

Further information can be found in *Advanced Design and Technology for Edexcel, Product Design: Graphics with Materials Technology,* **Unit 6.**

KEY POINTS

Represent and illustrate your final solution (20 marks)

This is where you put forward your **final design solution**. Make sure you address all the elements of the task and work to your specification. You need to represent and illustrate your final design solution, using:

- clear manufacturing and assembly details (at least *four* of each)   (8 marks)
- dimensions/sizes (at least *eight*)   (4 marks)
- details and quantity of all materials/components(at least *four*)   (4 marks)
- clear and appropriate communication techniques.   (4 marks)

There should be sufficient information in your drawings and notes to allow someone else to make it. The examiner should be able to understand how your final design solution is to

be manufactured. It should not be a pictorial illustration in full colour. You should use:

- detailed drawing techniques and annotation
- appropriate dimensioning (conforming to British standards)
- annotation showing how the product will be manufactured identifying specific processes
- details and quantities of specific materials and components (include a cutting list)
- reference to the scale of production.

Orthographic third angle drawings are not required in the design exam but you may wish to use them. Appropriate graphic techniques could include dimensioned drawings that show different views of the product, and exploded drawings that show any hidden details.

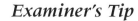

Examiner's Tip

The emphasis of this section is placed upon the use of clear and appropriate communication. Use drawing conventions such as isometric or orthographic and refer to specific materials, processes and scale of production.

Draw up a production plan

You need to

describe the production requirements of the solution including:
- ☐ assembly processes/unit operations
- ☐ sequence of assembly/work order with details of tools, equipment and tolerances
- ☐ quality checks at critical control points with quality indicators.

KEY TERMS
Check you understand this term

Production plan

 Further information can be found in *Advanced Design and Technology for Edexcel, Product Design: Graphics with Materials Technology,* **Unit 6.**

KEY POINTS

Draw up a production plan for your final solution (15 marks)

There is more than one way of producing a **production plan**. One good way of incorporating all the information required is to produce a simple flow chart. Make sure you address all the elements of the task. Your plan should include operations related to all of the following.

- processing (for example injection moulding, casting, lithography)
- assembly (for example screw on tops, nuts/bolts, binding)
- specific quality control checks (for example using a densitometer to check ink density).

Assembly processes/unit operations

Your plan must incorporate the manufacture of all the component parts which go together to make up your product. You need to identify the specific operations and commercial processes which will be used. *This does not include the designing stages or any modelling processes.* The nature of the processing and assembly you select will depend upon your chosen materials and the scale of production identified in your product design specification. Make sure that you use specific and appropriate technical terms.

Sequence of assembly/work order with details of tools, equipment and tolerances

Once you have identified your processes you need to organise them into the correct sequence. Simple flow charts are a good method of representing the sequence of operations. You should refer to specific tools, equipment and processes. You should address tolerances in your quality control checks.

Quality checks at critical control points with quality indicators

You should identify critical control points where quality checks will be made. These should be specific and you need to identify:

- at what point in the process the quality checks will be made
- what is being checked (for example print registration, print density, critical dimensions against tolerances)
- how it is being checked (for example visual inspection, densitometer, manual gauge or micrometer).

Do not use generalised statements such as 'the component is checked for quality'. You need to state exactly where and how will you check for quality.

 Examiner's Tip

Be specific. You will not gain credit for generalised statements. Address all of the areas as equally as possible for all components. Ideally you should be able to describe a minimum of five processing operations, five assembly operations and five quality control procedures.

Evaluate

You need to

evaluate your final solution against the product design specification and suggest improvements relating to quality of design and market potential.

 KEY TERMS
Check you understand these terms

Evaluation, Suggest improvements

📖 **Further information can be found** in *Advanced Design and Technology for Edexcel, Product Design: Graphics with Materials Technology*, Unit 6.

KEY POINTS

Evaluate your final solution against the product design specification and suggest improvements (10 marks)

Your evaluation and your suggestions for improvement are equally important, so divide your time accordingly. Make sure you address all the elements of the task and refer to your specification. One mark is awarded for each valid, justified point.

Evaluate your final solution against the product design specification (5 marks)

Your **evaluation** and evaluative comments should be *objective* (positive and negative points relating closely to specification) and *justified* (explained with reasons given to support points made). You should use your specification to evaluate your design against the same headings given in the first exam question. You should be critical. By identifying negative aspects of your design, as well as positive ones, you will find it easier to suggest improvements. Turn these headings into questions, for example will your product perform all the functions listed in your specification? You should also ask yourself:

- how successfully does the final design proposal match the specification
- why would customers be attracted to buy the product?

Suggest improvements (5 marks)

You should **suggest improvements** that are realistic and relate to the product design specification. Generalised, unjustified points will not be credited nor will comments related to the quality of your work. Your suggested improvements should relate to the success of your final design proposals. Again you need to refer to your specification. Consider, for example:

- suggesting modifications to improve the aesthetics, ergonomics or durability of your product
- suggesting changes to your design to optimise manufacturing processes
- changing your choice of materials or manufacturing processes
- recommending more use of CAM or automation for the manufacture of your product.

Examiner's Tips

- Remember that you are evaluating your final design proposal, not your initial ideas nor the quality of your work. No credit will be given for comments such as 'My drawings could have been better if I had used a ruler'.
- The marks for this section are usually divided equally between your evaluation and suggested modifications. Make sure that you provide at least *five* justified points for each. If you do not make any points you will not receive any marks.

PRACTICE EXAMINATION STYLE QUESTION

Individual drinks products are often packaged together and sold in multi-packs.
You have investigated:

- individual drinks containers and multi-pack packaging
- the range of materials and processes used to produce these individual containers and multi-packs
- the range of brand identities and surface graphics employed by drinks manufacturers
- the general aesthetic and functional requirements of drinks packaging.

Your task is to design an individual soft drink container and a multi-pack capable of holding **twelve** of these containers. As part of the task you will also need to design a brand identity and associated graphics for the surfaces of both the drinks container and multi-pack.

Your designs must be based upon **one** of the following brand names: 'Coola', 'Quench', 'Phizz', 'Swoosh', 'Brite'.

1 Analyse the design problem and develop a design specification, identifying appropriate constraints.

(15 marks)

2 Generate and evaluate a range of design ideas. **(15 marks)**

3 Develop, describe and justify a final solution, identifying appropriate materials and components. **(15 marks)**

4 Represent and illustrate your final solution. **(20 marks)**

5 Draw up a production plan for your final solution. **(15 marks)**

6 Evaluate your final solution against the product design specification and suggest improvements. **(10 marks)**

Total for this question paper: **90 marks**